The Triumph of *Babylon*

The Triumph of *Babylon 5*

The Science Fiction Classic and Its Long Twilight Struggles

BAZ GREENLAND

McFarland & Company, Inc., Publishers
Jefferson, North Carolina

Library of Congress Cataloging-in-Publication Data

Names: Greenland, Baz, 1981– author.
Title: The triumph of Babylon 5 : the science fiction classic and its long twilight struggles / Baz Greenland.
Description: Jefferson, North Carolina : McFarland & Company, Inc., Publishers, 2024. | Includes bibliographical references and index.
Identifiers: LCCN 2023057503 | ISBN 9781476692401 (paperback : acid free paper) ♾ ISBN 9781476651446 (ebook)
Subjects: LCSH: Babylon 5 (Television program) | Science fiction television programs—United States—History and criticism. | BISAC: PERFORMING ARTS / Television / Genres / Science Fiction, Fantasy & Horror
Classification: LCC PN1992.77.B24 G74 2024 | DDC 791.45/72—dc23/eng/20231218
LC record available at https://lccn.loc.gov/2023057503

British Library cataloguing data are available

ISBN (print) 978-1-4766-9240-1
ISBN (ebook) 978-1-4766-5144-6

© 2024 Baz Greenland. All rights reserved

No part of this book may be reproduced or transmitted in any form or by any means, electronic or mechanical, including photocopying or recording, or by any information storage and retrieval system, without permission in writing from the publisher.

Front cover images © 2024 Shutterstock

Printed in the United States of America

McFarland & Company, Inc., Publishers
  Box 611, Jefferson, North Carolina 28640
    www.mcfarlandpub.com

For Gem, who always believed in me
and always supported my inner geek.

A special thanks to Tony Black, who helped me get started on this journey with McFarland, Luke Winch, my cohost in our *Babylon 5* adventure that is *A Dream Given Form*, and Patricia Tallman, Peter Jurasik and Marshall Teague, who took the time to share their memories of *Babylon 5* with me and the wider fandom.

Table of Contents

Introduction	1
1. The Legacy of *Babylon 5*	5
2. Science Fiction Story Arcs	11
3. The Development of *Babylon 5*	19
4. Babylon Prime	25
5. A Chat with Peter Jurasik (Part 1)	32
6. From *Star Trek* to *Babylon 5* … and Back to *Star Trek* Again	41
7. Making "*The Lord of the Rings* in space" a Reality	47
8. The Great Publicity Machine	55
9. JMS's Character Trapdoors	63
10. The Diversity That Almost Was	73
11. A Chat with Marshall Teague	79
12. Season One: A Master Class in World-Building	90
13. Season Two: The Changing of the Guard	102
14. Season Three: Tearing Up the Television Rule Book	115
15. Season Four: The Race to the Finish Line	126
16. Season Five: Epilogues and Opportunities	139
17. A Chat with Patricia Tallman	151
18. The TNT Movies: Looking Back Before Moving On	163
19. The *Crusade* to Save Earth—and *Babylon 5*	170
20. *To Live and Die in Starlight*	179
21. *The Lost Tales* and What Could Have Been	183

22. *The Memory of Shadows*: The Big-Screen *Babylon 5*s That Never Were	188
23. A Chat with Peter Jurasik (Part 2)	195
24. The Canonization of Novels	203
25. The *Babylon 5* Community	212
26. Objects in Motion and the Possibilities to Come	218
Chapter Notes	223
Bibliography	235
Index	239

Introduction

What is the golden age of science fiction television? Is it the '60s, with the birth of genre icons like *Star Trek, Lost in Space* and *Doctor Who*? Or has that golden age emerged in the 21st century, as modern special effects match the visions of the ambitious storytellers? Classic shows like *Battlestar Galactica* have returned in the form of new, ambitious revivals and reboots, matched by innovative new content such as *The Expanse, The Mandalorian* and *Orphan Black*.

For me, there is only one answer: the rebirth of science fiction TV in the '90s. It was a time where my teenage self fully embraced geekdom. *Star Trek* got there first. Whether it was UK reruns of the original series on BBC2 during the weekends, or 6:00 p.m. showings of *Star Trek: The Next Generation, Star Trek: Deep Space Nine* and later *Star Trek: Voyager*, I found myself lost in the future, filled with aliens, starships, and all the wonders of the universe. Other shows made their mark too: *Space: Above and Beyond, Red Dwarf, Sliders, Quantum Leap* and, of course, *The X-Files* much closer to home.

But nothing quite captured my heart like *Babylon 5*.

I had heard about the show during its first couple of years but had dismissed it as an inferior *Star Trek* clone. But when Channel 4 started broadcasting season three at 6:00 p.m. on Sundays here in the UK, I gave it a go.

I was hooked.

Season three was the show at its absolute height, delivering on two fantastic years of world-building (though I didn't know that at the time). I looked in awe at my first Shadow ship as it went head-to-head with the *White Star*. I immediately fell in love with the characters. The rivalry of Londo and G'Kar. The weirdness of Kosh. The courageous Captain Sheridan, fiery first officer Commander Ivanova (I certainly had a crush on Claudia Christian at the time) and the noble Ranger Marcus Cole, who reminded me of Aragorn from my favorite book, *The Lord of the Rings*.

It would not be the first time *Babylon 5* drew on Tolkien's works for inspiration.

And that title sequence. "The Babylon Project was our last, best hope for peace. It failed. But in the Year of the Shadow War, it became something greater: our last, best hope … for victory."

What had I just walked into?

Then came "Message from Earth," "Point of No Return" and "Severed Dreams." Everything I had just watched for the last seven weeks fell apart in front of my eyes in the most spectacular way. "Interludes and Examinations" killed off Kosh! The Shadow War erupted. "War Without End" blew my mind! And that finale on Z'ha'dum! Season three left me on tenterhooks. It is still my favorite television season of all time.

The end of the Shadow War and the conflict with Earth in season four was staggering. I remember going to see *Alien: Resurrection* with friends at the cinema. We were huge *Alien* fans and couldn't wait to see the return of Ripley and the Xenomorphs. But on the way there, all we could talk about was Ivanova taking on the Earth-Shadow hybrid ships in "Between the Darkness and the Light" the night before (Channel 4 liked to mix up the schedules and showed the fourth season at around 10:30 on Thursday nights).

Season five was good, but a little disappointing. Where was Ivanova? Why was the telepath storyline dragging out? But it came back strong. The last five episodes were worth the wait. "The Fall of Centauri Prime" was hauntingly tragic, and I still remember that pit in my stomach and goosebumps on my arms watching "Sleeping in Light."

Babylon 5 stayed with me. I caught late night reruns on Channel 4, finally seeing what life was like under Commander Sinclair in season one. I bought all the seasons on VHS. On my A-Levels results day, I treated myself by popping into the video store and spending a whole $100 on the complete season three box set. That's how much I loved the show. I introduced new friends to *Babylon 5*. I got the TV movies. I stuck through *Crusade*.

But *Babylon 5* slipped away, when all I wanted was more. I was ready when *Legends of the Rangers* teased the possibility of future stories. I bought the DVD of *The Lost Tales* on the day of release and hoped dearly that this would be the first of many stories.

But alas, it was not to be. To quote my favorite episode, *Babylon 5*'s legacy has been something of a long twilight struggle. With the collapse of PTEN, the Prime Time Entertainment Network, J. Michael Straczynski was forced to wrap his five-year arc a whole season early. The promise of a spin-off series died in its infancy due to studio interference by TNT (Turner Network Television). *The Lost Tales* never continued, in part due to the writers' strike of 2008. Even the long-rumored movie, *The Memory of Shadows*, never materialized.

I find myself going back and rewatching the show I have loved dearly for almost 30 years, reliving all those magical moments. The Shakespearean levels of humor and tragedy that make up Londo and G'Kar's relationship, surely the greatest double act in TV history. The mighty Delenn, facing off against the Earth armada in "Severed Dreams" and leading the fight against the Shadows with Sheridan. The growing rebellion against an increasingly xenophobic Earth that seemed horrifyingly fantastical in previous watches and now feels disturbingly relatable in the current cultural climate. The dread and darkness of the Shadows. G'Kar's freedom speech. Garibaldi's betrayal and manipulation by Bester. Sheridan's interrogation. Ivanova's last stand. G'Kar forgiving Londo. Sheridan sending the *White Star* into Z'ha'dum. Sinclair's reveal as Valen. The Inquisitor simply known as Jack. The destruction of Babylon 5. So many moments that give me goosebumps just thinking about them.

While *Babylon 5* has struggled to continue, it has always been there in my heart. I spent years writing articles on TV and film for various websites. When an opportunity would arise, I would find a way to write about *Babylon 5*, even if I wasn't sure there were still enough fans out there to read my work. But people did read it. There were plenty of fans out there like me, who still watched the show and hoped for more.

When my attention turned to podcasting, I seized upon the opportunity to talk about *Babylon 5*. I found a cohost, Luke Winch, who loved the show as much as I did, and I've been delighted that fans everywhere have engaged with what we have had to say. *A Dream Given Form* is still going strong on the We Made This network.

I've even had the opportunity to talk to some of the cast too. I interviewed Walter Koenig at the Destination Star Trek convention about his role as Chekov. Walter had spent decades talking about *Star Trek*. Despite his obvious frailty, he answered my questions with plenty of enthusiasm. But when I snuck in a couple of questions about playing Bester on *Babylon 5*, his eyes lit up. Suddenly there was an energy that came out of nowhere, and he talked with such fondness of his time on the show. *Babylon 5* clearly meant so much to him, and there was a sparkle in his eye as he talked.

On *A Dream Given Form*, my first cast interview was with the delightful Patricia Tallman. We chatted about her playing Lyta Alexander, and her passion for the show—and the fans—was intoxicating. She shared some home truths too, particularly around her departure after *The Gathering*, but there was nothing but praise for *Babylon 5* and its cast and crew. As she said, it was the little show that could, living in the shadow of bigger genre giants like *Star Trek*.

Her words have stuck with me. So much of *Babylon 5*'s legacy has been about its struggle to survive. You only need to look at any discussion with J. Michael Straczynski to know that the show was made by the skin of its teeth. Every year, there was a question mark over its survival. Studio instability and cast exits that dramatically changed the direction of the show meant it was a miracle we got the show Straczynski made.

The show's inception, the struggles during production, and the attempts to continue the *Babylon 5* story are almost as epic a tale as the fight against the Shadows and the battle to save Earth.

I've been writing about *Babylon 5* piecemeal for years, but this is an opportunity to truly explore that "long twilight struggle." It's not always a happy story. The loss of several major cast members certainly casts a shadow over the show, and those stories make for a harrowing tale.

But there's also plenty of joy. Not just for me, but for all the fans who have remained with the show decades after it ended. Even those involved with the show, like Walter and Patricia, still have a clear passion and love for what was made. Its legacy lives on through the words and thoughts of fans and cast and crew alike. In a way, it has never gone away.

Babylon 5 was innovative. It was special. For me, was a show like no other.

1

The Legacy of *Babylon 5*

Babylon 5 has a rich legacy.

Yes, that's a bold statement to make.

What does it mean for a television show to have a legacy? Is it about popularity? Will 21st-century cultural zeitgeists like *Game of Thrones* and *Stranger Things* have legacies of their own, 30 years down the line? Perhaps legacy is about leading the charge, being the first out of the gate. Does George Reeves's *The Adventures of Superman* from the 1950s have a legacy because it was the first superhero TV show? What about accessibility to mainstream audiences? Does *The X-Files* have a legacy because it transcended from cult to mainstream television in the '90s?

Is it about the influence a show has on those who followed?

While all of the above may be true, the nature of influence might be the closest thematic definition of a television legacy. The *Star Trek* franchise arguably has a legacy; it wasn't the first show set on a spaceship, but it helped establish a format by which genre television could touch upon cultural and societal issues through the lens of something fantastical. It brought together a diverse cast, including a Black woman in a key position on the bridge, and was able to use the lens of science fiction to tell allegories covering everything from racial conflict ("Let This Be Your Last Battlefield") to an examination of the U.S.'s involvement in the Vietnam War ("A Private Little War"). While it technically wasn't the first instance, it also featured an interracial kiss on prime-time television ("Plato's Stepchildren").

With falling ratings, *Star Trek* was canceled after three seasons, but its popularity continued to grow through reruns and a return to Kirk and his crew in an animated spin-off and a series of films. In the '80s it spawned the first of many TV spin-offs in *Star Trek: The Next Generation*. Across 13 films and 11 TV series (to date), the *Star Trek* franchise has charted humanity's exploration of the stars. It is still going strong today and still has rich stories to capture the hearts of our imagination.

On a smaller scale, *Buffy the Vampire Slayer* is a show with a legacy. Putting aside the issues with creator Joss Whedon, it subverted audience expectations of gender roles, fused horror and real life in a way rarely seen on screen before, and developed season-long arcs that could be seen in everything from Russell T Davies's 2005 reboot of *Doctor Who*[1] to modern superhero shows like *The Flash*.

Buffy the Vampire Slayer brought about a renaissance of horror television—everything from *Supernatural* to current darling *Stranger Things*. It turned convention on its head with a blond schoolgirl revealed as a villain in the pilot episode, "Welcome to the Hellmouth," and then gave us a heroine in Buffy that led to the wave of strong female leads—from *Alias*'s Sidney Bristow to *Jessica Jones*. This was another show that used analogy to tell great stories. School was literally on the Hellmouth. Buffy's boyfriend actually does turn evil after she sleeps with him. It gave audiences something fresh and exciting and—like *Star Trek*—has been often copied but rarely bettered.

The Oxford English Dictionary defines legacy as "a situation that exists now because of events, actions, etc. that took place in the past." The story of *Babylon 5* as a TV show can certainly be viewed through the prism of that definition.

The narrative structure of the show is built on the events of the past. The horrors of the last great Shadow War left scars on the Minbari and the Narn. The rise of Valen a thousand years ago shaped Minbari culture, most significantly the character of Delenn. The Vorlon manipulation of other races and the creation of telepaths saw the show revisiting the trauma of the past, most fundamentally in the show's final season.

The more recent horrors of the Earth–Minbari war were explored through the trauma of Sinclair and his missing 24 hours at the Battle of the Line, and then with the appearance of war hero Sheridan to stir the pot. The genetic holocaust unleashed by Deathwalker left its mark on the League of Non-Aligned Worlds in the show's first season. The mystery of Babylon 4's disappearance was a huge mystery that had immense importance to the show come season three.

These past events shape the galaxy we see when *Babylon 5* begins and continue to influence decisions and actions throughout the course of the show. The very notion of Babylon 5, as a station where different races can come together to work out their differences and find peace, is a direct reaction to the conflicts that have scared the galaxy.

If you look at the development of the show, its creation was a reaction to the genre television that preceded it. It was an attempt to move beyond the shadow of *Star Trek*, something few sci-fi shows had ever successfully achieved. The move from episodic to long-form storytelling and series arcs

1. The Legacy of Babylon 5

were unheard of at the time. J. Michael Straczynski (JMS) wanted science fiction to be taken seriously by network television, without the sanitation of content deemed too adult or provocative.[2]

Over the course of this book, we'll explore the challenges of developing a science fiction series at a time when *Star Trek* was king on television, and how the development of another space station–based series, *Star Trek: Deep Space Nine*, impacted *Babylon 5* (and vice versa). We'll also look at the challenges of pitching a show that would take five years to tell its story and not have everything wrapped up each time the credits rolled. These are key ingredients in the building blocks of the show.

If there is one aspect of *Babylon 5* that enshrines the idea of legacy, it is the impact it had on television that followed. Genre television as it exists today is in part shaped by *Babylon 5*. *Lost*, *Battlestar Galactica*, *Buffy the Vampire Slayer* and *The Expanse*, to name just a few, owe something to *Babylon 5*, which opened the doors for networks to produce shows that embraced story arcs and long-form storytelling.

Most intriguingly, *Star Trek* has gone down the same revolutionary path *Babylon 5* took in the '90s. While credit must be given to the tremendous work done on *Star Trek: Deep Space Nine* (something we'll delve into), modern Trek like *Star Trek: Discovery* and *Star Trek: Picard* has moved beyond the episodic model of storytelling to tell longer, more complex story arcs that span a whole season or more.

J. Michael Straczynski's *Babylon 5* told science fiction stories that audiences had never seen. Its legacy as a pioneer in genre television cannot be underestimated.

Babylon 5's *Place in the Science Fiction Genre*

Babylon 5 is a show with a passionate and loyal fanbase, but it is rare that you will see it top the "best of" lists of science fiction television. Whether it is the distraction of dated CGI that was revolutionary at the time, the alienness of the show compared to the more human-centric shows like *Battlestar Galactica*, *The X-Files* and *The Expanse*, or the fact that it has always lived in the shadow of that almighty *Star Trek* franchise, there is a perception that it was doing great things but was very much of its time.

There certainly are elements that feel dated. The computer-generated imagery feels a little cartoonish by today's standards. The show was produced without the more expensive model work employed by the *Star Trek* shows and thus feels less timeless than its contemporaries, *The Next Generation* and *Deep Space Nine*. The clunkiness of some alien designs, like the insectoid N'Grath from *Babylon 5*'s first season, equally dates the show.

These issues of dating are largely cosmetic. When it comes to character work and storytelling, the show was ahead of its time. Conflicts and issues like Earth's xenophobia resonate today far more than they ever did in the '90s; more outlandish ideas like the Shadows are drawn from cultural references like *The Lord of the Rings*, which make it richer and more accessible to wider audiences. Whether social issues like alcoholism and drug addiction, or the issues of race, religion, politics, or media representation and identity, there is so much to relate to in a show that is three decades old.

It's almost a given that a character will come out of a five-season TV show very different from how they went it. But that was not always the case. With the rare exception of *Deep Space Nine*, the crews of the USS *Enterprise*-D and *Voyager* were largely the same after years of traveling the galaxy. There were events that shaped them, but they were still the same people we met in the first episode.

By contract, the characters of *Babylon 5* were different. G'Kar started as a vengeful villain and ended up as a spiritual leader. Londo went from being a joke among his people to becoming the Centauri emperor. Loyal Earthforce captain John Sheridan turned traitor, and then became president of the galaxy. Lennier went from bumbling aide to tragic warrior, and Lyta from loyal Psi Corps telepath to freedom fighter.

Sweeping story arcs changed the landscape of the galaxy. Earth rose into a xenophobic dictatorship and collapsed into civil war. The Minbari were broken and reborn under new leadership. The Vorlons went from mysterious aliens to allies, then enemies, before leaving the galaxy for good. Babylon 5 became a station about peace before switching to become the headquarters in two pivotal wars. Across the five seasons, J. Michael Straczynski's use of long-form storytelling revolutionized not just *Babylon 5*, but genre television as a whole.

Babylon 5 is a largely respected institution in the science fiction genre. It feels dated because it was the first, but it is recognized for everything it was trying to achieve and how it delivered its epic story arcs. *Babylon 5* will rarely top 10 lists because shows like *Battlestar Galactica* and *The Expanse* came after, building on what the show did. *Star Trek* and *Star Trek: The Next Generation* will largely hit higher in the ranks, because they were more popular and spring-boarded a whole franchise of TV shows and movies.

This is evident whenever you search for lists of greatest sci-fi TV shows. In 2020, *Rolling Stone* placed *Babylon 5* 29th in its 50 Best Science Fiction TV Shows of All Time.[3] While *Star Trek: The Next Generation* was a little higher at 23, *Star Trek: The Original Series* was first, *Battlestar Galactica* third.

> This show became a fan-favorite because it wasn't content to just use tales of outer-space diplomacy as a cover for ideological beard-stroking—this was unabashed hard sci-fi, full of its own self-contained mythology and blessed with a kick-ass make-up department.

Despite barely scraping into the top 30, *Rolling Stone* recognized the importance and maturity of *Babylon 5* as a piece of science fiction television. Along with the fun mention of a kick-ass makeup department—you only have to look at the Narn and Minbari to agree—it is the show's approach to mythological storytelling that earns its respectable place on the list.

That appreciation was reflected in *Paste Magazine*'s 2018 list of the 100 Best Sci-Fi TV Shows of All Time.[4] Noting that it was "a rare example of a series that carried out the exact number of seasons it initially planned, it was as such well-planned from the start and featured deep continuity," the article placed *Babylon 5* at 25th. In comparison, *Star Trek: The Original Series* was sixth, *Star Trek: The Next Generation* second, and the almighty *Battlestar Galactica* took top spot.

Similarly, Rotten Tomatoes took its "Tomatometer" data, culled from critics' reviews, a number of reputable "best of" lists, and some editorial discretion, to create their own list of the 100 Best Sci-Fi TV Shows of All Time. *Babylon 5* came in at 18, with *Star Trek: The Original Series* fifth, *Star Trek: The Next Generation* fourth and *Battlestar Galactica* once again in first place.[5] *Babylon 5* is regularly recognized among its peers, but rarely has the pulling power to climb the ranks of the top 10.

There will certainly be fans, this author included, who will rank it higher than its contemporaries and the shows that followed. You often have to look beyond the restraints of '90s technology to get there, but when you do, you are rewarded with rich storytelling and characterization and an understanding that the work *Babylon 5* did laid the foundation for all that followed.

Unlike more overt genre television stalwarts *Star Trek* and *Buffy the Vampire Slayer*, *Babylon 5*'s influences across genre television are a little less apparent, and as such are a little less recognized.

Babylon 5, *30 Years On…*

People are still talking about *Babylon 5* now. That's not bad a for a TV show that ran for five seasons and finished in 1998. There was a huge buzz when the show was remastered on HBO Max in 2021, not just because it was a chance for old fans to revisit the show and bring new fans to the franchise, but because it gave people the chance to reevaluate its impact on genre television.

The long-form storytelling, character arcs, the development of a complex mythology; these are all things television audiences now take for granted. Richard Edwards asked in his 2021 article for TechRadar, "Is Babylon 5 secretly the most influential TV show of the past 25 years?"[6] The answer may be yes. As Edwards points out, Straczynski was a showrunner before audiences even knew what a showrunner was, and *Babylon 5* laid the groundwork for multi-season arcs decades before *Lost* and *Breaking Bad* came along and popularized the model.

There is great interest in what *Babylon 5* was doing and what it might do again. Twitter discourse with Straczynski[7] is allowing fans to share their love of *Babylon 5* and chat with the show's creator just as he did during the '90s on the Usenet group rec.arts.sf.tv.babylon5 and similar groups, such as GEnie and CompuServe.[8]

Most significantly, in the age of TV reboots and revivals, the talk of Straczynski's planned *Babylon 5* reboot at the CW network had the internet abuzz with excitement—and trepidation. Would it be as good as the original? Would it be its own thing, separate from the stories Straczynski has already told?

As the show celebrated its 30th anniversary, the internet was still waiting for bated breath for news of if, and when, the reboot would come.

The age of podcasting is giving people the platform to share their love of *Babylon 5* like never before. The number is growing daily, from *Yum Yum*[9] to *Grey 17*,[10] *The Last, Best Babylon 5 Podcast*,[11] and of course my own podcast *A Dream Given Form* for the We Made This network,[12] not to mention popular YouTuber reactions like Medusa Cascade.[13] The conversation about *Babylon 5* feels more active now than it has done in years.

Ultimately, *Babylon 5* has long been too big to be a hidden gem, but not big enough to garner the same buzz as those top-10 listers. It is a curiosity and a cult favorite. But the conversation of late is changing. People are talking about the show again with excitement, passion, and praise.

It might be that *Babylon 5* will get even more recognition as people reevaluate its influence and impact on science fiction television.

2

Science Fiction Story Arcs

Babylon 5 existed long before *The Gathering* aired on the TNT network in February 1993. J. Michael Straczynski spent years developing the series, engaging with production companies and studios as far back as 1986 and writing the pilot in 1987.

As he describes it, "It took us five years to find a company that believed in this story long enough to let us tell it."[1]

There were two big reasons for this. He was told that no American space-based science fiction series other than *Star Trek* had gone more than three seasons in over 20 years. He would be lucky to get two seasons, let alone five. But that science fiction juggernaut wasn't the only hurdle. This wasn't a show that would follow the classic television model, and that was a risky unknown for everyone involved.

> The idea back then was that when the end of the episode comes up, you hit the reset button and start the next one fresh. Maybe you might get a two-parter, but that's about it. Stations and networks felt strongly about that because they didn't think the American public had the attention span to cover more than two episodes.[2]

As Straczynski describes it, there was no appetite for what he was calling a novel for television. You have to admire his ambition and ability to not compromise on his vision. This was a show that would set up a story that might not be resolved for a year or two. Sinclair's "hole in his mind" and the mystery of the missing 24 hours at the Battle of the Line would be teased in *The Gathering*, revisited in "And the Sky Full of Stars," discussed in season two opener "Points of Departure," and then only fully resolved in season three's "War Without End." Similarly, the disappearance of Babylon 4 would also take two seasons to resolve.

And these are just small examples in the grand scheme of things. The tease of the Shadows in season one's "Signs and Portents" would play out all the way through to the epic "Into the Fire," early in season four. Lyta would first make contact with a Vorlon in *The Gathering* but not learn about the truth of the Vorlons' plans for telepaths until season five's "Secrets of the Soul." There was a degree of patience required when it came to these story arcs, but the payoff was almost always well deserved.

Babylon 5 was a show built around several big mytharcs. The Shadow War. The rise of a xenophobic dictatorship on Earth. The conflict between the Religious and Warrior Castes of Minbar. The rising tensions with the Psi Corps. The more personal arcs often centered around characters who become spiritual figureheads in the fight against darkness—from G'Kar to Delenn, Sinclair to Sheridan—as well as Londo's personal rise and fall into darkness.

There are multiple mytharcs at play in *Babylon 5*. In his 2020 book *Myth-Building in Modern Media: The Role of the Mytharc in Imagined Worlds*,[3] A.J. Black delineates two distinct mythologies that can be applied to the five-year story arc Straczynski planned for the show: the monomytharc and the cultural mytharc.

Black notes that the monomytharc, which draws upon the 12 stages of Joseph Campbell's "hero's journey,"[4] concerns a protagonist whose path, traversing the constructs of initiation, rebirth and transformation, is internalized through external forces. In *Babylon 5*, several key character arcs follow this journey, most notably the leaders Sheridan and Delenn.

Sheridan is initiated into station life at the start of season two as a replacement for Sinclair and quickly finds himself battling the external forces of the increasingly corrupt and xenophobic Earth and the much greater threat of the Shadows. It is Sheridan's discovery of the Shadow threat in season two's "In the Shadow of Z'ha'dum" that is his true "call to adventure"; the realization that he needs to join Delenn and Kosh in their army of light against the darkness spreading across the galaxy. From this point in the show, he is no longer just the captain of a diplomatic space station. He is now a leader in the fight for the survival of everyone within and beyond Babylon 5. Kosh becomes his mentor.

The corruption of President Clark's Earth serves as a turning point for Sheridan, as his commitment to fight against the Shadows directly conflicts with his duties as an Earthforce captain. Season three's "Severed Dreams" acts as the moment he truly crosses the threshold, giving up his home, his family and his career to protect Babylon 5 in the coming war with the Shadows. It is a significant step in his journey, culminating in his death and resurrection at the hands of Lorien at Z'ha'dum.

This is a literal moment of rebirth for Sheridan. Lorien serves as the goddess persona of Campbell's monomyth and Black's monomytharc, guiding him to a higher purpose. Sheridan is never the same person again. He is transformed. The return from Z'ha'dum is a very literal interpretation of his journey to galactic savior and revolutionary in the wars that come to a head in season four. The Interstellar Alliance becomes the final boon, the glorious victory after all the ordeals Sheridan had faced. It's only natural that he takes his place as president of that alliance as the show heads into its final year.

Similarly, Delenn goes through her own monomytharc. Her initiation into the Grey Council and Babylon 5 comes prior to the events of *The Gathering*, but are explored through flashbacks that detail her own path to leader in the army of light against the Shadows. Her call to adventure can be reflected in her own literal rebirth and transformation to half-Minbari, half-human at the start of season two as a symbol of the alliance between both races in the encroaching Shadow War. She certainly faces her own trials, namely the breaking of the Grey Council and decision to ally herself wholly with Babylon 5 in season three's "Severed Dreams." She would also face her own past actions in season four's "Atonement," a revelatory episode that fills in the pieces in her own mytharc and would be expanded further in the TV movie *In the Beginning*.

Forever tied to Sheridan, Delenn becomes a leader in the Shadow War—and later the brief Minbari civil war—and a key player in the newly formed Interstellar Alliance of the show's final season. While multiple characters have their own internal monomytharc—particularly Londo and G'Kar—*Babylon 5* revolves heavily around the epic journeys taken by Sheridan and Delenn to fight the good fight and forge peace.

The cultural mytharc, which reflects our emergent concerns and cultural touchstones through we which define our place in the world, is also a cornerstone of *Babylon 5*'s overarching mythology. The rise of a fascist Earth under President Clark and the corruption at the heart of Earthforce also taps into the historical events such as the rise of Nazism, while also becoming increasingly comparable to real-world struggles as time progresses. Hatred, xenophobia, and the never-ending debate over cultural identity dominate Clark's Earth in *Babylon 5*, while also serving as a mirror to the real world. This extends to other cultural themes, such as the manipulation of the media and free speech, and the fear of the unknown and how that impacts the audience's understanding of the world we live in.

There are also hints of Black's third definition of mythology, the divine mytharc, in the control and manipulation of the younger races at the hands of the Vorlons and Shadows. The Shadow conflict becomes something of a holy war that drives the arcs of Sheridan and Delenn, as well as Sheridan's predecessor, Sinclair, who eventually becomes a spiritual figure of his own as Valen, a thousand years ago.

These grand mytharcs shape the narrative of *Babylon 5*, enriching Straczynski's universe in a way that science fiction television had never really achieved before. Kirk and Picard never really had their own monomytharcs in their TV shows, save perhaps for Kirk's path in the *Star Trek* movies. While the series would often use fantastical settings for cultural observations, these were singular events, rather than unfolding mythologies. *Lost in Space* had the narrative arc of trying to get the Robinson family home, but never had the depth of world-building seen by the likes of *Babylon 5* and beyond. The 1970s *Battlestar Galactica* probably had the largest sense of mythology, though this would be expanded to much greater effect in the reboot—the divine mytharc of the Cylons' plan forming a cornerstone of that series.

Even when framed through the journey back to Earth, *Lost in Space* and *Battlestar Galactica* still kept the arc as largely background detail, focusing instead on the episodic adventures of the week. But across its five-year arc, *Babylon 5* would change the perception of how we saw televised mythology forever.

The Five-Year Narrative

What is the five-year arc of *Babylon 5*? There are several long-form narratives vying for attention, but they are all ultimately tied to the events of the Shadow War. The Earth–Minbari war that preceded the show occurred during the Grey Council's search for the enemy. The corruption of Earth and the rise of Londo and the Centauri through seasons one to three were about the influence of the Shadows and their manipulation of the younger races. The Psi Corps and the telepath legacy were ultimately revealed to be cannon fodder, created by the Vorlons to fight the Shadows.

The Shadow War came at the show's midpoint, shaking everything up and plunging the galaxy into chaos. Even after its resolution early in season four, the Minbari and Earth civil wars and the Drakh revenge against the Centauri in season five were all centered on the fallout of the Shadow influence on the galaxy.

If season one was focused on world-building and seeding the Shadows into the story, season two saw their string-pulling result in catastrophic changes, like the fall of the Narn regime and the building of the army of light to fight the darkness. Season three would see the Shadows move openly, with the resolution of that war taking place in the fourth season. The fallout with Earth and the Minbari would likely have seeded through season five, had Straczynski been able to stick to his plan. But despite this pivotal change, the final year continued the theme of fallout from the Shadows in the actions of the Drakh and the fall of Centauri Prime.

The five-year arc did not go as originally planned. The unexpected

2. Science Fiction Story Arcs 15

departure of Michael O'Hare as Sinclair altered Straczynski's plan for the show. We'll explore that in more detail when we look at JMS's ingenious use of character trapdoors to replace Sinclair with Sheridan. The threat of *Babylon 5* ending with season four forced Straczynski to wrap up several plot threads much earlier than planned, making it more of a four-season arc and an epilogue season.

Despite these changes, *Babylon 5* still delivered a five-year novel for television, just as Straczynski had envisioned when he spent half a decade pitching the show to different networks. We might have had less Byron and his rogue telepaths and more expansion of the season four conflicts, but it told a complete story.

In his 1863 book, *Die Technik des Dramas*, German novelist and playwright Gustav Freytag coined the Freytag's Pyramid, the "definitive study of the five-act dramatic structure." The exposition, setting up events to come; the rise, building on the setup; the climax, where events turn, and the protagonists find themselves on the back foot; the return or fall, where the protagonist fights back; and the catastrophe, or dénouement.

While it might be simplistic to attribute this structure to *Babylon 5*, you could also argue that each season in fact falls under these motifs, beat for beat. Season one, "Signs and Portents," is all about world-building, adding the exposition around the different races and sowing the seeds for the Shadows. We learn everything we need to know about the fallen Centauri Republic, making Londo's action more understandable when he accepts Mr. Morden's offer of help. Humanity is given a rich and believable future; it is grimier than the utopian ideals of *Star Trek*, but it certainly feels more realistic, with politics and media just as much a part of everyday life as worker's rights and all the vices we still have today. By the end of season one, bigger events have been set up and the dominos are ready to start falling.

Season two is ominously titled "The Coming of Shadows," building on that world with an increasingly corrupt Earth and the Shadow influence leading to conflict and loss. The Centauri rise to absolute power, crushing the Narn. The Shadow influence is more keenly felt and the Nightwatch is born. The rising darkness is a key theme in many episodes, building on the worlds established in season one.

Season three is the climax—the titular "Point of No Return"—where Babylon 5 is forced to break away from Earth and the Shadow War begins. This is truly the climax to two years of careful world-building. Sheridan and his staff are forced to reject their careers and their homes to stand up against Clark and his fascist Earth. The Shadows move openly, and the galaxy is plunged into war. The dam well and truly bursts.

In season four, "No Surrender, No Retreat," the forces of good fight back, defeating the Shadows (and Vorlons) and freeing Earth from the tyrannical clutches of President Clark. It is the moment in which all those dark powers—be it Clark or the Shadows—fall from their lofty positions and the heroes return to reclaim the galaxy.

While it is largely an epilogue to the great conflicts of years three and four, season five, "The Wheel of Fire," is very much the aftermath. What happens when our heroes win? What happens when those allies of the Shadows seek revenge? Freytag argues that in a narrative structure, this would be where the protagonist dies; indeed, season five ends with the Alliance damaged, the Centauri in ruins, and the demises of both Sheridan and the station. We'll delve into each season in greater detail later in this book.

It is clear how Straczynski coined *Babylon 5* as a novel for television. Shows like *Star Trek* might go on for one season or seven, but while cancellation might leave a few plot threads hanging, the episodic nature of these stories would not impede what had already been told. *Babylon 5* was different. It needed the exposition, the rise, the climax, the return, and the catastrophe to tell its story. Ending the story before it was ready would leave *Babylon 5* unfinished. It would be *The Lord of the Rings* after Helms Deep, or *Dune* after Paul Atreides and his mother had been banished to the desert. The story would not be complete.

That made the development of *Babylon 5* such an innovative and challenging undertaking. That Straczynski delivered the five-year arc is a testament to his talents as a writer and everyone involved in the show.

And perhaps there was a little bit of luck too.

Long-Form Storytelling in Sci-Fi Today— from Battlestar Galactica *to* The Expanse

While *Star Trek: Deep Space Nine* was one of the first science fiction shows to start embracing *Babylon 5*'s use of long-form storytelling and multi-episode arcs, it was certainly not the last. *Babylon 5* revolutionized genre television to the point where solely episodic storytelling often felt like a thing of the past.

Space: Above and Beyond was something of a precursor to the likes of *Battlestar Galactica* 10 years later. Developed by Glen Morgan and James Wong, who cut their teeth on *The X-Files* for two seasons, it told the struggles of a group of space marines against alien invaders over the course of its single 23-episode season. As *Babylon 5* was entering its third season, *Space: Above and Beyond* mixed stand-alone missions with a longer story arc that was ultimately cut short by the show's cancellation. Like *Babylon 5*, and later the *Battlestar Galactica* reboot, it offered a darker, grittier, and more realistic side of humanity and explored the ramifications of war on its characters over multiple episodes. Had it aired even a decade later, it might have survived longer than it did. Instead, it remains another curious innovator in the move to more long-form storytelling in science fiction television.

Star Trek would fully go down that road in an attempt to save the dying television franchise with *Star Trek: Enterprise*. After two seasons of weekly adventures in the same vein as *Star Trek: The Next Generation* and *Star Trek: Voyager*, the final *Star Trek* show of the Rick Berman era launched an "innovative" season-long arc for its third season and brought a mix of stand-alone and multi-episode arcs for its fourth. It wasn't enough to keep the franchise afloat, but it made *Star Trek* more exciting again, and when it finally returned in 2017, both *Star Trek: Discovery* and *Star Trek: Picard* embraced season-long arcs.

But by that time, science fiction television had changed completely. From *Battlestar Galactica* to *The Expanse*, audiences were no longer treated to episodic adventures. The stories ran multiple seasons, telling epic mytharcs—the divine mytharc of the Cylons' plan for humanity and the monomytharc of Holden and the crew of the *Rocinante*. Wider genre television like *Lost* had spent six years telling the story of the mythical island and the survivors of Oceanic Airlines flight 815. These were compelling, character-driven stories and audiences were invested.

Straczynski's work on *Babylon 5* was widely recognized as being the gold standard for long-form storytelling. While he wasn't directly involved in the development of two of the 21st century's greatest genre shows, his influence was there from the word go.

> Ronald D. Moore sent me a copy of the *Battlestar: Galactica* pilot script to look at with an eye toward using our multi-year structure, and Damon Lindelof later told me that they borrowed our structure straight up for *Lost*. Those two shows further crystallized the five-year arc structure, ... that really made a huge impact even though initially you didn't initially see it happening in the mainstream shows.[5]

Of course, genre television is littered with the corpses of TV mytharcs. Just as *Space: Above and Beyond* died after a single season, so did the many attempts to take *Lost*'s crown after the show ended. *Invasion*, *The Event*, and *Flashforward* are just a few shows that attempted to get a slice of the *Lost* audience and failed. *Journeyman*, *Almost Human*, and even *Firefly* remain some of the most interesting one-season wonders—though at least Joss Whedon was able to follow up *Firefly* with a big-screen adventure in *Serenity*.

But whereas many attempts to tell televised mytharcs failed, others succeeded. The *Battlestar Galactica* reboot remains the gold standard for science fiction television in the 21st century. From the mystery of which character might be a Cylon to Baltar and Six's twisted relationship, the internal power struggles of the fleet, the Cylons' divine plan and the search for Earth, Ronald D. Moore's show became water-cooler television for many.

Moore joined a whole host of innovative showrunners who followed in J. Michael Straczynski's wake. Joss Whedon broke ground with *Buffy the Vampire Slayer* and *Angel*. J.J. Abrams launched *Alias* and *Lost*, before heading to the big screen with continuations of the almighty *Star Trek* and *Star Wars* franchises. Vince Gilligan gave audiences *Breaking Bad* and *Better Call Saul*, regarded as two of television's finest dramas. Russell T Davies brought back *Doctor Who* for the modern age, before handing over the reins to Steven Moffat (and eventually returning for the show's 60th anniversary). Noah Hawley gave us excellent dramas like *Fargo* and *Legion*. Shonda Rhimes built a television empire, from *Grey's Anatomy* to *Bridgerton*. And of course, credit must be given to Straczynski's contemporary in '90s science fiction television, *The X-Files*'s Chris Carter.

Straczynski ushered in long-form storytelling and story arcs and became one of the first significant showrunners on television. Science fiction was changed forever by *Babylon 5*. While it might not have directly influenced the shows that followed, *Babylon 5* laid the groundwork. It is because of Straczynski's vision for a five-year novel for television that the doors were opened for the kind of innovative and much-beloved television shows we've become used to over the last 20 or so years.

3

The Development of *Babylon 5*

"What was the spark that ignited your desire to create B5?"

That was the question posed to J. Michael Straczynski on the rec.arts.sf.tv.babylon5.moderated message board back in 1995, just as the second season of *Babylon 5* was airing its eighth episode, "A Race Through Dark Places."[1]

His answer was split into three points.

1. The approach to doing a science fiction television show within a reasonable budget. His experiences on *Captain Power and the Soldiers of the Future* had shown him that long-term planning was partly to blame, and he decided that instead of "[going] in search of new worlds, building them anew each week," a fixed space station setting would keep costs at a reasonable level.
2. He'd interviewed and known too many science fiction producers who knew absolutely nothing about the genre, didn't respect the genre, just wanted to collect the bucks and get out. He wanted to change that. Science fiction television *could* be taken seriously.
3. As a lifelong fan of grand science fiction sagas like *Foundation*, *Childhood's End*, *The Lord of the Rings* and *Dune*, he kept wondering: why hadn't someone done this for TV?

The answer, it turned out, was that we were waiting for Straczynski to come along. Before Oceanic flight 815 crashed on the mythical island and before the Cylons' grand plan for humanity. Before the war for the Iron Throne, before the hosts took over Westworld, and before Rick Grimes woke up in a zombie apocalypse. Before all that, there was the war against the Shadows and the dawn of the Third Age of Mankind.

It is interesting that Straczynski was also driven by practical needs just as much as his vision for an epic canvas of storytelling. While he would soon learn that his inexperience as a showrunner would create issues when it came to production on *The Gathering*, he had learned enough through his career to know that budgets mattered. *Babylon 5* was never going to get the money thrown at it that *Star Trek* would. There had to be practical solutions to tell the story he wanted to tell.

This serious approach to science fiction would extend right down to his "no cute kids or robots" mandate, though there would be exceptions to that (Straczynski would clarify that this related to the series regulars, in an effort to ensure there was nothing on the show like Wesley Crusher or the bots from *Buck Rogers*).[2] This was a future that would be gritty and realistic, not filled with trite, crowd-pleasing moments that had been a staple of much of science fiction television to that point.

The development of *Babylon 5* as an idea was very much an organic process, as Straczynski himself has documented extensively.

> Once I had the locale, I began to populate it with characters, and sketch out directions that might be interesting. I dragged out my notes on religion, philosophy, history, sociology, psychology, science and started stitching together a crazy quilt pattern that eventually formed a picture. Once I had that picture in my head, once I knew what the major theme was, the rest fell into place. All at once, I saw the full five-year story in a flash, and I frantically began scribbling down notes.

Babylon 5 may have taken more than five years to go through concept to pilot, but the journey to *The Gathering* was far longer than that. It was both an attempt to change the way audiences—and studios—saw science fiction television and the crucible through which everything Straczynski had built in his career would come to fruition.

In this chapter we will examine that career, looking at JMS's work as a writer that led to the development of *Babylon 5*, the success that followed, and delve into other factors that led to this five-year novel for television.

From He-Man *to* Murder, She Wrote

J. Michael Straczynski has had an extensive career as a writer. For fans of *Babylon 5* watching the show when it first aired, it was likely that they had already seen his words brought to life on screen through some of their favorite kids cartoons from the '80s.

Surviving a truly traumatic childhood—one that Straczynski would reveal in his fascinating, but somewhat harrowing autobiography, *Becoming Superman*—his love of comics sustained him into his adult life and ignited his love for the written word. Fueled by his admiration for the

3. The Development of Babylon 5

works of Harlon Ellison (who would later become a mentor and friend to Straczynski) and Rod Serling, he would achieve degrees in psychology and sociology before starting a career in journalism.

His first creative credit came when he pitched a script for *He-Man and the Masters of the Universe*, one of the juggernauts of children's animation. His first credit on IMDB is for the 1984 episode "Trouble's Middle Name." Straczynski would go on to write eight further episodes and his success would see him working with Larry DiTillio to develop the spin-off *She-Ra: Princess of Power*. After Filmation refused to give Straczynski and DiTillio credit as story editors, he moved on to *Jayce and the Wheeled Warriors*. He would also be one of the best writers associated with *The Real Ghostbusters*, the popular animated spin-off from the 1984 movie.

Straczynski moved into live action, working as script editor and writer of 10 episodes of the science fiction "kids" show *Captain Power and the Soldiers of the Future*. Having already written one episode for season two, he became story editor for the third season of the '80s reboot of *The Twilight Zone*. He would write 10 further episodes and be credited for adapting a classic story, "Our Selena Is Dying," by one of his idols, Rod Serling.

Prior to *Babylon 5*, Straczynski's live-action TV writing career would continue apace, with scripts for *Jake and the Fatman*, *Walker, Texas Ranger* and *Murder, She Wrote*. The Angela Lansbury crime drama would be his last regular writing gig before *Babylon 5* was picked up.

Heading to Epsilon Eridani

Straczynski's work as story editor on season one of *Captain Power and the Soldiers of the Future* set the foundation for the work that he would do on *Babylon 5*. It was his first experience of writing for live television and it allowed him to formulate the ideas for what would become *Babylon 5*. As he describes it in his autobiography, if his work on live-action science fiction show *Captain Power* was a set of training wheels, then *Babylon 5* was a Harley-Davidson.[3]

Straczynski wrote and pitched the pilot script for *Babylon 5* to *Captain Power*'s producers, Doug Netter and John Copeland, and they agreed to help sell the series. Both would come onboard for the show as producers along with Straczynski's cowriter Larry DiTillio (who would remain for the first two seasons).

With Netter and Copeland on board to help with the pitch, Straczynski assumed the whole process would take a few months. It took five years.

That process included a pitch to Paramount, which we will cover in a future chapter. The relationship between *Star Trek* and *Babylon 5* is worthy of its own discussion.

Warner Bros., who had partnered with several station groups to create the Prime Time Entertainment Network (PTEN), considered *Babylon 5* for one of two original series slots in its first year. To say it was a struggle to get the show made was an understatement, right down to Straczynski's pitch to the station executives. All his carefully conceived plans came crashing down when, minutes before the pitch, a broken molar forced him to mumble his way through the presentation.

Time Trax and *The Wild West* won the two coveted slots at PTEN. Fortunately, there was support from PTEN co-chairs Evan Thompson and Dick Robertson. A pilot was ordered, only for it to come crashing down when *Star Trek: Deep Space Nine* was announced at Paramount. For the first time, but not for the last, the development of the very similar, space station-based *Star Trek* series would put the creation of *Babylon 5* in jeopardy. PTEN, understandably, was cautious about putting money into a show that might be seen as a rip-off of the almighty *Star Trek* franchise. There was the question of whether it would gain any audience at all.

Through luck, determination, and the support of Thompson and Robertson, the pilot was made. However, the challenges did not stop there. Straczynski admits that his choice of director, Richard Compton, was a terrible mistake.[4] Without the experience of being a showrunner, Straczynski watched as Compton went with a very different approach than what the showrunner wanted, focusing more on smoke, lenses, and lightning rather than the actual actors.

> When filming on the two-hour pilot began on August 10, 1992, Richard kept modifying the alien prosthetics at the last minute to make some of them more cartoony, then pushed forward to upstage the scientifically accurate aliens that I wanted to feature. Each time I complained he said it was an accident, or that the makeup didn't look good on camera, and promised to fix it for the rest of the scene. But Richard knew that once he put the extras where he wanted them in the master shot, we couldn't change them later because the shots wouldn't match during editing.

In his rather frank account of the pilot filming in his autobiography, Straczynski talks about the fantastic work of the art department and production designer John Iacovelli being obscured by haze and shadows at Compton's insistence. Straczynski lost control of the very thing he had spent years developing and hated the final version. He believed this was the death of *Babylon 5* before it had even been broadcast.

And yet, somehow, it managed to survive Compton's attempts to sabotage everything Straczynski had worked for. *The Gathering* tested positively in focus groups. Better still, its 10.3 national broadcast rating was higher than the debuts of the other two shows PTEN had picked up to series.

Despite proving its worth, it still took three months for *Babylon 5* to get a full series order. Much of its unique concept had already been stolen by the debut of *Deep Space Nine*, and it wouldn't air its first season until January 1994, by which time the *Star Trek* series was already halfway through its second.

Babylon 5 began production in an abandoned hot tub factory in Sun Valley. It was far removed from the sort of big studios used by Paramount for the *Star Trek* shows, but it allowed Straczynski and his team to work largely without interference. Despite the threat of cancellation each year—and the collapse of PTEN in season four—work on *Babylon 5* pushed on. It proved itself as a piece of science fiction that could compete with the likes of *Star Trek*, while also introducing story arcs and a gritty, more realistic vision of humanity's future that had not been seen on science fiction television. Straczynski stopped getting studio notes after the second episode of season two.[5]

There would be other challenges, which we'll cover as we delve into each season, but the long struggle to get into production was achieved. *Babylon 5* was open for business.

A Career Beyond Babylon 5 … and Back Again

For the next seven years, Straczynski's career was dominated by *Babylon 5*, its spin-off TV movies, and the short-lived *Crusade*, which we will explore in much greater detail later in this book.

Aside from a brief return to *Murder, She Wrote* with the TV movie *Murder, She Wrote: A Story to Die For,* Straczynski's love of comics saw him move away from scripted television and into the worlds of Marvel and DC. Setting up his own company, Joe's Comics, Straczynski would create beloved titles such as *Rising Stars* and *Midnight Nation* before being asked to write for *The Amazing Spider-Man* in 2000. In the same year, he would also take up the offer to write the pilot script for the Showtime series *Jeremiah*, a show he would run for two seasons.

While *Jeremiah* proved to be a less than rewarding experience, Straczynski's career as a comics writer saw him flourish. Comics were where he found a love of stories as a child, and through comics, he established himself as a successful and celebrated writer.

Straczynski's *The Amazing Spider-Man* #36 won the Eisner Award at San Diego Comic-Con. Praised for the way Straczynski and the artists sensitively handled the events of 9/11 through the eyes of Spider-Man and other Marvel heroes, Straczynski's words resonated with readers everywhere. It remains an essential comic to this day.

> Only madmen could contain the thought, execute the act, fly the planes. The sane world will always be vulnerable to madmen because we cannot go where they go to conceive of such things. We could not see it coming. We could not be here before it happened. We could not stop it. But we are here now. You cannot see us for the dust, but we are here. You cannot hear us for the cries, but we are here.

He would also reinvent *Thor* in 2007, and his work would heavily influence the first Marvel Cinematic Universe *Thor* movie in 2011 (a film which features a cameo from Straczynski himself as the first man to try to lift Mjolnir), before working on his beloved *Superman* with *Superman: Earth One* in 2010.

After years of development, Straczynski would also write the Clint Eastwood–directed *Changeling* in 2008, based on the real-life case of Christine Collins, who took on the L.A.P.D. after they tried to pass off an impostor as her missing child. Straczynski would be nominated for a BAFTA for best original screenplay. He would also pen the screenplays for *Underworld: Awakening* and *World War Z* before returning to television and working with the Wachowskis on *Sense8* in 2015.

Straczynski's attempts to incorporate more diverse ideas into *Babylon 5*, such as the idea of the first transgender character in Delenn, or the romance of Susan Ivanova and Talia Winters, ultimately struggled to reach fruition, something we'll explore further later in this book. But with *Sense8*, Straczynski and the Wachowskis were able to create a far more progressive drama that resonated with the LGBTQ+ community, while telling a challenging and thought-provoking story. It only managed two seasons on Netflix before it was canceled due to high production costs. However, it was granted a final two-hour episode to wrap things up. *Sense8* proved that Straczynski was still a force to be reckoned with on television.

There have been many attempts to revive the *Babylon 5* franchise, and this book will certainly explore those struggles. But the fact that Straczynski returned to the franchise as the show reached its 30th anniversary, this time in a full reboot, showed that there was still plenty of magic to come from him, as he reimagined a future audiences fell in love with almost three decades ago.

4

Babylon Prime

Even with his revolutionary approach to creating a five-year story arc for television, not everything J. Michael Straczynski planned in his original pitch to Warner Bros. made it to the screen. Actors would come and go, and ideas would change.

Nothing lives in a vacuum, and when you have networks, cast and crew, audiences and all the other elements that go into the making of a television show, there are hundreds of different factors that could change the direction of the story.

As such, it's easy to see why so many TV shows prior to and post–*Babylon 5* are more content to think in the short- to medium-term. What does the next year of television look like? What characters do audiences most respond to? Could we use a plot point or character beat from an earlier episode and explore that more thoroughly?

This looser approach can be incredibly successful. James Marsters's Spike was only meant to be in five episodes of *Buffy the Vampire Slayer* and then killed off.[1] But he was so popular, with the crew and fans alike, that he lived on and became a regular from mid-season four onward—and in the final season of spin-off show *Angel*. In *Star Trek: Deep Space Nine*, a throw-away reference to a secret fleet in season three episode "Defiant" was used to create the epic two-parter "Improbable Cause" and "The Die is Cast," which would have huge ramifications for the show's Dominion plot moving forward.[2]

Even in *Babylon 5*, a novel for television all mapped out from the start, Straczynski admitted that sometimes "we were kinda making up the rules as we went."[3] The most significant change he made would occur when he was forced to wrap up the main conflicts in the show during the fourth season, after PTEN collapsed, leaving the fifth season to flounder before it found its feet again with the Drakh and Centauri threats.

It cannot be overstated how much the change of the lead character had a significant impact on the direction of the show. The original plans for Sinclair and Delenn feel a million miles from what we got on screen. Some elements were translated across to Sheridan's arc, but there are key differences too, some of which might have never seen the light of day even if Michael O'Hare *had* stayed on as Jeffrey Sinclair.

In this chapter, we will delve into the earliest days on *Babylon 5* and explore the original five-year concept for the show and proposed follow-up series *Babylon Prime*.

The Original Plan for Sinclair and Delenn

For any fan, the idea of looking back at the original plans for a show and comparing them to what we got is fascinating. Fortunately, *Babylon 5* fans were provided just that, in the form of the 15th volume of *Babylon 5: The Scripts of J. Michael Straczynski*. It contained a seven-page story outline given to Warner Brothers executives early in production on season one, drafted in response to a request to explain where the show was going. It's a detailed, but not necessarily complete idea of Straczynski's plans for the next five years.

Given that he had been developing the show since the late 1980s, this isn't the earliest draft of the *Babylon 5* story, but it remains the most complete version of his original plans.[4]

This memo would have been written in late 1993 or early 1994. As such, it is not surprising that there is little difference between outline's season one and the one that we saw on screen. Sinclair would try to figure out the hole in his mind from the Battle of the Line, Babylon 4 would return in "Babylon Squared," President Santiago would be assassinated, and Delenn would undergo her transformation. These events all take place largely as they did in that first full year on screen. As several online posters have noted, the only real omission seemed to be the lack of anything Bester and Psi Corps related.

The most notable, and understandable, difference between the memo and *Babylon 5* as we saw it was the continuation of Sinclair as commander of Babylon 5, something which also followed through into the plans for the follow-up series. This is not surprising, given that Michael O'Hare's difficulties that led to his departure weren't known to Straczynski until later in season one's production.

The second-year notes aren't too far removed from what we saw, despite Sinclair still being in command. Delenn would emerge half-human, though the reason for her change would be more overt than what we saw on screen: to become Sinclair's mate after the revelation at the Battle of the Line that he was the savior of the Minbari people. There is no

4. Babylon Prime

mention of Valen; it would be revealed early in season two that the Minbari have been gradually becoming infertile over the last 2,000 years. The savior, it seemed, would mate with a Minbari and their child would save the Minbari race.

Straczynski's note suggests two significant issues with this. The Warrior Caste of the Minbari would interpret this prophecy differently and believe a Sinclair/Delenn pairing would destroy their species. Catherine Sakai would continue to become a more prominent character, after her engagement to Sinclair in season one.

The "coming of Shadows" would play out similarly to what we saw in season two. While it is unclear whether there would be a Narn/Centauri war in the second year, Londo would continue to become complicit in his alliance with the Shadows, orchestrating a series of disasters and reversals for the Narn regime, undermining them in the buildup to the conflict that would follow. Kosh would reveal himself to all when he saved Sinclair's life at the end of season two, much in the same way as he did with Sheridan in "The Fall of Night."

The first big trajectory change, therefore, seems to be the motivations for the Minbari saving Sinclair at the Battle of the Line and Delenn's reasons for becoming half-human. Without Sinclair, those ideas were diluted. Delenn's actions would be more symbolic than practical.

It is also worth noting that the notes suggest a slower buildup than those we saw in the completed second season. Much of what took place in season two of *Babylon 5* on-screen appears to have been moved up from Straczynski's original plans for season three. The Narn home world would fall to the Centauri, with the help of the Shadows. However, G'Kar would appear to leave the show several episodes later, returning to the Narn home world to join the resistance.

In what might have been a variation of the Talia plot from season two's "Divided Loyalties," Catherine Sakai would be "mind raped" and leave the show. A traitor would also be revealed to be working against the station. With Sakai gone, the Sinclair and Delenn romance would begin. Audiences would also discover that the Vorlons had been manipulating the younger races, while the Shadows sought to rule the galaxy in rebellion against this manipulation.

There is no mention of Babylon 5 breaking away from Earth or the onset of the Shadow War, two events that would be pivotal to the third season and change the direction of the show forever.

The fourth season, therefore, is largely unrecognizable from the show we got. There are some similar narratives; Garibaldi would fall off the wagon and quit as security officer, just as he did in the televised fourth year. However, he would become a mercenary. The Shadows and Vorlons would wage a war against each other, but not directly, manipulating the younger races to do their bidding instead. It would plunge the galaxy into chaos. Finally, Sinclair would impregnate Delenn with their prophesied child and savior of the Minbari race.

The Vorlon and Shadow "war" would end in the fifth and final season, with the destruction of a huge Vorlon mothership (described as being hundreds of miles long) by the Shadows. With the Vorlons becoming extinct, the Shadows would end up ruling the galaxy from behind the scenes. Londo's involvement with the Shadows would become public knowledge as the Centauri attempted to claim Babylon 5 space.

Rather than offering any real resolution however, information would be leaked by the Vorlons, blaming Earth for the destruction of their mothership, that would make Sinclair appear to be a traitor. The Warrior Caste would launch a military coup on Minbar, forcing the Grey Council into exile and starting a second war with Earth. The Minbari would eventually attack and destroy Babylon 5. Garibaldi, Sinclair, Delenn, and their baby would escape just in time.

Had events played out as they did in this outline, *Babylon 5* would have been a more sedately paced show than the one we got. There is obviously a lot of detail missing—the outline only really refers to Sinclair, Garibaldi, Delenn, Londo, G'Kar, Kosh, and Catherine Sakai—so it is hard to understand without the context of the rich world-building and narrative nuance apparent in the show. Most significantly, it ends on a cliff-hanger, without the narrative triumphs seen in the fourth and fifth seasons of the show.

The original concept of *Babylon 5* feels very much like the first half of the story, with elements like the defeat of the Shadows and the formation of the Interstellar Alliance taking place in the follow-up series, *Babylon Prime*.

The Second Five-Year Arc

Straczynski intended *Babylon 5* to be its own series, with *Babylon Prime* to follow only if there was an appetite for it. It is surprising, then, that many of the elements that made it into the (admittedly condensed) third and fourth seasons of the show played out over a 10-year arc in his original plans. The five years of this version of *Babylon 5* would offer very little closure. The heroes on the run, Babylon 5 destroyed, and the Shadows ruling the galaxy make for a very dark climax.

But if *Babylon 5* ended on somewhat of a sour note, ultimately the failure and destruction of Babylon 5 as a station, then *Babylon Prime*

4. Babylon Prime

would be the triumphant fight against evil, playing out events that eventually took place in the third and fourth seasons of the televised run.

Assuming the episode "Babylon Squared" would have remained in season one, then the payoff would not occur until the first season of *Babylon Prime*. Sinclair, Delenn, and Zathras would use the Great Machine on Epsilon III, to travel back nine years and steal Babylon 4. However, unlike "War Without End" from season three of *Babylon 5*, they would bring the station to the future—the present—and use it as a base to start an alliance against the Shadows and their influence on the galaxy.

Renamed Babylon Prime, the station would move through space. However, the unstable time fields would have ramifications, with Sinclair aging into the older version we saw in "Babylon Squared." More significantly, Sinclair and Delenn's child would grow into an adult rapidly and become a messianic figure to the people of the galaxy, the leader of this new alliance.

Over the course of the series, Londo would capture Sinclair and Delenn and then betray the Shadows, setting them free. Possibly this would have played out as we saw in *Babylon 5*'s opening episode to season one, "Midnight on the Firing Line," where Londo had a dream of dying throttling G'Kar, and may have played out, again, similarly to the future events audiences saw in "War Without End."

Sinclair and Delenn's child and his allies would defeat the Shadows, while in a twist of events, the Minbari would lose their war against Earth. Sinclair would find his name cleared and would split up from Delenn, as she returned to the Grey Council on Minbar to help her people recover. And while Sinclair and Delenn's child would become the leader of a new Interstellar Alliance, Sinclair would retire to a completely uninhabited planet, where we leave him fishing.

Putting the narratives of both shows together, it seems that *Babylon 5* would have been much more of a slow burn, with big events like the outbreak of the new Earth–Minbari war and the Shadows destroying the Vorlons only taking place in the final season. *Babylon Prime*, however, feels like it was filled with many of the crowd-pleasing moments that resonated so much with fans in the third and fourth seasons.

Again, it is hard to say whether the original *Babylon 5* and *Babylon Prime* plans would have been better or worse than what audiences eventually got. The final version of the TV show certainly appears to be the more thrilling option of the two.

There is also a lot that is missing. Sheridan is the obvious example, but then, it was never the intention that Michael O'Hare would need to leave the show after one season. Again, the notes for *Babylon Prime* offer no mention of President Clark, Bester, or the Psi Corps. The entire Earth civil war is noticeably absent from both series plans, along with the role of the resident telepath (Talia and then Lyta), who in the televised *Babylon* 5 was a key weapon in the Shadow War and its fallout.

There may be reasons for this. Walter Koenig might not have been cast as Bester at this point, and it is possible his fantastic, villainous performance was what prompted so many memorable returns to the show. The Earth civil war may have been swept aside by the second war with the Minbari. With the death of most of the Vorlons in the fifth season of this version of *Babylon 5*, the telepath characters may have had a more limited role to play.

G'Kar is also a character that seems to disappear from season three of *Babylon 5*. While he might have reappeared in *Babylon Prime*, there seems to be nothing in those pages to suggest that he would become the beloved spiritual figure that emerged after the conquest of Narn. There is very little mention of other Earthforce characters, outside Garibaldi's fall from grace in season four. The Rangers are also noticeably absent, given the role they, and in particular Marcus Cole, played in the events of the show.

But of course, a scene page outline is just that, an outline. The richness of the world-building and characterization we saw on screen is hard to convey in a rough 10-year plan. The seven-page memo offers just a glimpse of what might have happened.

How Much of These Concepts Survived?

You can certainly see snippets of these ideas used in different ways on the show. Catherine Sakai's fate seems to be a mix of Talia's hidden personality and the loss of Anna Sheridan. Whether Sakai would have been the traitor alluded to in the plans for *Babylon 5*'s third season remains little more than conjecture but suggests that Straczynski always had a plan to use the hidden traitorous personality Control, for use whenever a key actor chose to leave—as we saw with Andrea Thompson (Talia). In any scenario, the loss of the commander/captain's life is narratively needed for a romance with Delenn to take place.

The Sinclair and Delenn romance, potentially seeded as early as the religious ritual in season one's "The Parliament of Dreams," is carried across to Sheridan and Delenn. There is no messianic child, though the unseen David is conceived by the show's end, and Sheridan himself takes on the role of president of the Interstellar Alliance. What role David would have played in the proposed *Babylon Prime* spin-off remains a mystery. That we got *Crusade* instead suggests that this idea was dead long before season five came along.

4. Babylon Prime

The conflict with the Religious Caste on Minbar, and the breaking of the Grey Council, can certainly be seen in the actions of Delenn and Neroon through the first four seasons of *Babylon 5*. This internal civil war was massively watered down and contained within just two episodes in the show's fourth season, likely the casualty of Straczynski's need to wrap things up by the end of season four. The infertile Minbari concept is replaced by "Minbari souls reborn in humans" angle. Garibaldi does quit his role as chief security officer in season four, though this is due to Bester's manipulation, not Garibaldi's return to the bottle.

Babylon Prime is less recognizable from the events of the TV show, though Sinclair and co. stealing Babylon 4 and Londo freeing Sinclair both follow similar paths to "War Without End." The Interstellar Alliance, it seems, was always the ultimate go-to; it would just have taken a lot longer to get there in this version—ten years rather than four.

The seven-page memo is a fascinating "what if?" scenario and is fun to explore and debate. But plans always change, and it's hard to imagine we would have got everything we saw in those pages. Even if O'Hare had stayed, it was a struggle to keep *Babylon 5* renewed every year. The fall of PTEN after season four would certainly have quashed plans for another six years of television.

So, while the memo remains a curiosity, perhaps it is better that fans got the complete story. Even if took just four years (and an epilogue season) to tell it, rather than a decade.

5

A Chat with Peter Jurasik (Part 1)

Who is the most important character in *Babylon 5*? Whose monomytharc is central to the narrative? As we have already explored, it could be Sheridan and Delenn, who bravely went against their own peoples to help fight a war against the Shadows, saved the galaxy, and forged peace in the Interstellar Alliance. But if the epic five-year arc of *Babylon 5* could be summed up in one individual's mytharc, then it might also be the long and tragic tale of Londo Mollari.

Babylon 5 is the story of fallen republican Londo Mollari, a Centauri ambassador who dreams of the glory days of old and emerges as a powerful figure, thanks to his alliance with Mr. Morden and the Shadows. While he seemed to be a villain for much of the show's run, there was good in Londo. Across the five seasons, he battled the darkness and found redemption, turning against the Shadows and becoming a founding member of the Interstellar Alliance.

But Londo's story was a sad one, and season five saw him pay the price for his actions. Achieving his dream of becoming the Centauri emperor, he found himself a puppet for the Drakh as they sought revenge against him, living a life of loneliness and despair to save his people. Salvation only came in his final moments, dying at the hands of his mortal enemy turned friend, G'Kar.

Londo Mollari was brought to majestic life by veteran actor of stage and screen Peter Jurasik. After starting out on Broadway in New York, Peter moved to L.A. in the '70s and picked up an amazing roster of TV and film performances. In addition to his award-winning performance as Londo in *Babylon 5*,[1] Peter is best known for roles such as Crom in 1982's *Tron* (a film also starring Bruce Boxleitner) and Sid the Snitch in *Hill Street Blues*. His sci-fi credentials also extend to '90s cult shows like *Third Rock from the Sun* and *Sliders*.

5. A Chat with Peter Jurasik (Part 1)

In an exclusive interview for this book, I had the opportunity to talk to Peter Jurasik about his time on *Babylon 5* and his memories of working with the cast and crew. This interview took place before the announcement of the 30th anniversary event, animated movie *The Road Home*, involving the surviving members of the *Babylon 5* cast.

There was so much to talk about that I couldn't possibly contain it all within one chapter. This is the first part of that chat, with the second half to follow later in the book.

BAZ: *Londo is one of TV's greatest characters, with an amazing arc over the five seasons the show. What was it like to play a character like Londo Mollari?*

PETER: Well, you know, I can't help but talk about the fact that I am gifted to be an actor, and a successful actor. I love acting. There are so many people who love to act. Any work that I do, I enjoy. Whether I'm reading on stage, or just doing a poem, or if it's a TV series, or a film. I love the work.

So, what [was] it like to play Londo? Well, in this case, he is one of maybe one or two characters in my 50 years as an actor, that is so rich and so nuanced. To see him grow and change, it was a complete and utter delight. I'm sure, Baz, you and the people who are reading the book understand that, especially on TV, characters are written to fill a slot. And so you're either the bad doctor, or you're the bad guy, or you're the good doctor, and you're the good guy. And once they get that character working, well, then they just stay with that, because that works so well in their storyline.

J. Michael Straczynski's scripts [for Londo] were such a gift. You talked about this wonderful arc. And, you know, he put me on to that, he told Andreas [Katsulas] and me a little bit at the beginning, a little bit about that arc that was happening, in what he referred to as the bible. And he talked to me about some arcs, and the character.

That's a dream come true for an actor. I was really lucky. I love work, no matter what I'm doing; good or bad, I'm happy to be working. And, you know, I enjoy the process of acting. There are some challenges when you don't have a great script. But these were wonderful scripts. When I got the pilot script, I stepped outside of our house—we lived in California then— and sat on the front porch and read the script. And my wife reminds me all the time that I said to her, which I rarely do immediately, that I would *love* to play this character. I want to play this character. I could tell by the nature of the writing, and how JMS had positioned the character at the start, that I wanted to be a part of him. So I can tell you, it's a gift for an actor.

B: *You mentioned that Joe gave you a bit of detail about Londo's arc at the beginning. He was quite a sympathetic, fallen hero at the start of season one. Did you know that he was going to become one of the primary villains of the show?*

P: Both Andreas and I were both quite aware. I had never met Andreas before. I had seen his work as the One-Armed Man [in *The Fugitive* (1993)] and I knew I knew of his work with Peter Brook. He had a sterling career. By coincidence, we both auditioned exactly at the same time, which was really just serendipity. There were hundreds of actors coming in. So we were lucky, that way. And even then, we talked about the fact that G'Kar was painted so dark at the beginning, and he was clearly going to be the villain. And I was painted the fool, the lost soul, the man stuck in the corner; that's how I like to look at it.

Both of us knew we didn't want to play *that* for five years. Joe let us know the plan, pretty early on. We did the pilot, and established the characters, but he let us know we were going to grow out of those. I didn't know I was going to become as villainous as Londo became, but I was glad to get out of that corner.

I was moved from one of the one of the poles—one of the extremes—towards center, that's how I look at it. And he took Andreas's character, who was on the other extreme—that really dark, villainous kind of character—and moved him center. So he let us know we were going to grow as actors, and if we wanted, the series bible was open to us to read.

B: *Did you know the big turning points were coming, like Londo's deal with the Shadows, starting the war with the Narn, the murder of Cartagia, or him becoming emperor? Or did you find these out in the scripts when you received them?*

P: No, I didn't know. Joe would have been happy if we wanted to sit down in his office and talk about the arc. But for me, as an actor, I think that would be really distracting for me. You start playing ahead, or playing for a result, and I wasn't gonna, you know? I knew that wasn't a good thing to do. You can't stay in the moment.

That's really one of the basic things you have to do as an actor, right? Play the moment and stay in the moment. Why am I here? What am I doing here? If I'm playing the future, or playing what's coming up, it doesn't help us very much. Being in the present is really, really good stuff. You need it as a person, and you need it as an actor.

Joe would have explained if I asked. Going into Joe's office was a really interesting event. I'll tell you a story. On *Hill Street Blues*, David Milch was the writer of my character. I played a character named Sid the Snitch. He was a goon; he'd do anything for 20 bucks. A real lowlife. David would follow you around a little bit on the set, and you would find stuff floating into your character, that you had been talking about, or that you were living. He was really on you, and listening to what you were doing.

Joe didn't work that way. Joe wrote the script and expected us to do that. If I didn't like something back on *Hill Street Blues*, I could go to Steve Bochco or David Milch and say, this is not working. Or I don't know why we're doing this. Or, you know, the classic "the actor says, my character wouldn't say this. I wouldn't do that."

But Joe wasn't about that. The first time I went in to ask him about a problem, how he handled that was great. He was so patient. He stopped what he did was doing and we sat in his office. I remember him either offering me a cup of coffee or something to eat. He made me feel really comfortable and then said, "Tell me about what you're thinking." I talked to him about the script—it was it was in the first season, I'm sure—and we talked about the dialogue. And he really listened, and I thought oh, well this is great. He's just going to make all my changes.

But at the end, he said, "That's great, Peter, I like how you're thinking about it, but we're not making any changes!" He just gave me a plain old "no, we're not we're not doing it." He didn't do it in a rude or a mean way. He just let me understand that he heard what I was saying, and he had listened to it, and acknowledged it, and gave me the thumbs-up and thanks. And "but no, we're not doing it. You're saying my words. You're doing my story." That's partly because he had the story all worked out in his [head], you know?

B: *It was quite revolutionary for television at the time, to have a five-year arc planned out in advance.*

P: Absolutely. I did, I don't know, maybe ten pilots in my career. So there was a lot of series work. And many, many guest roles, a lot more guest roles than I can even count. When you get cast in the role, they're going to nail you into that little frame. And they're going to make you stay in that, because it works for them as writers, to have a character they can use, to move this plot forward or this story forward. The idea, as you say, to have a character change. I mean, I don't know what to say, that completely surprised me.

We were as excited, probably as much as the fans or anybody else, when we got our scripts [for *Babylon 5*] each week. We'd look at them and think, wow, this is great. Look at the changes that are going on. He not only built that into the story, but he led us as characters that way. "Just stay with me here, watch what I'm doing and follow my lead. And I won't let you down at the end." Which he didn't, of course. He finished the arc for everybody.

B: *When I spoke to Pat [Tallman] and Marshall [Teague] about their time on* Babylon 5, *what struck me was how they talked about a deep camaraderie between the cast. Can you share some of your experiences working with your fellow cast members on the set of* Babylon 5?

P: I've been cast in a number of recurring roles, on four or five different series, and the idea that everyone's going to get along is just crazy. The idea that people are going to like each other. You put ten people in a room and give them a common project to work on—not everyone's gonna get along. But we were a lucky group, that way. That's all I can say. We were lucky, because we liked each other, and we supported each other and gave each other room.

Jerry Doyle was a smart son of a gun and had a really sharp, bright mind, and he could tear you apart with his tongue, if he wanted. Claudia is a wonderful, sweet woman. But she's smart and sharp, and you better have your wits on you, when you're hanging out with her! And Mira, just standing back from her, you could feel the presence of who she was. When she came to this project, as I always say about Andreas, she was already a star. I was a veteran actor, even when I came on to *Babylon 5*. We were lucky that we fit so well together.

We all had trouble in the first season with Michael [O'Hare], but we were unaware that he was not well. That was a bump in the road that we didn't understand. But when Bruce Boxleitner came in, he just fit, you know, just like a hand in a glove. He's a perfectly elegant guy. He and Bill Mumy, for instance, couldn't be further apart politically. They got along just great. What can you say about Bill? Bill Mumy is an established person, who has been around and done a ton of work. He appreciates the work and he's there to do the work. He's not there to, you know, to battle, or struggle or fight. He's there to do good work. Bruce was the same way. So, maybe it was just good luck. We have good people and I think we were lucky enough that we were all mature enough, or nice enough, or smart enough, or something enough, that we were not going to get into a struggle.

Stephen Furst and I were like two schoolgirls together. We just loved being with each other, as two actors. I had met him on the *Mary Tyler Moore* lot, when I was doing *Hill Street Blues* and he was doing *St. Elsewhere*. He and I ran into each other, and we knew each other, but we weren't buddies. But we became fast friends on *Babylon 5*, and we really adored working with each other. I think you can see it in a lot of the work, that we're having a good time, we're enjoying ourselves. Andreas and I were the same way. I did most of my work with them.

But the truth is, we were lucky. I really believe that, because you can just as easily end up on a set and say, I hate that person, and I can't stand seeing them. And God forbid you hate that person, and you have to have a friendly, or God help us, a romantic relationship with them. Well, then you're in real trouble! I've got to kiss the person I hate!

I can't tell you how Andreas and Mira connected, but I could tell you about how they worked together. I watched them work together. And I can tell you, they danced. They danced really beautifully again, whenever they had to work. So that tells you all you need to know.

When we were off screen, we were a really tight cast. We would eat together, have lunch together. Joe would usually come out and have lunch with us. So he set the tone. Also, the number one on the call sheet, Bruce Boxleitner, or Michael O'Hare, set the tone for that. That's why the first year there's a little rockiness. Because Michael was rough, as we didn't know anything about it. We didn't know about it.

B: *I guess that's because Joe sheltered Michael, protected him from what was going on?*

P: That's right. But Bruce set the tone. The producers set the tone. We had wonderful people like Doug Netter and John Copeland, as our producers. They were great. The makeup people, Optic Nerve and Greg Funk; those people were fabulous. All wonderful personalities and wonderful people. That's lucky!

B: *So, you mentioned Bruce Boxleitner. I know you were in* **Tron** *together, and you guest-starred in his show* **Scarecrow and Mrs. King.** *But did you know Bruce well, when he came on in the second season?*

P: I didn't know him well, but he and I are both contemporaries. We both landed in Hollywood at the same time. We're both the same age, and while we have different points of view on some stuff, we were friends, and we knew each other, and we were supportive of each other. We would run into each other here, there, elsewhere, in auditions. I didn't have a word with him on *Tron*. Not a word. But I knew him, and I hung out with him on *Scarecrow and Mrs. King*.[2]

As I said, the number one person, who's leading the cast, is an important person for balance and harmony. That person is very important because again, they set the tone for the cast. And he's perfect for that. He does it without any kind of pretense. He's got to play this perfectly nice character, which was a pain in the ass, when you've got to play the perfect individual, the captain. Thank God he had Joe writing, because eventually, he went through his arcs too!

But Bruce handled that easily. Not everybody can, as they say, put the ground on and walk and be comfortable doing it. But Bruce felt comfortable in the number one role and led us and kept it casual. He's a nice, elegant actor, and great guy to have. And, you know, I'm still friends with him. Not buddies. I was buddies with Andreas. I was a real buddy with Stephen, and Bill now. Bill and I are now close and real buddies.

B: *Let's talk about Andreas Katsulas. You said you became buddies off camera and on camera, you had so many amazing scenes together. What was it like working with each other?*

P: It's funny, because so many people comment on our relationship. But I haven't talked that much about [it], and well, I wish Andreas was here to talk about it with us. Because for me, it was such an easy relationship. Off camera, we just liked each other. He was a goofy, funny guy. And I'm a goofy funny guy. But what was really interesting about our relationship was that as actors, we had very different approaches to how we did our work. I don't want to go into what his acting techniques were or what his background was. I refer people to look at Peter Brook to understand the kind of actor he was. Andreas was a world-class stage actor, and he worked truly from the inside out. He would get ready to do the work. But he was not in any way one of these actors who said, "Oh, call me G'Kar, don't call me Andreas." Because when the scene ended, he was able to relax, and get his cigarette, and joke around and be a normal guy. But his working process was from the inside out of the character. He was always dealing was G'Kar's guts first, and then pushing it out.

I am practically the polar opposite. I work on a character from the outside in. I'm much more of a stage actor. That's how I was taught. So, for me, walk, talk, how I move. It's important. Now, how did that end up for he and I? Well, we ended up being [a] wonderful complement to each other again. We could have clashed. But in fact, we two people just fit together. A little ying and yang there. He loved how I approached the work, and I loved how he approached the work. I watched him do it, but I was not in competition, or anything like that. He was a completely generous actor. He was also a completely loose cannon, in the sense that he would do just about anything at any time. And that was a really, really wonderful guy to have around.

So, I would have loved to have heard what he had to say. But I think he would say he had a good time and really enjoyed being with me. We always looked forward to being on the set together. We didn't laugh as much as Stephen [and] I did. Because, as I said, we were like goofy little schoolgirls, giggling together. You know, I think people wanted to give us a little shot on the head. But Andreas was serious about the work. Not overly serious, but he liked to get it done and focus on it. He took it to heart as they said, he approached his character of G'Kar from the inside out, if that makes any sense to you. If you're an actor, that makes all the sense.

5. A Chat with Peter Jurasik (Part 1)

B: *The Londo and Vir relationship was just as special as Londo and G'Kar's. What was it like working on those scenes together with Stephen Furst?*

P: Well, again, how Joe brought Stephen onto the show, that was really, really smart writing from an actor's point of view. I saw what he did. He started Londo in one corner; he put me at one pole. Londo was a guy who was ready to fall; he was a drunk, he was lost. He was super troubled and all that. And because of that, he was also funny. He was comedic. He was a source of humor, you know, the poor sentimental republican Centauri.

By bringing Vir in, it was clear that he was going to handle comedy and allow me to move to a more serious tone. Stephen and I, we both love comedy. So we had a ball, doing comedy. We could make each other laugh pretty easily and we loved amusing each other during the work. So, working with him, that was part of the fun.

But what was great about Joe's scripts, and working with Stephen, is that we would have a great time doing the comedy, but when we had to move towards more serious stuff, it was easy to do. Stephen was already an established actor, had done plenty of film and *St. Elsewhere.* You know, he was doing scenes with Denzel Washington! And the guy could act, right? He did a lot of good work, and he was also a director. Stephen had that overview, going onto the set, he had this director's eye. So when we moved towards the more serious stuff, we moved pretty easily. I trusted Stephen a lot, and he trusted me. Again, that's really important. I also trusted him to let him set the tone for us. I would do my stuff, and I'd watch carefully what he was doing and giving me back. I knew that he had a great sense of his character. He understood the inside of Vir.

You know the famous story of him auditioning and coming into the audition. Right? And Joe said, well, that's Vir!

B: *Yes! He put hand soap in his hair to make it stand up, got soap into his eyes, and bumbled into his audition, apologizing for the hair. And Joe immediately found the actor he was looking for.*

P: Yes, that's it. Stephen had a lot of Vir in him. He understood that character. He had the energy of that character. He's the only actor I know who—I was laughing about this with a friend a month or so ago—we were talking about auditions and Stephen is the only actor I know who had an agent call for [a] Stephen Furst type. They were looking for a Stephen Furst type! Stephen said, "Hey, you're looking for a Stephen Furst type? I'm Stephen Furst!"

He did not get the role! He didn't get the role, of course, because he didn't get in to read for the role and there's something humorous about that. But he understood those Stephen Furst types. He got it. The character he played in *Animal House* was in a really interesting position, that character. He understood Stephen Furst types and did them really well. And Vir was the classic Stephen.

This was a guy who really understood acting, understood directing, and we also tickled each other. It was a funny bonus. We would laugh all the time. I'm sure that the directors and the technicians, at some point, were like how do we get rid of these two? They're having too much fun. Why are we paying them? These two are getting paid to do this?! We had such a good time with it. It wasn't like that with Andreas, not because I wasn't having fun, but it wasn't overt fun like that. We would giggle a lot and have a really good time.

B: *You talked about character arcs. Londo and G'Kar went from hero and villain to vice versa, and back again. Vir started as a kind of bumbling, almost clownish character to start with. Then we got to season four and all the stuff with the mad Emperor Cartagia, which was on a whole other level. So serious and so dramatic, but so beautifully done.*

P: Well, again, it all came out of Joe. You have those characters like Vir, who, as you said, was so bumbling at first. In the beginning, Londo was also bumbling. I see it as a line, moving left to right across the line. Comedy on one end, and drama on the other. And, you know, he started us way on the edge, on the comedy line. But he eventually got us to do stuff where, you know, Londo got Vir to kill the emperor, and said, "Yeah, that's okay. You're gonna be all right with that." I mean, that's great writing by Joe and a great challenge for us!

B: *You certainly rose to the challenge, because those performances on screen were amazing.*

P: We were having such a good time, and both of us appreciated a good script. It was good. All of us knew, at some point, "Hey, Joe's got this." That's a wonderful feeling.

My exclusive chat with Peter Jurasik continues later in the book.

6

From *Star Trek* to *Babylon 5* ... and Back to *Star Trek* Again

Star Trek has come up a few times in this book and will do so again. It's impossible to talk about *Babylon 5* without looking at the long, and influential, shadow the *Star Trek* franchise had over it.

With the successful return of *Star Trek* to the small screen in *Star Trek: The Next Generation*, the adventures of Captain Picard and the *Enterprise*-D were the crowning jewel of science fiction television heading out of the '80s. There was the occasional live-action series like *V* or *Buck Rogers in the 25*th *Century*, but nothing could compare to the juggernaut that was *Star Trek*.

Babylon 5 sits in the period when live-action science fiction television was in its renaissance, and it was competing in a busy field. *Star Trek* was still the only dominant space-bound series, while *Quantum Leap*, *Sliders* and *The X-Files*, those staples of early '90s cult television, focused on the past and present Earth (or alternate versions). *Babylon 5* had to compete under that shadow, only made more difficult by the emergence of *Star Trek: Deep Space Nine*.

To this day, the second live-action *Star Trek* spin-off is seen as something of a rival to *Babylon 5*, not least because of their shared premise. Both were space station–based science fiction dramas. Both were a bit grittier than *Star Trek: The Next Generation*. Both featured more nuanced characters and dealt with spirituality and war. The similarities are startling, leaving many fans of each series to believe the other was a direct rip-off.

Of course, that wasn't the case. There are many unique differences between *Babylon 5* and *Deep Space Nine*. But it is also hard to ignore similar concepts, with both launching in the very same year. There is more to the shared premises than you might realize.

The Babylon 5 *vs.* Deep Space Nine *Debate*

Which is better? *Babylon 5* or *Deep Space Nine*? It has been a long, ongoing debate (for the record, this author loves both) about which came first and who copied who. The short answer is *Babylon 5* did not do any copying. Straczynski had been developing his show since the '80s, and while *Deep Space Nine* had managed to broadcast a season and a half before the first full season of *Babylon 5* aired, his plans for the show preceded the first episode of the *Star Trek* spin-off. *Babylon 5* was its own thing and didn't need to look to that show for inspiration.

The longer answer is somewhat more complex and is shrouded with enough rumor and supposition that the truth will never really be made clear. Straczynski pitched to Paramount—the home of *Star Trek*—in 1989. There were rumblings of a deal before Paramount rejected the pitch, but it was Warner Bros. who picked up the project for their new Prime Time Entertainment Network (PTEN). This was announced formally in November 1991, shortly before production got underway on *Deep Space Nine* over at Paramount.

During his pitch to Paramount, Straczynski had provided the pilot script, the series bible and some concept art. Paramount knew everything and *may* have used some of those ideas for their *Star Trek* spin-off. Straczynski's then wife Kathryn was working as a paid writer's intern at Paramount and soon learned that the plans for *Deep Space Nine* were eerily similar to *Babylon 5*. In fact, it brought her internship to an end, as she was forced to step away from *Star Trek* altogether due to the conflict of interest with her husband's show.

A short while later, Straczynski received a call from his friend Walter Koenig, who gave all the details on the upcoming *Star Trek* project.[1]

> Joe, it's about an Earth-sponsored space station, identified by a name and a number, located in neutral territory, that serves as a meeting place for alien races, with a bar, a casino, a female second-in-charge, and a shape-changer.

In *Becoming Superman*, Straczynski noted that he had given all his development material to Paramount during the pitch, and everything had gone positively, and then there was radio silence. Given later statements that emerged, Straczynski suggests that Paramount Studio executives knew all about *Babylon 5* and let the material be used to develop *Star Trek: Deep Space Nine*.

This is backed up by an online comment in 2013 from Stephen Hopstaken, who worked in the publicity department for Warner Bros. In response to an *Io9* article looking at *Babylon 5* on its 20th anniversary, he wrote,[2]

6. From Star Trek to Babylon 5 ... and Back to Star Trek Again

I was told they purposely took what they liked from the B5 script and put it in the DS9 script. In fact, there was talk of leaving the B5 script intact and just setting it in the Star Trek universe.

There is no concrete confirmation as to whether these claims are true, and a response from Paramount is unlikely to ever come. But it is hard to deny that there are distinct similarities between the two shows. Given that Paramount had Straczynski's full production notes on *Babylon 5*, there was certainly the potential for that material to be used to develop *Star Trek*'s first space station–based show.

When Paramount got ahead of the game with *Deep Space Nine*, Warner Bros. almost canceled *Babylon 5*. Paramount was putting together their own syndicated network, which would compete with PTEN for the small number of independent TV stations. With $12 million being spent on the pilot of *Deep Space Nine*, compared to *Babylon 5*'s $3.5 million—and the weight Paramount carried—it was clear which one would come out on top.

Straczynski's request to Warner Bros. to seek legal action fell on deaf ears, and it was only through the efforts of Evan Thompson and Dick Robertson, the co-chairs of PTEN, that the pilot was made at all. Fortunately, the show survived this struggle. We have already covered the challenges of making *The Gathering* and getting the subsequent first season greenlit in a previous chapter. But framed through the rivalry between Paramount and Warner Bros., getting *Babylon 5* to series feels like something of a Herculean triumph against the odds.

Babylon 5 might never be as big as *Star Trek*, but it was able to hold its own. Unfortunately, the timing was terrible for *Babylon 5* as both shows' narrative similarities made it look as if it had copied *Deep Space Nine*. The debut of a warship in their respective third seasons, for example. The USS *Defiant* turned up in September 1994. Captain Sheridan was presented with the *White Star* in November 1995.

There is the flip side in the "who copied who" argument. *Babylon 5* was consumed by the Shadow War that broke out in the second half of season three—April 1996. That ran for a season and a half, counting the Earth civil war that followed. *Deep Space Nine* kicked off an ambitious two-year war arc with its season five finale in June 1997.

Did *Babylon 5* copy *Deep Space Nine*, and then did *Deep Space Nine* copy *Babylon 5*? Almost certainly not. They were their own shows, doing their own thing. If anything, *Babylon 5* remains the more influential of the two, with its use of long-form storytelling likely paving the way for narrative decisions in the later seasons of *Deep Space Nine*.

Perhaps these shared similarities come down to the very simple idea of a limited number of stories. There will always be variations of a theme—Shadows, Dominion, *White Star*, *Defiant*—but any narrative can be boiled down to a handful of plots. Christopher Booker's *The Seven Basic Plots: Why We Tell Stories* suggests there are just seven stories in existence: Overcoming the Monster, Rags to Riches, the Quest, Voyage and Return, Comedy, Tragedy, and Rebirth.[3]

Perhaps *Babylon 5* and *Star Trek: Deep Space Nine* truly follow the same story—Overcoming the Monster. In both shows, the protagonist sets out to defeat an antagonistic force (often evil) that threatens the protagonist and/or protagonist's homeland, be it the Shadows or the Dominion. Both Captain Sheridan and Captain Sisko lead the fight from their respective stations, both saving humanity from insurmountable odds. A station meant for peace becomes the center point for a grand, galactic conflict.

The nature of "copying" is something of a moot point. There may be only so many ways a space station–based series can go over the course of multiple seasons. Perhaps those similar narratives are all one big coincidence.

Or perhaps Paramount did copy Straczynski's work and made it their own. If they did, no one is going to admit it.

The Star Trek *Pitch*

The relationship between *Babylon 5* and *Star Trek* is a complex one. How much influence Straczynski's notes had on the development of *Deep Space Nine* is up for conjecture. But regardless, his use of long-form storytelling and story arcs surely helped pave the way for multi-episode narratives and the season-arc stories in science fiction television. And that impact did lead to a change in style for the *Star Trek* brand when it resurrected its TV franchise with *Discovery* and *Picard*. Episodic stories were out, and series-long arcs were most definitely in.

But J. Michael Straczynski almost had a more direct influence in the direction of the *Star Trek* franchise.

In 2004, *Star Trek: Enterprise* would enter its final season and the death throes of the *Star Trek* TV legacy that had started way back in 1987. The franchise was stale, and ratings were down. Something new was needed to shake things up.

In that same year, Straczynski and *Dark Skies* creator Bryce Zabel wrote a 14-page treatment for *Star Trek: Re-Boot the Universe*. The full treatment, available online,[4] makes for a fascinating look at how these writers might have set the franchise on a new path, going back to the beginning with Kirk, Spock, and McCoy. However, Paramount Pictures

6. From Star Trek to Babylon 5 ... and Back to Star Trek Again 45

was already on the same page, with the first steps toward what would become the "Kelvin" *Star Trek* movies already in development. As such, the idea was never pitched.

There are some distinct similarities between *Star Trek: Re-Boot the Universe* and the Kelvin movies. It was a reboot rather than the Next Generation of the *Next Generation*, focusing on new versions of the original trio, Captain James T. Kirk, Science Officer Spock and Dr. Leonard McCoy.

> We will start with a two-hour pilot that tells the story no one has ever seen: the circumstances that lead Kirk and McCoy (friends before this) to meet Spock for the first time. It will involve their discovery of a lost city on an uncharted world, nearly a million years old, and their encounter with the race that built it, a race long sought after by every civilized world for the tremendous advantages they could provide.

There are trademarks of the reboot movies in this pitch, mixed with some of the mythological approach to ancient races and civilizations we saw in *Babylon 5*. Straczynski and Zabel cite *The X-Files* as a key example of the approach this rebooted *Star Trek* might take, weaving in stand-alone stories, ongoing character development and "mythology episodes" to build a show that feels something of a hybrid of the '90s *Babylon 5* and *Star Trek* models.

The season one breakdown gives a full picture of how this might have worked, mixing mytharc with stand-alone storytelling. The approach would bring in respected science fiction writers, something that goes all the way back to Harlan Ellison—Straczynski's mentor and friend—who wrote one of the original *Star Trek*'s greatest episodes, "The City of the Edge of Forever." There would be a mix of reimaginings of classic stories and new. Straczynski and Zabel were looking to optimize the potential a *Star Trek* reboot would bring.

The pilot episode would deal with the coming together of Kirk, Spock and McCoy and their journey to the *Enterprise*. There would be four or five episodes of ongoing arc-driven narratives, the equivalent to the "mythology" episodes of *The X-Files*. Another four to five episodes would come from stories pitched by major writers in the science fiction and fantasy genre, adapted for screen. Another four to five episodes would reimagine episodes from the original *Star Trek* series, then a bunch of stand-alone adventures and a finale that would "drop a huge clue into play, and forces the *Enterprise* to take a stand, putting its very existence on the line."

The Kelvin movies opted for the safer route—a *Star Trek* not too far removed from the "prime timeline." In fact, J.J. Abrams's approach of making the 2009 reboot a sequel to the *Star Trek: The Next Generation* era as well as a prequel and reboot, would allow the new movies to spin off without ignoring fans of the old.

Straczynski and Zabel, however, were bolder than that. This was a full reimagining. Their pitch suggests that the look and feel of their *Star Trek* would be unlike anything committed to screen before. How might fans have reacted? Would it have been as radically different as Ronald D. Moore's *Battlestar Galactica* reboot had been from the old '70s TV series?

Star Trek: Re-Boot the Universe never got past the idea stage. Would Paramount have even considered it? It would have been a radical new version of *Star Trek*, drawing upon Straczynski's (and Zabel's) keen understanding of science fiction television, the approach to classic and modern storytelling, and the need for evolution.

Ultimately, Straczynski and *Star Trek* would always be at arm's length. But *Star Trek: Re-Boot the Universe* shows what his *Star Trek* might have looked like, if he ever got his hands on the franchise.

7

Making "*The Lord of the Rings* in space" a Reality

Why hadn't grand sagas like *Foundation, Childhood's End, The Lord of the Rings* and *Dune* been made for TV before *Babylon 5* came along?

From Middle Earth to the deserts of Arrakis, these sprawling epics had captured the hearts of readers, but nothing like them had really been seen on screen. 1984's *Dune* was considered something of a disaster for director David Lynch, though the ambition was admirable. Ralph Bakshi had adapted *The Lord of the Rings* in 1978, but this mix of animation and live action failed to tell a complete story, ending just after the Battle of Helm's Deep. *Childhood's End* would not get a live-screen adaptation until the Syfy miniseries in 2015. *Foundation* wouldn't appear until Apple TV's 2021 adaptation, when it became one of the streamer's prestige dramas.

While the BBC radio dramatization of *The Lord of the Rings* was culturally successful, it wasn't until Peter Jackson's movie trilogy in 2001–2003 that we would get an adaptation worthy of J.R.R. Tolkien's source material. Denis Villeneuve would have better success than Lynch with Frank Herbert's *Dune* in 2021. A sequel, covering the second half of the book, was quickly commissioned and released in 2024.

There's an obvious answer to why Villeneuve's *Dune* was more successful than Lynch's, or why it took Isaac Asimov's *Foundation* almost 80 years from the publication of his first short story to live-screen adaptation. Technology.

Peter Jackson and Wētā Workshop revolutionized computer-generated effects with the making of *The Lord of the Rings* in the same way that Industrial Light and Magic did with *Star Wars* back in the '70s and '80s. *Dune* and *Foundation* had epic narratives but needed the advancement of technologies to bring them to life effectively on the big and small screens.

When it came to developing *Babylon 5*, Straczynski's ambitious plan to tell an epic five-year saga set in space had another hurdle to cross. Was there enough money to bring his vision to life? Was technology advanced enough that Earthforce, Minbari, Shadows, Vorlons et al could be brought to life in a strikingly visual way? Could these worlds that lived in Straczynski's mind be effectively translated onto the screen?

The Cost of Making Science Fiction Television

Science fiction television was expensive, even without the whole host of aliens, ships and planets that would feature in any given episode. Epic space battles were unheard of. Even *Star Trek* steered clear of anything too grand; the movies resorted to skirmishes between two or three ships (as seen in climaxes to *Star Trek II: The Wrath of Khan* and *Star Trek VI: The Undiscovered Country*). The epic Borg invasion at the heart of *Star Trek: The Next Generation*'s "The Best of Both Worlds" two-parter was really just a series of skirmishes between the *Enterprise* and the Borg cube, with the massacre of the Federation fleet taking place off screen and leaving a graveyard of ships behind.

So how would Straczynski enable *Babylon 5* to convey the Shadow War in all its might? Or the fall of Narn? Or the Earth civil war? Or even the arrival of the Vorlon fleet in *The Gathering*? These were grand concepts never seen before on screen.

Any TV series set in space was produced using miniatures and motion control photography. This was expensive and production was arduous. The idea that *Star Trek: The Next Generation* made 26 episodes a season[1] feels something of a miracle. It was the most expensive dramatic series of its time, with an average cost of $1.3 million per episode.

Straczynski knew that the sort of money Paramount were throwing at the *Star Trek* franchise would never be made available to *Babylon 5*. PTEN's budget for their shows was between $600,000 and $800,000 per episode. Already, the idea of competing with a show like *The Next Generation* was a hurdle—and that was before *Deep Space Nine* came along.

There were two solutions that Straczynski came up with. First was the decision to set the show on a space station, making more use of standard sets week after week to keep production costs down. Indeed, there is very little of the world outside *Babylon 5* in the show's first season.

Second was the decision to abandon the use of conventional models and motion control.[2]

> We decided that *Babylon 5* would use computer-generated imagery on a scale never preciously attempted in television. The risks were substantial since CGI was still in its infancy, used mainly to create video transitions and primitive

7. Making "The Lord of the Rings *in space*" a Reality 49

3-D shapes; pulling this tech into actual production would mean rolling the dice on a new and unproven technology.

In *Becoming Superman*, Straczynski notes that Warner Bros. was immediately skeptical about making a show using CGI, a large cast, heavy prosthetics, and stunts on the PTEN budget. As Straczynski described it, *Star Trek* was the only space-based science fiction series to last more than three seasons in 25 years. How would he tell a grand sci-fi arc over five seasons?

Once again, the odds were not in Straczynski's favor, but his vision and determination won through. *Babylon 5* became a grand saga for television.

The use of CGI was a risk that paid off, but also became the show's Achilles heel. Some shots look stunning to this very day—the Minbari ships, the White Star, the Vorlon and Shadow vessels—and Babylon 5 itself holds up incredibly well. But with the advancement of technology, some of the CGI used dates the show. The shots of Mars and the shuttle train inside Babylon 5 look like something out of an old computer game. Which makes sense, when you realize that many of the effects shots were produced on Commodore Amigas.[3]

In many ways, you have to take the use of dated CGI with the same pinch of salt as the polystyrene planets of '60s *Star Trek* or the rubbery alien suits of classic *Doctor Who*. The storytelling is strong, but the effects didn't always match the ambition of those tales. Given that *Babylon 5* was made in the '90s and not the '60s or '70s, it's frustrating that the "bad CGI" can pull the viewer out of the episode. Especially when *The Next Generation* and *Deep Space Nine*, with their expensive use of model work, hold up much better on repeat viewing.

Like old *Star Trek* or *Doctor Who*, there will be potential new viewers put off by the dated effects. This may be one of the reasons *Babylon 5* doesn't rank as high as its *Star Trek* contemporaries in those "best of" lists. But if the price of making *Babylon 5* was taking a risk on untested CGI technology, then the payoff was certainly worth it.

The Epics That Influenced Babylon 5

Babylon 5 has sometimes been referred to as "*The Lord of the Rings* in space," which is both an honor and a disservice. There are certainly influences from J.R.R. Tolkien's books in Straczynski's grand space saga, but JMS drew upon a whole range of literary sagas when it came to building *Babylon 5*.

Every piece of fiction is influenced by what came before. *Doctor Who* drew upon *Quatermass*, *James Bond*, *Hammer Horror* and even *The*

Return of the Pink Panther in its classic era, while the 2005 revival saw Russell T Davies openly acknowledging the influences of shows like *Buffy the Vampire Slayer*, with its season-villain arcs as a foundation for each year.

The X-Files was certainly influenced by *The Twilight Zone*, with its anthological approach to the strange and mysterious stories of the week, and *Kolchak: The Night Stalker*, which saw a reporter—Kolchak—investing strange cases involving the supernatural. Just as influential was the iconic *Twin Peaks* at the beginning of the '90s, which fused criminal procedural and the supernatural for more mainstream audiences. From the mystery of who killed Laura Palmer to the Black Lodge, there was a strange and surreal mythos that permeated the real world of the small Washington town. Thematically and aesthetically, *The X-Files* feels like a natural successor to this show and was another revolutionary in bringing genre television to mass audiences.

Given his love for grand storytelling, it is no surprise that Straczynski cited the *Foundation* series, *Childhood's End*, *The Lord of the Rings*, *Dune*, the *Lensman* series, and even the poem "Ulysses," as key influences on the story of *Babylon 5*. Great storytelling takes from other sources and makes it their own. And Straczynski took from some of the best.

"Ulysses"

> Tho, we are not now that strength which in old days
> Moved earth and heaven, that which we are, we are;
> One equal temper of heroic hearts,
> Made weak by time and fate, but strong in will
> To strive, to seek, to find, and not to yield.

There is more to Jeffrey Sinclair's discussion with Delenn in *The Gathering* than a mere quoting of a classic text. "Ulysses" by Alfred, Lord Tennyson is a favorite not only of the station's commander, but J. Michael Straczynski too.

"Ulysses" is the story of man longing for adventure, for that which makes life worth living. We see how an old adventurer is not ready to settle even at his age and always yearns for one more quest. He is a warrior of Troy, a man with great honor, who has spent his life at sea and longs to return, to explore until his dying breath. He might be old, but his vigor is the same. He will always continue to explore and discover.

Sinclair, and later Sheridan, are *Babylon 5*'s Ulysses. Sinclair holds the works of Tennyson close to his heart; his then-girlfriend Catherine Sakai notes in "The Parliament of Dreams" that she had to memorize it after she spent a year living with him. He is haunted by his past and the events of the Battle of the Line, but seeks adventure and the wonders of the universe. Despite the great loss of life that befell humanity in the Earth–Minbari war, he still has hope. He believes in humanity's journey to the stars and the wonders it will hold. This is reflected in one of Sinclair's best speeches, defending the purpose of Babylon 5 on its second anniversary, in season one's "Infection."

> Ask ten different scientists about the environment, population control, genetics, and you'll get ten different answers, but there's one thing every scientist on the planet agrees on. Whether it happens in a hundred years or a thousand years or a million years, eventually our Sun will grow cold and go out. When that happens, it won't just take us. It'll take Marilyn Monroe, and Lao-Tzu, and Einstein, and Moributo, and Buddy Holly, and Aristophanes, and—all of this—all of this—was for nothing. Unless we go to the stars.

Sinclair's words echo Ulysses. Humanity can't be content to remain on Earth. They need to explore, to go to the stars.

Despite the events surrounding President Clark, the Nightwatch and the Earth civil war, *Babylon 5* is still something of an optimistic look to humanity's future. They build communities in the stars; this, Delenn notes, is humanity's greatest strength. Characters like Sinclair, Sheridan and Ivanova do not break, do not yield to the insurmountable odds they face. From the horrors of the Earth-Minbari conflict to the Shadow War, they fight the good fight, becoming heroes of legend.

Sheridan, another war hero like Ulysses, continues where Sinclair left off. He believes that the best of humanity will be found by looking out to the stars and not within. Babylon 5 is the statement by which humanity will achieve that journey. Not from Earth, the island of Ithaca in Tennyson's poem, but by working together with other races and building a better future.

The Lord of the Rings

> We walk in the dark places that no one else will enter.
> We stand on the bridge, and no one may pass.

If "Ulysses" is a subtle thematic influence on *Babylon 5*, then *The Lord of the Rings* is much more overt. *Babylon 5* takes place on the brink of the Third Age of Mankind, where Rangers walk in dark places, preparing for the war against the coming darkness, and the flaming eye in space rules from Z'ha'dum, home world of the Shadows.

Straczynski clearly has a deep love for Tolkien's mythology and uses the themes and ideas presented in *The Lord of the Rings* as a basis for the Shadows and the coming war.

The Rangers are the most direct homage to Tolkien, Minbari and human warriors that stand on the front lines against the darkness. Lifted from the Dunedain, they are most prominently represented by Marcus Cole, the Ranger of seasons three and four. His look and demeanor are similar to Aragorn's Ranger persona—Strider—and despite the futuristic, military trappings in which he finds himself, Marcus certainly feels as if he would be right at home in Middle Earth.

The motto of the Rangers, spoken by Marcus in season three's "Grey 17 Is Missing," is also evocative of two key moments from the novels. "We walk in the dark places that no one else will enter" is not too dissimilar to Aragorn's "Lonely men are we, Rangers of the North, hunters—but hunters ever of the servants of the Enemy" from the Council of Elrond. "We stand on the bridge, and no one may pass" is clearly a reference to Gandalf's battle with the Balrog in Moria during *The Fellowship of the Ring*.

There is also a direct homage to the flaming Eye of Sauron and the black riders of *The Lord of the Rings* in the representation of the Shadows on-screen. The piercing scream of the Shadow vessels is designed to evoke the cries of the Nazgul, while Ivanova faces the flaming eye at Z'ha'dum on two occasions. While it is a defense system, there is an unnerving horror element too. In season four opener "The Hour of the Wolf," Ivanova, Delenn and Lyta are enticed by the flaming eye to land on the Shadow home world. The corruption of Sauron's power is startlingly similar to that of the Shadows.

There are other, less obvious ideas that represent a love for Tolkien's work in the show. The Shadow home world of Z'ha'dum is evocative of the fallen kingdom of Moria—Khazad-Dum—while Lorien, from season four, shares his name with the great elven kingdom that was home to Celeborn and Galadriel. The idea of the First Ones leaving the galaxy to go beyond the Rim mirrors the elves leaving Middle Earth to go to Valinor. Both Frodo and Sheridan, the central heroes of the respective stories, would leave their life for Valinor/the Rim in the final chapters.

In fact, the Minbari often feel like a spiritual representation of the elves from *The Lord of the Rings*, not least through the representation of Delenn. Her romance with Sheridan—a Minbari and a human—draws upon the great loves of Beren and Luthien from *The Silmarillion* and, of course, Aragorn and Arwen from *The Lord of the Rings*.

Straczynski also acknowledges Tolkien's work when a techno-mage loosely quotes Gandalf through the character of Gildor Inglorion: "Do not meddle in the affairs of wizards, for they are subtle and quick to anger."

7. Making "The Lord of the Rings *in space*" a Reality

Ultimately, the showrunner has noted that these similarities are just that. There is no attempt to tell *"The Lord of the Rings* in space."

> Of course, I've read and enjoyed Tolkien. But as I've said, I have no interest in doing LoTR with the serial numbers filed off.[4]

While *The Lord of the Rings* may be the most direct homage on the show, the influences of many great epics helped shape Straczynski's work on *Babylon 5*. There are analogies to be drawn between his favorite science fiction story *Dune* and *Babylon 5*, represented through the Padishah Empire and the Centauri, the Psi Corps and the Bene Gesserit, the Vorlons and the Spacing Guild, and the Narn and the Fremen.

The legends of King Arthur also play a role in the show. Season one's "Grail" features the quest for the Holy Grail in the halls of Babylon 5, while season three's "A Late Delivery from Avalon" has a Battle of the Line survivor believing himself to be King Arthur reborn, with G'Kar and Marcus his new Knights of the Round Table.

The idea of younger races like ascending to some higher plane of existence is reminiscent of Arthur C. Clarke's *Childhood's End* and is represented in everything from Jason Ironheart in season one's "Mind War" to the doomed Ralga race from TV movie "River of Souls," captured by the Soul Hunters at their moment of ascension.

Babylon 5 is not *The Lord of the Rings* in space, just as it is not *Dune* or King Arthur or *Childhood's End* reconceptualized. It is its own science fiction epic that stands shoulder to shoulder with these other epics. It takes ideas from the very best and molds them into its own story.

Babylon

Babylon 5 finds its roots in historical influences just as much as literary ones. American presidents are reflected in the narrative of the show, from the opening narration to seasons one and two—"Babylon 5 is our last, best hope, for peace" mirroring Abraham Lincoln's famous 1863 speech to Congress that the United States was "...this last best hope of Earth." Similarly, it is easy to draw parallels between the assassination of JFK in 1963 and the assassination of President Santiago in the season one finale, "Chrysalis."

World War II is a strong influence on the portrayal of Earth in *Babylon 5*, particularly the Nightwatch and their "Blitz mentality," not to mention the rise of xenophobia and hatred that is eerily similar to the rise of Nazism and the Third Reich—which feels even more disturbingly more relevant in today's social climate. Sheridan references the dilemma

Churchill felt over the bombing of Coventry as he debates what to do about Morden, after learning about the Shadow threat in season two's "In the Shadow of Z'ha'dum."

It's also clear that Straczynski also drew upon ancient Rome and the bloody rule of Emperor Caligula when he created the Centauri. The decadence of a fallen empire reborn makes the parallel clear across the first three seasons of the show. But it is the arrival of the mad Emperor Cartagia in season four that is perhaps Straczynski's most obvious—and fun—use of Roman history to shape the fate of the Centauri empire.

> I picked Babylon for the station, because a lot of what happens in the Babylon 5 story comes out of Babylonian creation myth, which says that the universe was born out of the conflict between order and chaos.[5]

The name "Babylon 5" is not without coincidence either. The fall of Babylon 5, the magnificent idea of a place where races could come together, transforms the station into a place of war across the show's third and fourth seasons.

While it is not apparent early on, the Babylonian creation myth is a key part of the *Babylon 5* mythos, as seen through the roles the Vorlons and Shadows play in the galaxy. The Vorlons' sense of order is undone by the Shadows sowing the seeds of chaos with races like the Centauri. Ultimately, their manipulation is revealed to all in season four's "Into the Fire." This is a pivotal episode that lays bare the hypocrisy of the Vorlon and Shadow ideas of order and chaos and sees the gods cast out of the galaxy by the younger races.

In any TV show, film or book you will find other cultural and literary influences. *Babylon 5* is no different. Straczynski understood what made science fiction and fantasy epics like *Dune* and *The Lord of the Rings* crucial to the cultural mythos and created *Babylon 5* as an example of how to translate epic stories to the small screen successfully. It wasn't without its challenges. Studio and audience expectations of episodic and long-form storytelling, and the challenges around technology and budget, made the production of *Babylon 5* a daring feat of science fiction television.

But Straczynski succeeded. He strove to seek, to find, and not to yield, and he built something that remains a tentpole example of how to make a science fiction epic for the small screen.

8

The Great Publicity Machine

How do you market a show like *Babylon 5* to domestic and international audiences when science fiction is a dirty word? That was the challenge the show faced in the early '90s. Before audiences even had the opportunity to decide whether *Babylon 5* was worth watching, the show needed to find a home to be broadcast on first.

In the U.S., most local stations had already signed on as PTEN affiliates, taking on TV packages for broadcast. That included *Babylon 5*. However, just because they had paid to air it didn't mean that it would get the prime time airing it deserved.

Broadcasting *Babylon 5* internationally was another challenge. Was there an appetite for a TV show set in space that wasn't a *Star Trek* series? Would international broadcasters pay for a show that risked getting little engagement on their own networks?

As with everything *Babylon 5*, the great publicity machine was another long twilight struggle against the odds to convince networks to broadcast the show. Much of that effort came from fans of the show.

Earl Green oversaw promotions for two local PTEN affiliates in Arkansas and Wisconsin. He worked tirelessly to ensure *Babylon 5* had a home—and a decent time slot—on those networks.

In this chapter, I'll chart Earl's efforts to ensure *Babylon 5* stayed on the air.

Selling Babylon 5 *on the Home Turf*

In late 2022, I chatted to Earl Green about his association with *Babylon 5*. He was a fan from the very beginning. In the early days of online debate and discussion, and before *The Gathering* even premiered, J. Michael Straczynski was interacting with the online community. As part of this early '90s online presence, Earl witnessed Straczynski's efforts to align audience expectations with the reality of what kind of show *Babylon 5* was going to be. For many people, their only reference point for anything science fiction on the small screen was *Star Trek*.

In those early days of *Babylon 5*, Straczynski had to "market" his own show to potential fans. No show outside of the *Star Trek* franchise had ever been openly marketed as a piece of science fiction TV. Even classics like *Lost in Space* would be classed as a "family drama."

Marketing *Babylon 5* was a unique challenge, and without people like Earl, the show might not have gotten the reach it did.

BAZ: *You oversaw promotions for two stations that were affiliates of Warner's Prime Time Entertainment Network. What did that role entail?*

EARL: Promotions at the local station level are about understanding what gets eyeballs on your particular station and trying to figure out how to get those viewers to sample other programming on the same station. A lot of the time, with syndicated programming, you take what the syndicator has already prepared (usually sent via a satellite feed in the dead of night) and put a local "tag" on it, something that identifies that show as "belonging" to your station.

B: *As a fan of the show, did you feel the pressure to ensure that the stations picked up* **Babylon 5***?*

E: In both cases, these stations had already signed on as PTEN affiliates before I worked there and were PTEN affiliates until PTEN ceased to exist at the end of 1997. For a small station with a modest budget, once you were signed on for a package like that, it was always going to be easier to just carry the shows—even if that meant that you were airing the material from PTEN [or] Universal Action Pack in the worst time slots possible—than to try to negotiate an exit from that contract.

So, I expect there were really very few instances of stations dumping PTEN altogether. Burying the shows in the dead of night, sure, but that's always cheaper than going into legal proceedings to sever the contract.

B: *What was the general reception to* **Babylon 5** *on these local networks?*

E: On the fan end of things, it seemed to be somewhere between enthusiasm, bewilderment, and a bit of derision. Even with the benefit of hindsight and an understanding of where VFX technology was going into 1993, I think it's safe to say that the effects, even though they won an Emmy, were a little underwhelming compared to the competing sci-fi franchise (there really was only one).

They showed huge promise, but there was a long way to go. The movement of the "camera" POV in a lot of the early Video Toaster–generated CGI is kind of ... video game-y, for lack of a better way to put it. There was

8. The Great Publicity Machine 57

criticism of the CGI, the acting, the sets, and what I noticed is that a lot of it really was entirely relative to what *Star Trek* was doing at the time (both *The Next Generation* and *Deep Space Nine*, which had just started at the beginning of 1993).

There was already, thanks to the press, a kind of competition between the two different space station shows, and some of the more strident elements of *Star Trek* fandom just weren't tolerant of this interloper challenging their favorite franchise or brand. There was some bewilderment in that you could clearly see how the pilot was setting up a larger story, and yet there was no series forthcoming for nearly a full year. It was easy to think that the show just wasn't coming back, that it hadn't gone to series—if you weren't paying attention to what Straczynski was saying on GEnie and CompuServe.

But there were fans like me, who had been paying attention all along, who were rooting for *Babylon 5*. I always found some of the strident opposition to it baffling. In those days, before the syndicated action hour market really heated up, and decades before you have streaming services spewing genre programming all over the place, why would anyone not want another show that tickles their love of sci-fi?

At the first station where I worked (Fort Smith, Arkansas, Fox station KPBI), the station management absolutely hated *Babylon 5*. The owner had signed onto PTEN because of the Wild West documentary[1] (also produced by Douglas Netter) and the rock 'n' roll history documentary that were among the initial offerings. Because he remembered the original 1970s *Kung Fu* series as being a western, he tolerated the new *Kung Fu* spin-off.

But *Time Trax*[2] and *Babylon 5* were shows he never would have picked up on their own; he had a real blind spot for sci-fi, never mind what the viewers might want to see. If *Time Trax* and *Babylon 5* hadn't been part of the PTEN package that he picked up expressly for that other programming, he wouldn't have aired them. There was that much resistance to it. (Obviously that has more to do with his personal taste than with the quality of any of the shows. It's ironic that he started another station in 1994 and chased the United Paramount Network [UPN] affiliation, knowing that UPN was pinning its entire success on a *Star Trek* show.)[3]

But it's also a good thing that he did that: because UPN had no promo material ready, absolutely none, for stations that were joining the network in the fall of 1995, months after it launched, I had to create my own from whole cloth to announce our new station was now the home of *Star Trek: Voyager*. The campaign I created won some awards, got noticed at the network level, and landed me my next job at the UPN station in Green Bay.

B: *What were your favorite pieces of marketing material for* Babylon 5?

E: In the first season, each station got a copy of the "Universe Today" newspaper as used in the early part of season one; I'm pretty sure they just printed up extras, there wouldn't have been enough screen-used ones to send to every station carrying the show. The body copy was lorem ipsum, but the headlines were relevant to the show, with one asking, "Is something living in hyperspace?"—keep in mind, this was very early in season one, so the whole Warren Keffer character arc hadn't happened yet. In fact, that character hadn't even been conceived. Where did that reporter get their info? Or were they listening to the Earth Alliance equivalent of Art Bell?

Keeping the Dream Afloat

In the U.S., there were four big networks competing for airtime in the '90s: National Broadcasting Company (NBC), Columbia Broadcasting System (CBS), American Broadcasting Company (ABC) and Fox Broadcasting Company (Fox). Local stations had five channels, meaning that all other shows, including local content, would be vying for this fifth slot. PTEN sold content for this "fifth channel" and, for a time, successfully took a share of the audience that might otherwise gravitate toward the "big four."

In 1993, UPN was founded. Paramount had originally planned to be part of PTEN, and the decision to step away is what might have led to *Babylon 5* being rejected by Paramount in favor of their own space station–set *Star Trek* series, *Deep Space Nine*. Chris-Craft Industries' United Television, who had been one of the owners of PTEN, switched their focus to UPN instead.

Suddenly, PTEN and UPN were fighting for the same "fifth network" real estate. PTEN lost. Many PTEN-affiliated stations objected to the amount of advertising driven by two competing networks, particularly as this drastically reduced the amount of marketing that could be levied against their own local content. PTEN backed out of its commitments for several series and eventually ground to a close in 1997. PTEN was sold off to MCA, Comcast, and Raycom Media. *Babylon 5* no longer had a home.

American basic cable television channel TNT saved *Babylon 5* from cancellation, picking up broadcast rights as well as a fifth season and follow-on TV movies. But in the days leading up to the conclusion of season four—the last season to be produced under PTEN—there was a question mark over whether local stations would even air the conclusion to Straczynski's epic science fiction drama.

8. The Great Publicity Machine

Why bother? The contract with PTEN was almost done. Did it matter if the last few episodes were given a decent time slot? There was a very real danger fans would not see the outcome of the Earth civil war and everything *Babylon 5* had built toward since the pilot.

Earl Green moved to the Green Bay, Wisconsin, UPN station, WACY, in August 1997. At that time, the final five episodes of *Babylon 5* season four were yet to air. Fans had just witnessed Sheridan's torture at the hands of Earthforce in "Intersections in Real Time" and were reeling from Garibaldi's betrayal. With the Earth civil war in full swing, the narrative stakes had never been higher.

As a fan of *Babylon 5*, Earl was faced with the challenge of convincing WACY to broadcast those final episodes with the attention they deserved. I asked him about that struggle.

E: When I arrived at the Green Bay UPN station in August 1997, I only had the evening schedule to worry about. The daytime schedule was all syndicated children's programming, which was an interesting experiment; someone else was assigned to be the promo writer/producer just for that programming. All I had to worry about was 4:00 p.m. through 6:00 a.m. It's exceedingly rare for a local station to bother to promote anything after, say, *The Tonight Show*'s time slot. So, all I had to worry about was 4:00 p.m. through 11:00 p.m.

As I was trying to get accustomed to how this station did things, I noticed that they had a ton of syndicated programming scattered all over the place: PTEN, Universal Action Pack, the syndicated reruns of Showtime series like *Stargate SG-1*, *Outer Limits*, and *Poltergeist: The Legacy*. Ironically, we were also the *Star Trek: Deep Space Nine* station, both first run and reruns. Our program director had also picked up other first-run syndicated action shows that qualified as sci-fi: *Team Knight Rider*, Gene Roddenberry's *Earth: Final Conflict*, and Disney's series version of *Honey, I Shrunk the Kids*.

I asked why we weren't "blocking" this programming—i.e., regularly scheduling it with similar programming that would attract the same audience. Instead, like quite a few other stations, these syndicated shows were scheduled in the dead of night. I think the plan was to show blocks of reruns of *The Simpsons* and *Coach* during prime time. Every night.

So I drew up a plan for a sci-fi block, most nights of the week. Two new shows at 7:00 p.m. and 8:00 (central), *Deep Space Nine* reruns at 9:00. And then we could get our *The Simpsons* fix at ten. Now, at this point, I'd been there for about a month, and I was suddenly telling them how to schedule things, which wasn't my job; my job was to promote the schedule what had already been set.

But I felt very strongly that the schedule could be better, and that we could aggressively promote all this action programming, which fell under sci-fi, or horror, or some combination of the two. While our NBC sister station downstairs did its best to own every male viewer interested in football (keep in mind, this was Green Bay, Wisconsin, we're talking about—the Packers were practically the local religion), we could pick up every other male viewer that didn't care about football.

It was a hard sell, especially since I was this brand-new guy basically trying to do my job and telling the program director how to do his. I pissed a few people off. But I pushed hard for it and bet my job on it—if rebranding our UPN station as the sci-fi station didn't pop a decent ratings number, I knew I was probably headed back to Arkansas in very short order.

The UPN 32 Prime Time Invasion campaign launched that fall. When we got the Nielsen ratings in November 1997, they showed that we were suddenly one of the ten fastest growing UPN stations in the country.

Now, we get to the point about the last episodes of the fourth season.

I made it a point to include *Babylon 5* in the "Prime Time Invasion" launch plan,[4] because I knew that the audience that we were trying to get on board for our programming block would appreciate that those last few episodes weren't buried in the dead of night. I got management sold on the "Prime Time Invasion" idea, but *Babylon 5* was the biggest fight: as one member of station management put it, "I don't want to run a free commercial for a cable channel." (Meaning TNT, which would be picking up *Babylon 5* in both new episodes and reruns at the beginning of 1998.)

I had to remind all involved that putting these last four weeks of the show in prime time was part of us demonstrating to a desirable demographic that we were going to treat their favorite shows well, and not dump them in a 2:00 a.m. Thursday time slot. (That demographic, by the way, was males 18–45 who tended to be geekier, better educated, less sports oriented, and thus had spending power our advertisers would find attractive.) We should not only run the show in prime time but shout from the rooftops that we're running them in prime time.

Finally, they gave in—I must've really been a real force of persuasion back then—[and] as soon as those five weeks of new shows were done, *Deep Space Nine* took its place on the schedule.

Wining and Dining to International Markets

While Earl was working to ensure that *Babylon 5* got the attention it deserved in the U.S., there was also the need to broaden the reach of the

8. The Great Publicity Machine

show internationally. As part of the Warner Bros. remit, *Babylon 5* was sold to global networks alongside '90s shows like *Friends*, *ER* and *Murphy Brown*.

Fortunately, *Babylon 5* was not as much of a hard sell as it might have been in the U.S. The show had no trouble being marketed to several English-speaking countries, such as England and Australia. Science fiction was big business in countries like Italy and Holland too. This may even explain why *Babylon 5* was marketed as sci-fi when few shows outside *Star Trek* ever had been.

The revolutionary approach to *Babylon 5*, as a serialized five-year novel for television, was also less of a hard sell internationally. Global networks were used to that kind of storytelling. In the UK, British sci-fi such as *Doctor Who* and *Blake's 7* had always certainly been a little bit more serialized.

But despite the appetite for science fiction outside the U.S., there was still considerable effort required to sell the show overseas. The Warner Bros. marketing team flew people from all over the world for Internationals—screenings of the shows Warner Bros. was trying to sell, alongside a considerable dose of parties, wining, and dining.[5] Warner Bros. content was also brought to big international conventions, where shows would be sold to buyers from all over the world. Warner Bros. needed to sell their content overseas, as they would rarely break even if they were only broadcast nationally.

While overseas uptake didn't play a factor in the decision to cancel or renew shows in the U.S., it was still an important cog in the publicity machine.

Casablanca *in Space*

But what of the actual marketing material itself? Looking back over old promotions, you will find glossy fact sheets with blurbs about *Babylon 5* and full cast list and stills from the show that provided details on the characters and actors. All highly informative and professional content, the sort of material you would expect when marketing to domestic and international networks.

But perhaps the most curious piece of marketing is the press kit that went out prior to *The Gathering*, before many of the characters had even been cast.[6] Given that Straczynski was striving to make a science fiction TV series that would be taken seriously, it is remarkable that the press kit was nothing short of glossy and sensationalist in its presentation, with artwork that would not be out of place in '50s B movie science fiction—it was

Chris Foss meets Bob Layzell in style, and the descriptions were equally fantastical.

> The outermost reaches of space are dominated by five potentially hostile federations, including the Earth Alliance. Intrigue, smuggling, murder, espionage, mistrust, collusion and spying are commonplace.
> In this time of uneasy peace and constant threat of war, a lone territory exists where all five federations' starships are assured safe passage. Smack in the center of this sector is a space station; a neutral port-of-call, a space-borne Casablanca filled with heroes and thieves, rogues and healers. Its name…. Babylon 5.

It is still arguably *Babylon 5* in its core concept, wrapped up in a swagger of *Buck Rogers* meets *Barbarella*. So why the very different tone?

Distinguishing itself from the almighty *Star Trek* franchise, *Babylon 5* needed to garner attention from the press to help sell the show and convince PTEN to pick it up for a full season. The press pack promised violence, murder, and sleaze—it was *Casablanca* in space, and everyone loved *Casablanca*. It was not a million miles away from the adage, "sex sells."

It also speaks to the challenges *Babylon 5* faced in marketing a show that was new and revolutionary. Local networks didn't want it. The idea of a five-year novel for television was unheard of. Outside of *Star Trek*, science fiction was a dirty word. There was a huge mountain to climb before audiences could even watch the show.

Straczynski recognized this when he pitched his glossy *Casablanca* in space. When the show finally got on the air, it was fans like Earl Green who kept the show in the public consciousness. The great *Babylon 5* publicity machine never stopped churning.

9

JMS's Character Trapdoors

Planning a five-year arc is no mean feat. There are so many factors that could derail the story plan, from budget restraints to dwindling audiences, network changes, cast departures and that all-important threat of cancellation.

One of the biggest challenges J. Michael Straczynski faced when it came to making a five-season novel for television was the need for certain characters to go through multi-season journeys. Londo, G'Kar, Delenn, Sheridan: these are characters who end up in very different places from where they began.

But what if the actors playing these characters were no longer available?

Babylon 5 had some major cast alterations over the course of its run, not least the replacement of its lead character. While the '90s *Star Trek* shows had a relatively stable cast—each losing one lead in their runs and replacing them with another—the crew of the space station Babylon 5 is hugely different. Even between the pilot movie, *The Gathering*, which aired in February 1993, and the first episode of season one in January 1994, the cast changes were noticeable. The loss of Sinclair a year later was a seismic shift in the show and one that Straczynski navigated admirably.

When it came to replacing Takashima with Ivanova, Lyta with Talia (and then Lyta again) and Sinclair with Sheridan, Straczynski had a plan. His character trapdoors were an ingenious and fascinating concept. Every character had a trapdoor, a way for Straczynski to accommodate a cast member's exit and replace them with a character who could serve that original purpose. He needed a station commander who would be sympathetic to aliens, question Earth and be instrumental in the conflicts to come. He needed a telepath who would become a superweapon in the Shadow War. While Sinclair/Sheridan and Lyta/Talia share some similar traits, they also work as their own characters, with their own agency, while still allowing the story to be told as planned.

What might have happened if Mira Furlan or Peter Jurasik had left the show? Would Lennier and Vir have filled those roles? Would *Babylon 5* have played out differently, or would Straczynski have largely kept to his vision?

No story remains intact from concept to execution; you only have to look at the ideas for *Babylon Prime*. But the use of character trapdoors is worthy of a deeper examination, and this chapter will delve a little deeper into the events around some of the most significant cast changes and consider what purpose Straczynski's trapdoors served in the continuing story of *Babylon 5*.

It's All Change at the Top: Sinclair to Sheridan

What if Captain Picard had been killed after his assimilation as Locutus of Borg at the end of *Star Trek: The Next Generation*'s third season? Or Buffy had stayed dead at the end of *Buffy the Vampire Slayer*'s first run of episodes? What if Scully never returned after her abduction early into the second season of *The X-Files*? These cast departures would have irrevocably changed those shows forever. They might not even have survived.

But let's consider what might have been. Riker as captain with Shelby remaining as his first officer? A new slayer taking the lead—Kendra the Vampire Slayer, anyone? Would Mulder have found a new partner to help investigate the paranormal and unexplained? These changes *might* have worked. They might have been successful. But those shows would have been very different too.

It can happen. One of the biggest shows on television, *NCIS*, continued after the departure of the almighty Leroy Jethro Gibbs (played by Mark Harmon) in its 19th season. *Batwoman* ran for two more years with a completely new lead, Javicia Leslie, when Ruby Rose's Kate Kane dropped out of the show after season one. In fact, *The X-Files* replaced Mulder for a while in season eight, with Robert Patrick's John Doggett partnering with Scully before taking the lead himself (though it's notable that the David Duchovny-less ninth season fared less well and led to the show's original cancellation).

With the unplanned departure of Michael O'Hare at the end of season one, *Babylon 5* was in a trepidatious place. While the show was an ensemble, Sinclair's reserved, diplomatic but often compromised leader was the guiding force. The alien ambassadors were yet to drive the narrative, as Londo and G'Kar would do in season two, and the bigger threats with Earth and the Shadows were still in their infancy.

9. JMS's Character Trapdoors

At the end of 2258, and the seismic changes in the season one finale "Chrysalis," Sinclair was the character who would lead the charge in the bigger events to come. As Straczynski looked to prep the sophomore season of *Babylon 5*, he was forced to write a brand-new character who would fill Sinclair's shoes. A station commander—or captain—who would quickly become disillusioned with Earth and its increasing xenophobic tendencies, all while becoming a leader in the coming war with an enemy few knew about.

Before we look at how Sheridan filled that role, it's important to understand the nature of O'Hare's departure from the show. While filming season one, his struggles with mental illness came to light. Battling delusions and paranoia, filming became a struggle for the lead on *Babylon 5*, forcing Straczynski to enact one of his infamous trapdoors to keep the show on track.

It's a harrowing and tragic story, and one that speaks to the courage of O'Hare in trying to keep the show alive while facing his illness. Just as remarkable was how Straczynski provided support to his lead actor even though it threatened to destroy the show he had fought so hard to build.

The creator of *Babylon 5* revealed the truth about the departure of Commander Sinclair from the show at a fan convention in 2013, shortly after O'Hare's death.

> Into the first year of working with Michael, I began to notice problems. ...he began to manifest symptoms of psychosis, where he began to talk about messages to him in the papers, that the FBI was following him, that he was getting secret messages in the television broadcast.
>
> And I realized that he was heading for a psychotic break. My psychology background came into play. And I didn't know what to do. Because most of the time he was fine. But every so often, when he was stressed, out would come delusional behavior. What do I do? What do I do? My first show, first season, if I tell Warners about this, they'll pull the plug.[1]

For the showrunner and the lead actor, this was a huge dilemma. This was Straczynski's big break, to launch a show that he had spent five years pitching[2] and that would not make it past his first season if the truth came out. But Straczynski knew he couldn't tell Warner Bros. He couldn't force his actor to take medication, but he could stop the show in its tracks to give O'Hare the time he needed. O'Hare begged Straczynski not to pull the plug, recognizing that he would be responsible for the show shutting down and people losing their jobs.

And so, a deal was made. Straczynski assigned someone to work with O'Hare—Macaulay Bruton, who would also appear on the show as Garibaldi's aide and traitor Jack—and was ready to bring everything to a halt if things got worse for the actor. As Straczynski describes it, O'Hare "held on by his fingernails for that season."

O'Hare's determination to keep going was certainly admirable, but not sustainable. Straczynski took the bold decision to remove O'Hare from the show and replace the character of Sinclair with a new lead. But this was clearly not a decision taken lightly, and Straczynski continued to support O'Hare even when he stepped away from *Babylon 5*.

> We finished the season up and I pulled him up into the office and I said you and I both know this is getting worse. We both know you're not going to make it to another season for the way things are, and I want to move on from you as commander of the station. Don't worry about it. Whatever your rent needs are for the while, I'll take care of it. Food, I got it covered. We will get you treatment, we will get you better.

Straczynski spent the next two years supporting O'Hare and his family, to ensure he got the care and medication he needed. When this worked, the showrunner was able to bring O'Hare back for the season three two-parter "War Without End," allowing a way to close off Sinclair's arc and introduce the notion of him being Valen.

But had O'Hare not suffered mental illness and remained on *Babylon 5*, would his role have played out similarly to Sheridan's across seasons two through five? As noted in *Babylon Prime*, the ten-year trajectory for Sinclair was quite different, and yet it shared a lot of similarities with the condensed Sheridan mytharc. The second year would likely have played out almost as closely. Sinclair had already demonstrated his ability to work around the rules, one that could have easily led to the same secret rebellion Sheridan became involved with by the end of season two and beyond. He had also built up a strong relationship with Delenn, which could have conceivably led her to reveal the truth about the Shadows we saw with Sheridan in season two's "In the Shadow of Z'ha'dum."

There would have been differences, however. No Anna Sheridan and the fate of the *Icarus*, for one. Sinclair's fiancée Catherine Sakai *was* destined to have her mind wiped, leading the way for a Sinclair and Delenn romance. There is no doubt that Sinclair would have been a leading hero in the fight against the Shadows and the corrupt Earth. His role in becoming Valen would likely not have happened at all, but there is a symmetry in his disappearing into the past and Sheridan going beyond the Rim in the finale, "Sleeping in Light."

Broad strokes aside, Sinclair and Sheridan are quite different in personality. You could buy Sinclair ultimately becoming the president of the Interstellar Alliance with his skills in diplomacy, but he suffers as an action hero in his season one appearances, and it is hard to imagine him raging against Kosh and the Shadows in the high-stakes drama of seasons three and four. He is a far more reserved character, and you could imagine Straczynski writing events differently to play to O'Hare's strengths.

There's also a warmth and energy to Bruce Boxleitner's performance as Sheridan that wasn't always there in Sinclair, and the show certainly plays to that actor's strengths over the course of his four seasons on the show. Some of that reserve may come down to O'Hare's own struggles when filming the show, but the personality differences are clear.

Season two was possibly the biggest hill for Straczynski to climb. He had to introduce a fresh-faced captain in the first episode and have him on the cusp of betraying everything he stood for 22 episodes later. Thanks to Boxleitner's engaging performance and Straczynski's writing, *Babylon 5* absolutely achieves this, building in some character shortcuts like Sheridan's love of conspiracy theories, the reveal of his side mission by General Hague and some major events that culminate in his disillusion with his superiors in "The Fall of Night." It would have been a far easier journey for Sinclair to take. Fortunately, Sheridan is all set on the same path by the end of 2259, ready for the shattering events of "Severed Dreams" halfway through season three.

It also helps that Sheridan has a more direct tie to the show's main threat, the Shadows, than Sinclair ever did.

> The character of Sinclair was tied primarily to the Minbari part of the story: the Battle of the Line, the missing 24 hours, the Minbari Soul aspect. I really needed someone who had a tie to the Shadows and to give him that added layer on top of everything else that he'd gone through seemed to be stretching credulity to the breaking point.[3]

Straczynski used his character trapdoors to great effect with the exit of Sinclair and the arrival of Sheridan, so much so that it almost seems planned, given his "phrasing" of Sinclair's departure back when the show was still on air.

As for the secrets surrounding his departure, Straczynski summarized O'Hare's conviction perfectly in 2013.

> Look, keep it to my grave. So, if anything ever happens to me, I want people to know that is the problem and that's why I left. Because people need to know that if there's a problem in their family, that if this can happen to an actor, a star of a show, the commander of a space station, it can happen to anyone and it's not a scandalous thing, it can be dealt with. So, if anything ever happens to me, I want you to be free to talk about this.

O'Hare's life was a tragic one, but not without admiration and beauty. He stuck with the medication, got married, and had a kid. He even returned to acting. Sadly, it wasn't to last, and he stopped taking his medication and disappeared off the grid. O'Hare ended up in a halfway house, under medication, before succumbing to a heart attack in 2012, aged 60.

With the help of Straczynski, he helped bring *Babylon 5* to life and kept it going even in the face of unimaginable struggles. In that sense, O'Hare is as much the hero of the story as Sinclair.

Traitors and Seconds in Command: Takashima, Ivanova and Lochley

Lieutenant Commander Laurel Takashima originally had a much bigger role on the show. Sinclair's second in command only appeared in 1993's pilot movie, *The Gathering*. The character was recalled to Earth (along with Doctor Kyle and telepath Lyta Alexander) following the events surrounding Kosh's assassination attempt.

Tamlyn Tomita chose not to return for season one, preferring to find alternative acting roles not based around military characters. Her delivery of lines in the pilot is also something of an issue, with some parties at Warner Bros. finding her unlikeable, unsympathetic, and harsh. The studio requested that her dialogue be replaced with something softer, which Straczynski fought against and lost.

So Takashima became something of a footnote in *Babylon 5* and was replaced by fan favorite Lieutenant Commander Susan Ivanova, brought majestically to life by Claudia Christian. Interestingly, Ivanova did not follow the same path planned for Takashima, who would have been revealed as a traitor, under the influence of the Psi Corps through a secret implanted personality. Her role in the attempted assassination of Kosh would have been exposed and she would have been replaced by Ivanova later in the story. Moving Ivanova into the second-in-command role was a quick and effective use of Straczynski's trapdoors, ready for season one.

But it is interesting that Takashima's traitor storyline still exists in the show, albeit through other characters. Garibaldi's aide Jack, played by Macaulay Bruton, would appear in multiple season one episodes and then shoot Garibaldi in the back as he uncovered (and failed to stop) the assassination attempt against President Santiago. One presumes Takashima would have been the traitor in "Chrysalis."

The idea that Takashima was a traitor certainly casts *The Gathering*—and the Lieutenant Commander's role in those events—in a new light. There are a number of "coincidences," such as Varner having easy access to the station and Sinclair getting stuck in the transport tube on the way to

9. JMS's Character Trapdoors

meet Kosh, which makes more sense when you realize Takashima had the opportunity to stall him from her post in C&C.

Whether Takashima's personality would have been wiped entirely remains a mystery. Particularly as this was the method by which Catherine Sakai would have been written out of the show, to make room for the planned Sinclair-Delenn romance. But it seems that Control was there from the start, seeded in Takashima at the very beginning of *Babylon 5*.

Jumping forward four years, the last-minute negotiations for season five (a surprise to many, given *Babylon 5*'s expected cancellation after four seasons) resulted in the departure of Claudia Christian. There is a lot of conjecture about the nature of Christian's departure, from contract negotiations to being actively forced out. But the loss of Ivanova left Babylon 5 without a commander for its final season.

Enter Tracy Scoggins as Captain Elizabeth Lochley for season five. It is clear that she was a last-minute addition, getting very little storyline outside of her past as Sheridan's ex-wife and a brief bit of exploration of her past in mid-season five episode "Day of the Dead." Unlike Ivanova, she remains something akin to a recurring character on the show, though Straczynski would use her more effectively in the subsequent TV movies and canceled spin-off series *Crusade*, where she would recur (and appear in the credits).

It's unclear what Ivanova's role would have been in the final season. Perhaps her latent telepath abilities and hatred for the Psi Corps would have played a pivotal role in the Byron telepath storyline, though as this largely served to expand Lyta's character, little can be drawn from this. Ivanova would appear in the finale, "Sleeping in Light," but that was an episode held over from season four, serving as a far more effective coda to her story, grieving for Marcus and taking command of the Rangers.

Perhaps, then, Lochley served her purpose: to give Babylon 5 a new captain while Sheridan moved on to the business of running the Earth Alliance.

Trapdoors to Replace Trapdoors: Lyta to Talia (and Lyta Again)

The telepath that becomes a superweapon in the Shadow War is something that Straczynski sets up from day one, as Lyta Alexander delves into Kosh's mind to uncover who tried to kill him and becomes connected to the Vorlons forever after. With the departure of Patricia Tallman as Lyta after the pilot episode, Andrea Thompson's Talia Winters would replace her. When Thompson left, Straczynski essentially reversed the character trapdoor, bringing Lyta back into the fold to fulfill the telepath storyline in seasons three and four.

The reason why Tallman left after *The Gathering* has been something of a mystery for years, with Straczynski suggesting that Tallman left after contractual differences,[4] to studio executives wanting to replace her.

When I interviewed Tallman back in 2022 for my podcast *A Dream Given Form*, I asked her if she thought she would return to *Babylon 5* after *The Gathering*. Her response revealed a very surprising answer.

> We were all told that we were part of the series. I didn't end up in season one because there was a producer at Warner Bros, who I wouldn't sleep with. I talk about this now. He got me off the show.[5]

It's a horrible story and one we have heard countless times before. Thankfully Tallman can speak about it now. While the producer in question will likely never be revealed, it adds some context to her departure.

With the unfortunate circumstances surrounding Tallman's departure, Straczynski brought in Thompson's Talia Winters as the resident Psi Corps telepath for season one. While it is likely Lyta's contact with Kosh in *The Gathering* would have awakened her heightened abilities, for Talia, this change comes in the form of Jason Ironheart in season one's "Mind War." A telepath and former lover of Talia's who has been experimented on by the Psi Corps, Jason gains enhanced telekinetic abilities that make him a danger to himself and the station. As well as the debut of the terrific Walter Koenig as Psi Cop Bester, this episode also has Jason pass on his abilities to Talia, and we see a glimpse of that change when Bester returns in season two's "A Race through Dark Places."

However, frustrated with the lack of storylines and a desire to move away from genre television, Thompson decided to leave right before the Shadow storyline got *really* interesting. Straczynski needed a superpowered telepath, so seizing the opportunity to bring Tallman back as a "guest" was something of a masterstroke, using the trapdoor to replace the character with the character they replaced! Straczynski even framed Tallman's return as an opportunity to "get several crucial parts of the story back on track."[6]

Straczynski did not need studio approval for a guest star, and so was able to navigate any of the difficulties with the unnamed producer. Tallman returned in season two's "Divided Loyalties" and twice in season three before becoming a series regular for the final two years of *Babylon 5*. At that point, there was little the producer could do to prevent Tallman's permanent status on the show. Lyta would go on to play a pivotal role in the defeat of the Shadows and Earth, before getting her own focus with Byron in season five.

Other Trapdoors and Possibilities

There are other, less notable character trapdoors executed by Straczynski. With the departure of Johnny Seka's Dr. Benjamin Kyle after the pilot, Richard Biggs's Dr. Stephen Franklin replaced him as the resident doctor on *Babylon 5* through the five full seasons. Ironically, Franklin leaves the station at the end of season five to replace Kyle as Head of Xenobiological Research on Earth. Kyle's role beyond *The Gathering* has never been laid out, so it is unclear whether he would have followed a similar trajectory as Franklin.

The replacement of Mary Woronov's Narn attaché Ko'Dath with Caitlin Brown's more popular Na'Toth feels like less the execution of a character trapdoor and more a case of finding an actor and character that works on the show. Brown, too, would leave after season one, citing the difficulties of managing daily prosthetics (though she would reprise her role for a one-off appearance in season five), to be replaced by the less successful Mary Kay Adams as Na'Toth in season two. Adams didn't have the same impact as Brown and would be quietly shuffled off after two episodes. Ultimately Na'Toth contributed little to the overall story, and it is unclear what, if anything, was changed about her story as the show progressed.

As for other trapdoors, here we enter the realm of supposition. The core alien ambassadors were never replaced, with Mira Furlan, Andreas Katsulas and Peter Jurasik all delivering masterful performances as Delenn, G'Kar and Londo across the five seasons of the show. In theory, Bill Mumy's Lennier could have taken on the mantle of Minbari ambassador in Delenn's name, though it's unclear what would have happened to the Sheridan romance plotline (I presume there was never any intention to be *that* openly progressive in the mid-90s). Still, it's impossible to imagine anyone else fulfilling the role of Delenn, thanks to Furlan's magnificent performance. A combination of Lennier and Neroon might have worked. John Vikery certainly had the gumption to bring out some of Delenn's more fiery qualities, if Neroon became a bigger player in the Shadow conflict and Minbari civil war.

It's also impossible to imagine *Babylon 5* without G'Kar and Londo. There are certainly no pivotal Narn characters that could have easily taken on G'Kar's role as spiritual leader and savior of his people. Perhaps Na'Toth, or Marshall Teague's Ta'Lon, who would ultimately replace G'Kar as ambassador in season five. For Londo, Vir is a more obvious example of how Straczynski might have activated his character trapdoors, but it is hard to imagine him taking on the more antagonistic qualities we saw from Londo in seasons two and three. Maybe there is a world where William London's Lord Refa fulfilled that villainous Centauri ambassador role, with Vir rising to the challenge to save his people from the darkness.

And finally, there is Security Chief Michael Garibaldi, who, narratively speaking, is replaced in *Babylon 5*. Straczynski was looking for a second in command and saw an opportunity for Jeff Conaway to restart his career following his issues with addiction, something Jerry Doyle also struggled with before and after *Babylon 5*. If Doyle had chosen to leave before the end of the show, Conaway's Zack Allan would have been the obvious replacement—he does become chief of security early in season four.

Lead characters are replaced all the time, and rarely does a TV show survive it. *The X-Files* was never the same when Mulder and Scully weren't at the heart of the story (hence their return in the 2016 revival). On the flip side, *The Walking Dead* lasted just fine without Andrew Lincoln's Rick Grimes; perhaps a zombie apocalypse narrative with a high body count helped make that more palatable. *Babylon 5* was a show where multiple characters were significant to the five-year plan and still lost key roles during the show's run, its lead commander included. But thanks to Straczynski's clever use of character trapdoors, the show, and its story, remained on track. More or less.

10

The Diversity That Almost Was

The fight for on-screen representation is a struggle that rages to this very day. Be it race, gender or sexual orientation, there is a long journey from having relatable, engaging characters on screen to having characters that truly represent the audience watching them.

Sci-fi has always been able to push boundaries in terms of representation. The tangential line between real life and fantasy allows sci-fi to create characters and stories that might (sadly, but inevitably) be less palatable in "mainstream" television.

Back in the '60s, *Star Trek* showed us an enlightened future where a Black woman was an officer on a starship and an Asian and a Russian man worked side by side with their "white American" colleagues. That isn't to say this representation was perfect. Nichelle Nichols understandably grew frustrated with the limited characterization of Uhura; she didn't even get a first name until the 2009 reboot. The same could be said for George Takei's Sulu and Walter Koenig's Chekov, who didn't get any real sort of focus until the movies.

As progressive as it was, *Star Trek* was still a product of the '60s. It's horribly sexist at times and leans into cliché stereotypes. But it was *trying*. Martin Luther King, Jr., recognized what Uhura represented and convinced Nichols to stay. This led to the famous interracial kiss between Kirk and Uhura in 1968's "Plato's Stepchildren." It wasn't the first kiss of its kind on U.S. TV (Nancy Sinatra kissed Sammy Davis, Jr., in 1967's *Movin' with Nancy*), but it was important. Even so, there was studio interference, with William Shatner famously ruining every other take where they didn't kiss, forcing them to use it on screen. Of course, being sci-fi, it was made more palatable by having Kirk and Uhura kiss due to "alien interference."

Did that make it more "acceptable" for white audiences? Perhaps. But there's no denying the statement it made. Jumping forward to the '90s, *Star Trek* attempted to bring some diversity by having a multi-racial cast in *The Next Generation*. But it had its problems. The men in skants were quickly dropped, and there was still the sexist approach to putting female characters in catsuits that ran through Deanna Troi to Seven of Nine and T'Pol in the early 2000s. The question of sexuality and representation also reared its head in the '90s era of *Star Trek*. Attempts to create a queer character were continuously shot down, particularly Jeri Ryan's Seven of Nine, who would only find herself in a queer relationship in 2020's *Star Trek: Picard*.

Star Trek would experiment with representation of gender. *The Next Generation*'s "The Outcast" features a planet of genderless humanoid aliens, and a character persecuted for defining themself as female. Jadzia (and later Ezri) Dax was seen as a transgender hero due to the Trill's ability to move from male to female hosts during its lifetime. But it would take "modern" *Star Trek* to finally fly the flag for representation in *Star Trek: Discovery*, which features two primary characters, Stamets and Culber, in a gay relationship and later, the first nonbinary character in Adira.

But *Star Trek* isn't the only sci-fi franchise to experiment with representation on screen. In film, Anita Pallenberg played lesbian Great Tyrant, Black Queen of Sogo in 1968's *Barbarella*, while 1983's *Born in Flames* dealt with themes of sexuality, class and racism, primarily through Adele Bertei's white lesbian Isabel and Honey's African American character of the same name. In TV, the '70s version of *Battlestar Galactica* would feature characters of different race in Terry Carter's Colonel Tigh and Herbert Jefferson, Jr.'s, Lieutenant Boomer, though the reboot would take things further as it experimented with reverse gender casting and a broader representation of race and sexuality representation, too.

In *Babylon 5*, J. Michael Straczynski would attempt to reflect diversity in the show's characters. There is a version of the show where Delenn was the show's first transgender character and Ivanova and Talia would have been in an open same-sex relationship. But various factors, not least potential interference from the studios, quashed any notion of these ideas playing out on screen.

When it came to representation of race and gender, *Babylon 5* fared better. Both Jonny Seka and Richard Biggs would play chief medical officers of color as Kyle and Franklin, while the first officer (and later captain) was always female, in the form of Takashima (also Asian), Ivanova and Lochley. There was a conscious decision to bring a more representative core cast that reflected the audience watching.

Was it enough? As a white cisgender heterosexual male, I wouldn't presume to make that definitive judgment. But *Babylon 5* always felt more authentic, a greater representation of where humankind might be over two hundred years into the future. It wasn't the Utopian idea of *Star Trek*—particularly the often-sterile era of *The Next Generation*. *Babylon 5* allowed humans to be fallible. It recognized that greed, ambition, bias and even hatred would still be part of the human condition.

Babylon 5 showed, even despite the rise of a xenophobic Earth, that some things had changed for the better. Women were in equal positions of power, from captains to senators and even the Earth president. There did not appear to be any racism toward fellow humans, despite xenophobic tendencies toward other races, and you would regularly see people of non-white races in positions of power and influence.

This even extended to religion. In one of *Babylon 5*'s most strikingly powerful scenes, season one's "The Parliament of Dreams," Commander Sinclair uses an expression of religion and spirituality by presenting station personnel and civilians to ambassadors that represent the multitude of human beliefs. It remains one of television's most unique and inclusive statements on the broad spectrum of human faith.

Few sci-fi shows would represent human religious and spiritual belief in such an open manner. In the world of *Star Trek*, religion seemed largely a thing of the past, abandoned alongside war, famine, and the pursuit of wealth. Even *Deep Space Nine*, the one show in the franchise to examine spirituality beyond the scope of the story of the week, framed religious exploration through the "alien" beliefs of the Bajoran people.

But in *Babylon 5*, spiritual and religious faith would often inform our understanding of the characters, and not just the alien beliefs such as those represented by Delenn and Lennier in the Minbari Religious Caste. From Franklin's (fictional) Foundationist beliefs to Father Theo and the Trappist Monks in season three and Ivanova's very real struggles with her Jewish heritage, humans were at least partly defined by their religious beliefs.

But if gender, racial and religious representation was handled effectively within the show, there were moments where the reality of what we saw in *Babylon 5* buckled against the altogether more progressive ideas Straczynski had for the show.

The First Transgender TV Character That Never Was

Prior to *Babylon 5*—and indeed in the years that followed—a transgender character was not something many expected to see on-screen. There were notable cinematic exceptions, from John Lithgow's former football player Roberta Muldoon in *The World According to Garp* (1982) to Vanessa Redgrave's Emmy-nominated portrayal of professional tennis player Renee Richards in 1986's *Second Serve*. The one small screen exception was David Duchovny's FBI Agent Dennis/Denise Bryson, who appeared in *Twin Peaks*' second season (and reprised the role in the 2017 revival), though it's hard to know if this was played more for laughs and leaning into the show's weird vibe or was a genuine attempt to present a trans character on TV. Certainly, Denise Bryson's appearance in the revival suggested she had settled into her identity as a woman.

Had he succeeded, Straczynski would have created one of the first genuine transgender characters in television in Mira Furlan's Minbari ambassador Delenn. In addition to her transformation from full Minbari to half–Minbari, half-human at the end of season one, Straczynski envisioned the character transitioning from male to female.

This was never to be, though not for the reasons most would assume. Delenn's rather severe look in *The Gathering* was part of the plan to have Furlan play a male Minbari. Given the softness of her voice, Straczynski planned to use voice modulation to make Delenn sound more masculine. Unfortunately, the results were terrible, and the idea of a male ambassador was dropped, with Delenn's look in subsequent seasons becoming much softer and more "feminine."

It is remarkable to think how forward thinking Straczynski was in his approach. Presumably the fact that Delenn was an alien would have made the idea of a character transitioning more palatable to less enlightened audiences. One also wonders if Straczynski would have been able to cast a transgender actress too, as hinted in a Twitter discussion back in 2018.

> Though the flip side is that by having Mira play Delenn as male, then transition to female, we would have been able to present the first transgendered character in SF TV, though alas not played by a transgendered actress given studio roadblocks at that time against the idea.[1]

JMS would go on to create the remarkable transgender character Nomi, played by trans actress Jamie Clayton, in Netflix's *Sense8*, which he developed with the Wachowskis, both transgender themselves. What was remarkable about Nomi was that she wasn't a character whose function was completely dominated by her identity as a trans woman. While it was important, her role as a hacker and a member of the "Sense8" cluster was what propelled her story forward. Her loving relationship with Freema Agyeman's pansexual Amanita was her rock, her happiness, and was presented in a very normal manner. As with much of *Sense8*'s LGBTQ+ representation, Nomi and Amanita's relationship was neither sensationalized nor treated any differently from the other romantic pairings on the show.

Around the same time that Straczynski tried to create TV's first transgender character in Delenn, Terry Farrell's Jadzia Dax of *Deep Space Nine*, and her successor in Nicole de Boer's Ezri Dax, were cited as a transgender representative for many people, with many of the Trill symbiont's previous hosts being male. It's a shame that when Farrell left at the end of season six of *Deep Space Nine*, the producers didn't consider a male actor to play the next host, making this idea more evident. Though given that Farrell was one of only two female leads on the show, it's understandable why another female host was picked.

In recent years, *Doctor Who* has taken strides with the characterization of Time Lords shifting gender during the regeneration process. Steven Moffat brought back the Master as Missy, played by Michelle Gomez, paving the way for Chris Chibnall to cast a female Doctor when he took over the show. Jodie Whittaker's Doctor is in many ways a transgender icon for the modern age, and the theme of representation continues with the transition to a Doctor of color in Ncuti Gatwa.

At the time of writing, the planned *Babylon 5* reboot is in its infancy, and details are sparse. But given Straczynski's experience on *Sense8*, there may be a chance for a transgender character to appear on the new version of the show. Not necessarily the character of Delenn—the reboot will be a complete reimagining—but the idea of genderfluid aliens is not as extreme as it might have been back in 1993.

The First Non-Heterosexual Lead Character on Television?

In 1997, Ellen DeGeneres made history with her sitcom *Ellen*, as the titular character came out as gay. It was a big deal, followed immediately by the actress revealing her own sexuality to the world. There had been queer characters on TV before, but not lead characters.

While Claudia Christian's Susan Ivanova wasn't the lead on *Babylon 5*, she was one of the primary characters. And while her brief, often doomed romantic relationships were with men, she did enter into a relationship with Talia Winters late in the second season.

Except it was never explicitly stated.

Susan and Talia always had a difficult relationship. Susan's mother was a telepath who was driven to suicide by the Psi Corps. Talia was a member of that organization. To Susan, Talia represented everything she hated. And yet, despite that, there was a bond that grew between the two characters, possibly because of the chemistry between Christian and Andrea Thompson on screen.

This came to a head in 1995's season two episode "Divided Loyalties." There is a tenderness to their scenes and the very strong suggestion that they spend the night together when Talia wakes up in Ivanova's bed to find her gone. Unfortunately, Talia's mind is wiped by a latent, traitorous personality, essentially killing the Talia that Susan, and the audience, knew. It's a heartbreaking climax to their doomed relationship.

It would have been braver if Straczynski had been more explicit in the script for "Divided Loyalties." That there is no "kiss" suggests he knew studio interference would quash an overt attempt at queer representation on the show, as noted by Straczynski himself in the *Lurker's Guide* notes for the episode. (*The Lurker's Guide to Babylon 5* is the ultimate fan website and may be found at http://www.midwinter.com/lurk/.)

> I didn't show a kiss because, in my experience, it's easier on all around if one steps into the shallow end of the pool first and walks into the deep end rather than diving in and splashing everybody in the process.[2]

Three months later, *Deep Space Nine* would break barriers with the kiss between Farrell's Jadzia Dax and her former host's wife, Lenara Khan, played by Susannah Thompson. It is presented as something of a passing moment of passion from Dax's previous male host to his wife, allowing the show to "get away" with a kiss between two women. Regardless of the clever acrobatics to get around possible studio interference, it was still an important step for the LGBTQ+ community.

But *Babylon 5* didn't completely let go of the relationship between Susan and Talia. While Straczynski hinted at playing things slow and safe in the depiction of their possible romance, he firmed things up with Susan's admittance of her true feelings for Talia during a Minbari rebirth ceremony in season three's "Ceremonies of Light and Dark."

"I think I loved Talia."

Susan Ivanova might not have said the words "I am bisexual," but as a leading character in 1996, this was an important step in queer representation, a whole year before *Ellen* (and Ellen) came out to the world.

Straczynski's ideas for the show and the reality of what he could achieve show an awareness of the need for diversity and representation on *Babylon 5*. In some areas, such as gender and religion, he succeeded, while buckling against more progressive (for the time) ideas around gender and sexuality.

Perhaps, with the reboot, Straczynski may have free rein when it comes to characters who truly represent the broad community of the audience watching.

11

A Chat with Marshall Teague

In late 2022, I chatted to Marshall Teague for my podcast, *A Dream Given Form*, with my co-host Luke Winch.[1]

A former U.S. Navy officer and deputy sheriff, Marshall moved into acting and had an extensive career spanning more than four decades of television and film. From *Knight Rider* to *The A-Team*, *Roadhouse* to *The Rock*, Teague has countless roles under his belt, but is best loved by *Babylon 5* fans as the man behind recurring Narn warrior Ta'Lon.

Marshall's first role in the *Babylon 5* universe was Nelson Drake in season one's "Infection," where full-body prosthetics turned him into a deadly Ikkaran weapon. In season two, he played the then unnamed Ta'Lon in "All Alone in the Night," returning four more times in seasons three and five. His final *Babylon 5* franchise role was Captain Daniels in an episode of the canceled spin-off, *Crusade*.

Marshall's acting career was extensive, but he still finds the time to talk about the legendary Narn warrior and *Babylon 5*. His admiration for the show, and J. Michael Straczynski's work, was clear the moment we started talking to us. He is a fan of both the show and the fans.

LUKE: *You've had an extensive acting career spanning four decades, and* **Babylon 5** *fans will know you for playing the role of the Narn Ta'Lon. Where does Ta'Lon compare to all the other actor roles that you've had?*

MARSHALL: Ta'Lon was unique, in that I always look at Ta'Lon as a very wise old samurai warrior. You know, very aged, but also very knowledgeable. And understanding that extreme violence at any second, though he can do that, is not necessary all the time. He has a very wise way of knowing when, where, and how to do it. By the same token, using his time and mind as the same weapon. Not quite as good as G'Kar, mind you, but in that realm, hopefully.

BAZ: Babylon 5*'s legacy has endured with fans for decades; from Comic Cons to social media. What do you think keeps* **Babylon 5** *alive* *in that cultural landscape and what has it been like to be part of that experience?*

M: I always like to use a comparison. And the comparison I will use is *Star Trek* and *Babylon 5*. *Star Trek* was always jumping from planet to planet, world to world, meeting people very shortly. Hi, how you doing? Gotta go. And on the other hand, *Babylon 5* brought all these civilizations together, I guess, to coin the phrase "under one roof." Even though it was several roofs. Everybody had to learn to live together, instead of just being in their own world and saying, "Okay, this is our world, we're going to do it this way." But when you're mixed with 20, 100, 200 other civilizations like that, I think it makes you become a little more diplomatic, and smarter, because you really have to learn to deal with everyone.

And it doesn't always work out. I mean, we try it today, and it doesn't always work out. But the idea behind *Babylon 5* was bringing people together, instead of having them go into warp speed, and jump someplace else for a short time. Try to solve their problems and leave. With *Babylon 5*, you couldn't leave the problem. You had to deal with the problem and hopefully come up with a solution that was good for everybody.

So that's how I would compare *Babylon 5*. Very, very smart. I think Joe Straczynski wrote this very intelligently. If you notice in the episodes, he always made you think. He made you look at both sides of the fence every time, or both sides have a lot of fences, in some cases.

L: *Some of the social and political themes of* Babylon 5 *really resonate with some of the problems that we're having now, in the U.K. and the U.S.*

M: Very similar. Very, very similar. I mean, you could jump into almost any episode and compare it to what's going on right now. There were social troubles in *Babylon 5*, not unlike what we're having today. The difference is in *Babylon 5*, which we should do more today, is that they tried to work together, instead of everybody standing on their side of the river and throwing things across. They said let's build a bridge and figure out a way to work this out. And try not to blow up the bridge in the process. It's very, very pertinent as to what's going on today.

L: *You first came into* Babylon 5 *playing Nelson Drake in season one's "Infection." What was your experience, coming onto the show and that process of prosthetics that you had to go through?*

M: Wow! That was a process. Prosthetics had been done, obviously, for a long time, but not quite to that scale, for television anyway. This was the first full-body prosthetic, if my understanding is correct, to be used at a television show. And of course, you've got to understand that for *everybody*, this was new.[2]

11. A Chat with Marshall Teague

Did they have a few hiccups? Yeah, everybody does. But there was a certain dedication. It was kind of like an unspoken rule. Everybody that came on there to work on *Babylon 5* had the same feeling: this is really something good. We want it to succeed. So they put forth the best effort you could ask for. And of course, having a guy walking around in this very large prosthetic suit, I think it woke everybody up.

How do you work with this? To take that bite in the first show of having to work with a human being inside a suit that for nine hours at a time. They couldn't take me out. Once it's on you, it's on you. For nine hours. Because it took four and a half hours to get me into the suit. Everything had to be blended because they didn't want to see any seams. So that takes a lot of time and patience. This group working with you in the makeup department, even though this was new, their professionalism was off the chart. They knew it was hard.

They had to learn, as I learned, that the internal temperature of that suit was around 104, 105 Fahrenheit. Now on the day we did the action shoots, where we did fights and things like that, the temperature got up to about 112. I lost 11 and a half pounds a day, wearing that suit.

Toward the end of the first day, they realized that when I walked, they were hearing a slushing sound, like water, all over the place. I sweated so much that I didn't have to go to the bathroom. It's not that I did it in the suit. No, I didn't, let me clear that up right now! I didn't have to go because there was nothing to go there. Everything that I consumed sweated off me and into the boots. So, I was walking around with that much fluid in the boots. Finally, somebody said "Oh man, what's that sound?" The sound guy did, I think. "I'm hearing something, it's a squeaking squishy sound." And they finally realized, ah man, that's Marshall. His feet are full of water!

So, the makeup came over and took me over to the side, because they didn't know what they were going to get from this one. And the first question they asked is did you do it in the suit?! They punched holes in the boots, and water just ran out. They had to have a person with a mop and a bucket come over and start mopping me up. I was just sweating so much. I was drinking constantly through a straw, and it just continually came off.

Finally, on the I think it was the third day, they located a cool suit. A vest circulated cool air. But those first couple of days were rough, because I honestly couldn't consume enough fluid. They learned a lot. I learned a lot. And we got through it.

B: *"Infection" was the first episode shot after the pilot episode, and there had been several months between production on* The Gathering *and the start of season one. What was the vibe, coming onto the show, when they were gearing up for a whole season of television?*

M: Everybody was a little nervous because they didn't want to fail. But they didn't quite have it together. How fast do we move? Can we move this wall? Where do we stand the guy in the suit because he can't really sit down? Lean him up against this wall here. We'll come to him later. That kind of thing. It was confusing and exciting. I think they really knew they had something very special.

When you read the script, and you're looking around at these magnificent sets that they built, you figure this all came out of the brain of Joe Straczynski. He never left his office because he wrote constantly. He was on his computer writing the next episode all the time. But he knew it. He had every single movement in his head already. And people were trying to catch up to his mind. Which they did. They got it together, once they understood the way he thought, and the way he saw things, they worked together very hard, to make it happen.

But there was confusion. There's always confusion. On the first day of any show that you do. There's always that first day, when everybody's sitting around going "okay, what do I do now?" "Where can I go?" "What do you need?" That kind of stuff. And it was a lot of fun to listen to, you know, after they finally opened up my ears a little bit!

B: *Amazing. So, as well as the Akkaran killing machine, in "Infection," you've done a lot of other prosthetics work, playing aliens on shows like* **Star Trek: Deep Space Nine** *and* **Voyager.** *Were any of these prosthetics as challenging as that first role on* **Babylon 5?**

M: Not even a bit! You've got to understand, they had to cast my entire body. I had to lay in this stuff, for 45 minutes, while it hardened and all I had to breathe through were two straws that were stuck into my nose. That's how it worked. So, you're lying there—literally—you can't move. They say, "don't move." "Okay." "Are you okay?" "Yes, I'm fine." "Can you breathe?" "Yes, I can." "All right, we'll be back and get you in about 45 minutes for lunch!" They took off and went to lunch, and I'm lying there in a box waiting. And they came back, and they said "how long has it been? Oh shit! He's still in there!"

But they had the perfect form. And they built that from me. My suit fit well, let me put it that way. Everything that was designed for the suit fit exceedingly well. Took a while to get in it, but it really fit well. You know, there was rumor that the first cast they did on me ended up in Planet Hollywood. They had it in a big plexiglass case. This suit of me sitting in there when people walked in. So that was the first thing they were greeted with. Oh, hell! What the hell is that!

L: *When you came back to play Ta'Lon in season two, the vibe and the confidence in the crew must have been very different from when you came on in that first season.*

11. A Chat with Marshall Teague

M: Very solid. They were very solid at that point. Everything had a purpose. Everybody had something that they had to get done. The people knew that if they were moving to the next scene, there was always a group there, setting that already in advance. We're shooting from here, here, here, and here. This is gonna be a first shot, like this. They just knew it. They knew what they were doing. There was no hesitation from anyone, there just wasn't. It was so tight. I mean, so tight, that everything had a precise time as to when they wanted it to happen, to give the actors and the performers the time they needed to not feel rushed, to get it done, and get it done well. So that's the difference.

Don't get me wrong, in the first episode, they were very courteous. They wanted you to get it done. But there were all these angles and things they were having to shoot because, you know, some of the rooms we shot in were kind of rounded at top. So, it was about getting it all together, and not bouncing sound off of it. Same for the lighting. You'll notice that there's a lot of shadows and cuts. They wanted to look like they had lit the whole place up. They wanted you to have a shadow, the same thing you would have in any room. I can only compliment the crew, really, and the cast. It was one great, wonderful machine to work in.

L: Brilliant. So, let's talk a little bit about Ta'Lon. I know that JMS wrote everything down. But did you have any input in terms of how Ta'Lon acts, or was it all JMS?

M: We had an episode where Bruce Boxleitner and I were captured. I think it was "All Alone in the Night," and it was a gladiatorial battle that we had to do for the entertainment of this group that captures people. And of course, they gave us swords. Well, I've been in martial arts now for over 50 years. And I've studied weapons and I was fairly good with a sword. When we finished the episode, Bruce said, we have Narns on Babylon 5, but we need to kind of keep this character around, because he's different. Joe had thought about that, but he didn't know where to go with him. I mean, Ta'Lon didn't even have a name in that episode.

So, I went in and talked to Joe about it. And he said, "What would you like to do, if you had a character?" I said, first of all, I don't want to carry a ray gun. I don't want to carry a blaster or transport things and beam me up Scotty. I want to be different than everybody you have on here, and I want to carry a sword, because that is what he lives by. That's part of his thing, his warrior mentality. And he said, "Well, you've got these kinds of swords." I said "No, no, no. More of an Asian, Japanese style sword." He said, "Do you have one?" I said "Yes, but it's a real one. It's a 15th-century katana." He said, "You bring the sword, I'll create the role."

And I walked in with the sword. He looked at it and he said, "Oh, yeah, oh, yeah!" So that's where that came from. Ta'Lon, he came up with. And obviously, the sword went with me, everywhere. Home at night. Back to the office. When it was over, everybody asked, "Can we keep that sword?" "Er, no!" I still have it. It's exactly the way it was, the day I left for the final time. I've had a lot of people try to buy that sword. It's not for sale!

L: *That homage to the samurai code, the samurai bushido. Was that something that JMS injected in there, or did you have input into that as well?*

M: I did. He said, "You've studied martial arts?" And I said, "Yes, I've been doing it ever since I was a little tiny tyke." He said, "Why don't we bring that into his personality? That aura that surrounds him?" I said, "You do know that samurai usually carry two swords. In this case, he should have just the one." He said, "What would you call it?" I said, "I would call it darkness. Because if he draws it, you know the drill, drawing the blade means blood is gonna be spilled somewhere."

I would have loved to have played more Ta'Lon on the show. I was very happy with the episodes I did get to do. And I've received over the years, thousands of correspondences, saying they would like to see more of Ta'Lon. And that's a heck of a compliment, for something's just a recurring role. It did make an impact.

B: *I think it was partly because he was so striking. Because of the nature of the storylines that happened on the show, the Narns were quite loud and quite aggressive at times. Whereas he was just this calm, serene presence among all the other characters.*

M: Exactly. Well, I think people recognize that a person who screams and yells a lot, to me, comes across a bit as a coward, or afraid, because they're trying to intimidate you with loudness. I'll do this and I'll do this! They're basically just running their mouth. In my perspective, some of the most dangerous human beings that I have known in my life—because I used to be a deputy sheriff also—are usually the quietest people you've ever met. They would sit there and just look at you and smile and nod their head.

I felt that was that was his strength, rather than his weakness. If you noticed in most of his scenes, when he would walk into a room, people would back up. He didn't have to say a word. He didn't have to do a damn thing! He would walk into the room and look at you. And it came across in the way it was written. Joe did a marvelous job of his presentation with Ta'Lon and where he put Ta'Lon. Ta'Lon was not a pawn. He was a very strong character and he placed him in very strategic positions of strength that worked with the program.

B: *So, when you were on season two's "All Alone in the Night," did discussions happen straightaway about how Ta'Lon would return to the show? Or was it envisioned as one-off role until Bruce suggested more appearances?*

M: It came to be, by how that particular episode started forming, with Bruce and myself. This coming together of two warriors, if you will. Even though Sheridan and Ta'Lon had to indulge in basically mortal combat, there was a respect that came across from the downbeat. And I think Joe saw that. He [thought,] "I'm gonna use this!" I always say kudos to Joe Straczynski. Not only for bringing me back, but for creating a character that was so strong and caring. He actually cared a lot. People might have called him an old softie. He wasn't a softie. But he cared deeply about what he stood for, and what G'Kar stood for and what other leaders stood for. He respected that. And he demanded respect in return, without having to say a word. So that was pretty cool!

B: *Absolutely. So, you spent a lot of time working with the late, great Andreas Katsulas in those later seasons. What was that experience like?*

M: It was absolute pleasure. We would get up at, say, four o'clock in the morning, to go into makeup. It didn't take as long to put on our pieces as, say, "Infection" did. It was maybe an hour and a half, and then you know, relax. We would talk and then he would go out and smoke a cigarette and I'd go out with him, where we talked and then we'd come and sit back down. The makeup ladies were great. Sometimes we fell asleep! They were there, putting all this on you, and you were just sound asleep, taking a nap. But the second they put our contact lenses into our eyes, we were not Andreas and Marshall. We were G'Kar and Ta'Lon.

And we never came out of character, the entire day. No matter what. We would go to lunch, and I would always stand behind him until he got his meal, and he would sit down to eat before I would sit. Everybody would look at us and say, "Aren't you guys taking this a little bit far?" We never paid any attention to them at all! This is the way we are. It comes across on film. The second they took the contacts out, we went right back to being Andreas and Marshall. That's just the way it worked. It was never spoken. It just became that.

I highly respected Andreas. You're talking about a classically trained actor. Brilliant at how he would go about bringing his message to you. As an actor, I learned something every day from working with him. I use it to this day. If I watch an actor that I have respect for and get an opportunity to work with, like Sean Connery; when I worked with him, I got to watch him work and watch how he worked. I've been very blessed to work with about, oh, I don't know, 15 Academy Award–winning actors and actresses.

And I found most of them to be just priceless to be around. I got along fine with them. I mean, I was Marshall, and you know, Jack Warden, he said just call me Jack Pots! Or just common Jack. Andreas said call me Andre, whatever. Just don't call me late for lunch!

Yeah, you pick things up, and if you don't, you're a fool! The day you think you've got all the answers is the day you need to leave this profession. Because you don't. The day you say you can't learn anything else. That means you're working on your ego alone. And you just screwed yourself!

L: *It's a great philosophy for life. Every day is a learning day.*

M: It is, and I try to do that every single day. It could be the smallest little thing and you look at it, you go, wow! Where did that come from? And you put it away. Hold on to it. Someday it'll come out and say, hey, remember me? Remember that time? Yes, you might want to use that. So you do.

L: *Thinking back to when you were talking about the caring nature of Ta'Lon. There was one scene that popped into my head as you were saying that, and that's the scene where G'Kar comes back to his quarters and Ta'Lon has been standing outside his door, waiting patiently. That really showed his loyalty and love, and dedication for G'Kar.*

M: I remember that day, very well. There's not a lot of people that can say after 25 years that you can remember that day and what you were doing at that moment. I can remember almost every moment he and I spent together. Whether it was his third cigarette or his fifth cigarette of the day. I would go outside with him, and we would sit on a wall. You've got these two red-eyed spotted-headed guys sitting on a wall. One's smoking a cigarette and the other's got a sword hanging over his back!

B: *What does it mean to you when people say they love the character of Ta'Lon?*

M: Any time someone says, "Hey, I dug the character you played," first of all, that means I did my job right, and did it good. I don't like to say well, because "well" is a kind of a statement. I went and did it well; I don't know if it was any good, but I did it. To say you did it good means you were all in on it.

There was a great lesson taught to me years ago, by one of my first acting coaches. I was such a new guy. I was so new. She was 83 years old, and at one point she was the head of talent for MGM, for about 16 to 18 years. When I tell you she gave Clark Gable his screen test, that tells you how far back she went, and the talent she saw. She worked with me, and she taught me two very important lessons.

One, the camera is a truth machine. You can't be playing the part

11. A Chat with Marshall Teague

of dog and think cat, because meow comes across instead of bow wow. And the second lesson she taught me was, it's not personal, it's just business. Don't lie and do your job. And do it good. Not well. Do it good. Big difference.

Her name was Lillian Sidney. Lillian Burns was her name, but she married George Sidney. George Sidney was a director, and he did a lot of the Elvis films. When I met her, she was all five foot two of her, and glasses that were so thick. [She] pointed her little hand at me and said, "You are going to learn Shakespeare; you're going to learn about the art of Shakespeare."

I ended up going to England, years ago, with money I had saved. I didn't get a job, but I went to the Academy, and I worked there painting sets. They would say, "Yank, you're understudying this role." I knew I wasn't going to get on stage. I knew that. But I did get on one night. I did the prologue from *Henry V*, and I got the job that night because the guy playing the role came in so pissed, drunk out of his mind. He nearly hung himself with his cape! So, the stage manager told him to go home, and said, "Here's the cloak, Yank, you're going on!"

Later on, there was a bar down the street, around the corner. I think it was called the Lame Duck at the time, and a lady named Maeve ran it. I was there. Nothing against the people that worked in the theater, but they never asked me to sit with them. But I walked in after that performance, and one of the young actors reached out and grabbed my arm. I looked down at him and he said, "Not bad, Yank. Not bad." That was my payoff for a year and a half. I couldn't have asked for any more than that. It was brilliant and I hold it very dear to my heart.

In four decades of doing this, I've had a lot of stories with a lot of people. For me, talking about Ta'Lon is something that is very dear to my heart. How many people can go along and say, "I had a job." "What did you do?" "It's nothing, I just played a little role." No. There are no little roles. There are only small actors. If you did your job good, and you put everything you could into it, bravo.

L: *So, picking on your excellent memory recall, do you have a favorite episode or moment from* Babylon 5?

M: Yes. There was a scene where G'Kar and I were working together. I think it was when he was getting ready to leave, and I was trying to explain to him what he meant to me. I said, "I carry my sword in my hand. You carry your sword in your heart and in your mind." It was a statement by Joe, but also, it made you want to reach out and hug that person and say this is how much you mean to me. In fact, Andreas *did* mean that much to me.

In our last scene, in "Objects at Rest," G'Kar is a hologram. He had already gone. Those scenes stand out in my mind as the pinnacle of the relationship between two people, that were trying to bring their people, and other people, together. Joe wrote those scenes and when you read it, it was easy to do, because all you do is drop the piece of paper, look the person in the eye and tell them the truth.

B: *That final scene was such an amazing moment. Ta'Lon wasn't in that many episodes over the course of* Babylon 5; *there were only a handful of scenes between Ta'Lon and G'Kar. But you got* that *relationship, you got* that *connection. Those words* meant *something.*

M: Yes. G'Kar stopped Ta'Lon from killing a group of people in one of their earlier episodes together. When we were filming that scene, when there was a mutiny against G'Kar, I stepped up and drew the sword. The actor said, "Can you draw that sword pretty quick?" I said, "Oh yeah. I'm going to put it right at the side of your neck. When you hit your spot, don't move." That was the introduction, and I remember Andreas saying, "Remind me never to piss you off!"

B: *So, at the end of season five, Ta'Lon took G'Kar's place as the Narn ambassador of Babylon 5. If the show had continued, or Ta'Lon's story had continued in* Crusade, *or the TV movies, where would you have liked to have seen Ta'Lon go next?*

M: Follow in the footsteps of G'Kar but using his own mind and his own way of going about it. He would always have G'Kar on his shoulder, talking to him. He would have to make the decision the way he thinks. I'm not sure that Ta'Lon would have taken the sword off. He may have set it down when he talked. When he walked in, the sword would have been more like a scepter, that I would set down, to bring peace to the table. I think that's how I would have approached that.

My understanding is that Joe is going to bring *Babylon 5* back. A new version of *Babylon 5*. And I wish him well. I hope that the young actors that will be in that look at it with the same integrity that we looked upon ours. I mean, if he called me and said, do you still have the sword? I'd say, it just so happens I do!

B: *Would you return in the reboot, if asked?*

M: If they asked me, of course. Because of my love for the show and my respect for Joe and his writing.

B: *If you were to play a new character in the* Babylon 5 *reboot, what kind of character would you like to be?*

M: You know, actors like to have their face seen. I'm no different. I do too. However, having said that, most people said they recognized it was me under the makeup, the moment they saw me, because of my eyes. They said

11. A Chat with Marshall Teague

you have a way of looking at people, that other people don't. Even with the red eyes, and all the makeup, the second I walked into the room, people said, "That's Marshall."

Would I like to play another type of character to Ta'Lon? I don't know. I really can't answer that because I loved the character I played. It doesn't bother me to wear head gear. They don't make you act. They are just utensils you place on your body to help you act. I've played werewolves, I've played a dinosaur person on *Star Trek: Voyager*.[3] A Jem'Hadar on *Star Trek: Deep Space Nine*.[4] You can't rely on prosthetics to do your job. It doesn't. You have to act with and through the mask. In *Phantom of the Opera*, he was always covered, but the performance was so brilliant. But I don't have a problem with it. It doesn't matter if it's a prosthetic. It's just another character you're playing.

I don't know if you guys know this, but all the alien heads on *Babylon 5* were made off my head.

B: *Really?*

M: The original bust, they made of my head, because I have a very distinct jaw line. Because I had very distinct cheeks and head size. They said you have the perfect noggin! They made all the other character masks off of it. I was told that, and I said, seriously? All those aliens are me? They said, "Yes, you have the perfect noggin, so we made all those heads off of it."

B: *So, there's a bit of Marshall Teague in all the aliens on* Babylon 5*?*

M: Yes. Whether I'm there or not, I'm there. That's another backdoor compliment. So many things come out of a single show, sometimes a person playing a character is actually you, and you don't even realize, until years later. I like to say my footprint is in *Babylon 5* in more places than you would know.

L: *So, final question, is what does* Babylon 5 *mean to you?*

M: I think I just described it! I never thought of any job I did as run of the mill, regardless of its size. I was in the movie *Roadhouse*, with Patrick Swayze.[5] I didn't have a lot of dialogue, but what do most people remember about that movie, more than anything? Me and Patrick Swayze fighting. And they remember my character, because he was the badass of badasses and the fights we had in the bar. I was on *Walker, Texas Ranger* eight times, playing different roles, and I was always the bad guy![6] Eight different characters on the same show. No one else can say that. It's about taking what you're given and giving back 150 percent. That's how I look at every role I've ever played.

You guys doing this, and appreciating *Babylon 5*, I'm tickled to death to be here talking to you about it. It's been a pleasure.

12

Season One

A Master Class in World-Building

A great first season of television lays the foundation for all the events that will follow, creating enticing new worlds and characters while also setting expectations for years two, three and beyond.

There are many great first seasons of television. *Buffy the Vampire Slayer* and *Dexter* designed the models for the villain of the season and continued to build on that model with each year that followed. *Twin Peaks* introduced dreams and the supernatural to its crime procedural format early on in its first year, establishing themes that would pay off in season two. *The X-Files* defined classic monster-of-the-week formats in episodes like "Squeeze," while also layering in the alien conspiracies to build a greater mythology within the format of the show. *Lost* laid the groundwork for intricate character storytelling through its use of flashbacks, while *Alias* wove the fantastical Rambaldi mythology into the weekly spy drama to build a complex and tense narrative of global conspiracies, secret organizations, and dark family secrets.

The first season of *Babylon 5* might not be up there with the likes of *Dexter* or *Lost*'s memorable first seasons, but it is arguably just as successful. J. Michael Straczynski delivers a master class in world-building, setting up the human and alien worlds and teasing plots that would not come to fruition until years later.

But he also keeps the show grounded and episodic. Much of season one feels like a mirror to *Star Trek*. Outside of the two-parter "A Voice in the Wilderness," the majority of episodes are self-contained and seem, at first glance, to have little impact on the next. There are substantial mythology episodes, such as "Signs and Portents" and "Babylon Squared," but even these have a self-contained narrative that wraps up the core story by the credits, while teasing bigger things to come.

Straczynski understood the audience and what people expected from

12. Season One

their weekly science fiction drama. He knew that people weren't ready for the kind of serialized drama that they would lap up in later years with *Lost* and *Battlestar Galactica*. A degree of patience was needed. So season one of *Babylon 5* took its time, painting a world unlike the utopia of *Star Trek*, while still following an episodic format people were comfortable with.

This was a season where the crew were talking about politics and the media news cycle. Where people hung out at casinos and drank and worried about the price of station rentals. Where dock workers went on strike for better rights and rogue telepaths were hunted down by a seemingly psychopathic police force. This was darker and gritter and more real, a far more believable vision of the 23rd century than Kirk's travels on the USS *Enterprise*.

A good first season can be just as rewarding in rewatch, and the first year of *Babylon 5* is a great one. Every episode has a reference or setup for bigger things to come. Straczynski painstakingly laid the groundwork for all the grand events of seasons two, three and four. Londo and G'Kar's bitter rivalry. Earth's rising xenophobia and troubles with Mars. The divide between the Minbari Religious and Warrior Castes. All of this is cleverly seeded in season one.

Naturally, there are heavy hitters too, in terms of the five-year arc. "Signs and Portents" reveals the Shadows for the first time. "Babylon Squared" deals with the disappearance of Babylon 4, which will play a huge role in season three. "Chrysalis" ends with the assassination of President Santiago at the (then unknown) orders of Clark. But these were just the tip of the iceberg that *Babylon 5* had to offer.

Over the course of this chapter, we'll explore those seeds in greater detail and examine the clever manipulation of the *Star Trek* episodic structure. But first, let's look to the pilot, where *Babylon 5*'s story all began....

The Gathering

The 1993 pilot is something of an oddity in the *Babylon 5* mythos. Except for Jerry Doyle's Michael Garibaldi, none of the main Earthforce crew are on the show for more than one season. Many of the regulars, like Vir and Lennier, would not turn up until the first full year. Lyta would be replaced by Talia, before replacing her later in the show's run. Cast changes are expected over a show's run, but from *The Gathering*, only Garibaldi, Delenn, Londo and G'Kar stay the course for five seasons.

The general aesthetic is different too. Some of this is down to the choices made by director Richard Compton, such as the focus on harsh lighting and smoke over characters and set, which we explored in an earlier chapter. Others are the simply creative choices made by Straczynski, such as the softening of G'Kar's look or the abandonment of the idea to make Delenn transition from male to female.

Arguably, there is a more of a tonal difference between the pilot and season one opener "Midnight on the Firing Line" then there is between season one and the rest of the series. Certainly, there is the sense that Straczynski had more control after the events of the pilot, and the focus on the excellent character work and world-building helped.

But *The Gathering*, despite the odd choices made by Compton, has plenty to offer too. The attempted assassination of Vorlon ambassador Kosh may serve as the catalyst, but there are moments that will have huge resonance later on. Sinclair's hole in his mind will play into the missing 24 hours at the Battle of the Line, explored in season one's "And the Sky Full of Stars" and his destiny as Valen, while the bitter history between the Centauri and Narn is quickly established through G'Kar's attempts to incriminate Londo.

There are also plot points that were inevitably altered by the change of cast between the pilot and season one. Laurel Takashima was meant to be a traitor and the framing of Sinclair makes a lot more sense when you watch her actions through this light. As explored in an earlier chapter, her traitorous storyline would move to other characters like Garibaldi's aide Jack and Talia Winters.

The loss of Takashima, Kyle, and Lyta as a result of Tamlyn Tomita, Johnny Sekka and Patricia Tallman's departures from *Babylon 5* would also have some advantages. The two people to get closest to Kosh would immediately be recalled to Earth, casting simple actor departures in a much more sinister light and playing into the rise of the xenophobic Earth across the rest of the show.

Looking at the original scripts for *The Gathering*, there are also some interesting ideas that would recur in different forms throughout the series. The original 1989 pilot script that Straczynski shopped to Warner Bros. featured Garibaldi trying to get hold of his dying father back on Mars, and there were many more scenes between the security chief and Sinclair. The assassin was an actual shape-shifter and Londo was a part-time pickpocket. Dr. Kyle was Dr. Chakri Mendak. Sinclair is not put on trial but finds a whole innovative way to solve the attempted assassination of Kosh. We would also meet Kosh's life-mate, Velana, who played an important role in the pilot.[1]

Of course, things always change in the development process, and even the script written in 1992 has a scene that was ultimately cut but would get more focus in season three's "Dust."[2]

SINCLAIR: Garibaldi ... what we've got?
Intercut between Sinclair, the Traveler, and Garibaldi, who is also behind cover, with two of his men.
GARIBALDI: Dust-dealer. Small time, given the way he tried to smuggle the stuff in here. I think we can take him out—
SINCLAIR: No, it's too crowded, somebody's bound to get caught in the crossfire. Let me talk to him. But get a backup team outside stat.

There are two versions of the pilot episode of *Babylon 5*. The original version of *The Gathering* aired on February 22, 1993, on PTEN. Due to the collapse of PTEN after season four, *Babylon 5* moved to TNT for its fifth and final season in 1998. Straczynski oversaw a special edition of *The Gathering*, which aired on TNT immediately after *In the Beginning*. This version was much more in keeping with Straczynski's vision. Scenes were edited to move at a faster pace, and 14 minutes of footage was restored to add exposition and character development.

Most notably, the new version of *The Gathering* added the prophetic line "Entil'zha, Valen," spoken by Kosh when he first meets Sinclair, foreshadowing the station commander's destiny revealed in season three's "War Without End."

The trip through the station's alien sector was cut and Tamlyn Tomita's lines were restored to their undubbed version. Warner Bros. had demanded her lines be completely redubbed as they sounded too "harsh." *Babylon 5* composer Christopher Franke, who scored the rest of the series, also replaced the original music by Stewart Copeland.

The Gathering is just the first step toward a bigger world. It didn't go as smoothly as Straczynski would have liked, and there were more changes and delays than he would have liked in getting from the pilot to season one, but it tested well with audiences and proved that *Babylon 5* could be a success, outperforming all other PTEN shows in the ratings when it made its 1993 debut.

Breaking the Mold

Eleven months later, season one made its debut with a revamped cast. Claudia Christian replaced Tamlyn Tomita in the new second in command role of Susan Ivanova. Andrea Thompson made her debut as Talia Winters, replacing Patricia Tallman's Lyta Alexander. Richard Biggs's Doctor Stephen Franklin replaced Johnny Sekka's Benjamin Kyle and Julia Nickson was in as Sinclair's new love interest Catherine Sakai. Along with the debut of Vir (Stephen Furst), Lennier (Bill Mumy) and Na'Toth (Julie Caitlin Brown), the core cast was complete.

Over the course of season one, *Babylon 5* seemed at first to deliver a similar format to now-rival *Star Trek: Deep Space Nine*. Each week, audiences would encounter new visitors and threats to the station, but the story would be wrapped up in a 45-minute run time. From Soul Hunters to rogue telepaths, Ikarran superweapons and the search for the Holy Grail, *Babylon 5* seemed to be another episodic show.

There was also the analogical approach to storytelling. One of the season's most powerful episodes, "Believers," sees Dr. Franklin battle against the wishes of two alien parents to heal their sick child, an overt take on the challenges surrounding Jehovah's Witnesses' beliefs. "Deathwalker" would look at a war criminal's experimentation on prisoners that mirrors the Nazi treatment of the Jews.

Babylon 5 appeared to be Straczynski's take on a largely familiar science fiction territory. *Star Trek*, particularly in the era of *The Next Generation*, had a model that worked. *Babylon 5* was following a similar path.

Or was it? Straczynski understood that a degree of patience was needed to introduce audiences to multi-year story arcs. While at first glance, it wasn't too dissimilar to *Deep Space Nine*, *Babylon 5* was actually setting up all the foundations for the big events.

The opening episode, "Midnight on the Firing Line," set up the rivalry between Peter Jurasik's Londo and Andreas Katsulas's G'Kar. This would be a cornerstone of the show and inform Londo's path to the Shadows in "Signs and Portents" and his actions in the destruction of the Narn base through his new allies in season closer "Chrysalis." In the second episode, "Soul Hunter," Sinclair would learn that Mira Furlan's Delenn was a member of the Grey Council and start an investigation into her true purposes, a storyline that would be bolstered by his experiences in "And the Sky Full of Stars" and his eventual path to becoming Valen. Earth's xenophobia would be established in the early episode "The War Prayer." Even those simple stand-alone stories would have great importance down the line.

The first season of *Deep Space Nine* was a little more focused on world-building in its first season than its predecessor, but only the finale, "In the Hands of the Prophets," could be seen as an arc-based episode. Season one of *Babylon 5* had "And the Sky Full of Stars," which set up Sinclair's destiny; "Signs and Portents," which introduced the Shadows; and two-parter "A Voice in the Wilderness," which established the Great Machine on Epsilon III. It also introduced the mystery of Babylon 4 in "Babylon Squared" and then blew everything apart with the growing Shadow influence and President Santiago's assassination in the finale, "Chrysalis." There are multiple "important" episodes in *Babylon 5*'s debut season.

The world-building was important. Straczynski quickly and subtly tweaked the "*Star Trek* model" to layer in a rich mythology. There would be ramifications from the events of those important season one episodes, though only "Chrysalis" would bring the most overt change of direction immediately. In season two, Straczynski would build on the episodic and mytharc model, with more episodes that had greater importance to the overall storyline, particularly in the home stretch of its sophomore run.

But he could only do that with the foundations he built in season one. Fans of *Babylon 5* soon came to realize that events that happened one week might have greater significance in the next. These were characters that were quickly changed by their season one journeys.

Londo transformed from the laughingstock of the Centauri court to a man with great influence. G'Kar was not the villain that we were presented with in those opening episodes. Sinclair had grown more disillusioned by Earth by the time Santiago was killed. It was rare to see characters so altered by the events around them after a single season of television, especially back in 1994.

Babylon 5 was different. It was about to prove that characters could evolve and change and be affected by the events that unfolded each week. But of course, season one was just the tip of the iceberg. Far bigger changes were yet to come.

Seeding the Five-Year Arc

We've already talked about world-building in season one. But what is not apparent until a rewatch is just how many moments seed the bigger things to come. There are snippets of information, dreams, references and even news items that seem just a part of the rich tapestry of *Babylon 5* at first glance. They have little to no relevance to the plot of the week but have huge relevance to the overall story. Here are some of the most notable seeds.

Episode 1: "Midnight on the Firing Line"
- Londo's dream features his death at G'Kar's hands, which will take place in the future glimpsed in season three's "War Without End."

Episode 6: "Mind War"
- The debut of the Psi Corps, pulling the strings in the government, which leads to "Chrysalis" and the reign of corrupt President Clark.
- The debut of the First Ones at Sigma 957, who would be recruited in season four's "The Summoning" to fight in the Shadow–Vorlon conflict.

Episode 8: "And the Sky Full of Stars"
Several of the headlines in Garibaldi's newspaper foreshadow future stories:
- "Psi-Corps in Election Tangle"
- "San Diego Still Considered Too Radioactive for Occupancy," which hints at the San Diego Wastelands, shown in "Spider in the Web" (season two, episode six).
- "Is Something Living in Hyperspace?" which sets up the Shadows, who would work in secret and debut later in season one's "Signs and Portents."

Episode 13: "Signs and Portents"
- Not only would the episode debut Mr. Morden and the Shadows, but it also revealed that the Minbari had chosen Sinclair to be the commander of Babylon 5.

Episode 16: "Eyes"
- The witch trial against Sinclair by Colonel Ari Ben Zayn would also act as a revenge plot by the off-screen Alfred Bester from "Mind War" and build on the mystery of Sinclair's involvement with the Minbari.

Episodes 18 and 19: "A Voice in the Wilderness (Parts 1 and 2)"
- Mars's disillusionment with Earth is hinted at in earlier season one episodes and brought to the fore in this two-parter. This sets up the rebellion that ignites with President Clark's martial law declaration in season three's "Point of No Return" and the rebellion and underground movement in season four.
- This episode also sets up the Great Machine on Epsilon III and new host Draal, who would have importance in the fight against the Shadows in subsequent seasons.

Episode 20: "Babylon Squared"
- The return of Babylon 4, the debut of Zathras, and Sinclair's destiny are all set up here and will play an important role in season three's "War Without End."

Episode 21: "The Quality of Mercy"
- The alien healing device will play an important role in saving Garibaldi's life in season two's "Revelations" and Marcus sacrificing his life energy to save Ivanova in season four's "Endgame."

While episodes like "And the Sky Full of Stars" and "Babylon Squared" are considered important episodes in the overall mytharc of *Babylon 5*, it is the smaller things, like the newspaper headlines, that are blink-and-you'll-miss-it moments but are richly rewarding when revisited with the knowledge of bigger things to come.

A Note on Viewing Orders

As is often the nature of television broadcasting, many episodes aired out of the original intended order. On a more serialized show like *Babylon 5*, this could prove problematic, but fortunately, this is only noticeable in the first and fifth seasons and the spin-off series *Crusade*, which we'll review in more detail later.

There are a number of ways in which season one—and later seasons—could be viewed, but there are two timelines that are most effective. The "JMS Viewing Order" (aka "The *Lurker's Guide* Master List") was compiled from J. Michael Straczynski's interviews, notes, and discussions. The *Lurker's Guide* put forward this viewing order, and it is one of the most widely recognized alternatives to the broadcast run.

However, there is an even more detailed chronological run, the *Babylon 5* Historical Database. This was compiled by Terry Jones during the show's run. Terry submitted the detailed series chronology to reference editor Fiona Avery in 1999 and it was approved by Straczynski himself. The *Babylon 5* Historical Database was created by looking "inside" the episode to determine the chronology rather than when PTEN decided to air an episode. It was published in Titan's *Babylon 5* magazine and later in the book *Across Time and Space: The Chronologies of Babylon 5* from Synthetic Worlds.[3]

The JMS Viewing Order for Season One:

- "Midnight on the Firing Line"
- "Soul Hunter"
- "Born to the Purple"
- "Infection"
- "The Parliament of Dreams"
- "Mind War"
- "The War Prayer"
- "And the Sky Full of Stars"
- "Deathwalker"
- "Believers"
- "Survivors"
- "By Any Means Necessary"
- "Signs and Portents"
- "Grail"
- "Eyes"
- "A Voice in the Wilderness—Part 1"
- "A Voice in the Wilderness—Part 2"
- "Babylon Squared"
- "The Quality of Mercy"
- "TKO"
- "Legacies"
- "Chrysalis"

The Straczynski-approved *Babylon 5* Historical Database Viewing Order for Season One (with chronological dates):

- "Midnight on the Firing Line"—February 2258
- "Soul Hunter"—Wednesday, March 2–Thursday, March 3, 2258
- "Infection"—Tuesday, March 8–Wednesday, March 9, 2258
- "Born to the Purple"—Tuesday, March 22–Friday, March 25, 2258
- "The Parliament of Dreams"—Wednesday, March 30–Sunday, April 3, 2258
- "The War Prayer"—Sunday, April 3–Thursday, April 7, 2258
- "And the Sky Full of Stars"—Monday, April 11–Wednesday, April 13, 2258
- "Mind War"—Sunday, April 24–Tuesday, April 26, 2258
- "By Any Means Necessary"—May 2258
- "Deathwalker"—May 2258
- "Believers"—June 2258
- "Survivors"—June 2258
- "A Voice in the Wilderness, Parts 1 and 2"—June 2258
- "Babylon Squared"—Tuesday, July 12–Wednesday, July 13, 2258
- "Legacies"—July 2258
- "Grail"—July 2258
  NOTE: "Babylon Squared," "Legacies" and "Grail" are before "Signs and Portents" and ordered on the basis of Delenn receiving the Triluminary and beginning construction on the Chrysalis device (shown at different stages of construction throughout).
- "Signs and Portents"—Wednesday, August 3–Friday, August 5, 2258
- "TKO"—August 2258
- "Eyes"—September 2258
- "The Quality of Mercy"—September 2258
- "Chrysalis"—Friday, December 30, 2258–Sunday, January 1, 2259

There are a few subtle differences between the lists, but the most significant change from the broadcast order is the back half of season one. "TKO," which deals with Ivanova's grief over her father, is placed near the end of the season, while "Legacies," which features the debut of Delenn's Warrior Caste rival Neroon, takes place after "A Voice in the Wilderness" two-parter in both orders.

The biggest difference between these versions is the placement of "Signs and Portents," the key mythology episode that introduces series villains, the Shadows. This happens much later in the *Babylon 5* Historical Database version, making the link between their debut and their return in season finale "Chrysalis" far closer thematically (chronologically, they still take place four months apart).

As season one keeps events largely self-contained, the changes to the viewing experience make for a subtler but richer experience for fans, offering the first season of *Babylon 5* the way Straczynski intended it

The Unmade Episodes of Season One

As with any TV series, there are always episode ideas that never get as far as the production stage. Some were little more than one-line concepts; Straczynski confirmed an idea for a season one episode where Takashima would have returned, on the run from something chasing her from the Rim.[4] Others, like "Festival," were ideas that got to the script stage and were abandoned; in this instance elements from "Festival" were reworked in season one's "The Parliament of Dreams." And then were two proposed scripts by Straczynski's mentor Harlon Ellison.

One story that went under two possible titles—"The World Below" or "Midnight in the Sunken Cathedral"—would have been set deep within the darkest parts of *Babylon 5* and focused on a whole subculture with its own rules, regulations, and leaders, where travelers could look for new opportunities to start new lives on other worlds.

But the most interesting idea was the episode that went under the working titles of "Demon in the Dust"/"Demon on the Run," which would have been a direct sequel to Ellison's 1964 *The Outer Limits* episode, "Demon with a Glass Hand." As a huge fan of *The Outer Limits* and Ellison's work, Straczynski was keen to develop the episode, particularly as the plan was to have Robert Culp reprise his role as Trent, an android from the distant future who would arrive on Babylon 5 after being on the run for over three hundred years.

Despite their friendship and Ellison's involvement on *Babylon 5* as a conceptual consultant, he never wrote a full script for the show—though season five's "A View from the Gallery" and "Objects in Motion" were based on his stories. The idea that an episode of *Babylon 5* could act as a sequel to one from *The Outer Limits* is fascinating and a little out there. But given Straczynski's use of cultural influences in *Babylon 5*, it might just have worked.

Supplemental: A Season One Review

Having reviewed TV content online for several years, I thought it would be fun to indulge in a review of each season as a supplement to these chapters.

The first season on *Babylon 5* is better than you remember. It doesn't have the big, grand, epic moments of late season two's Narn–Centauri war, the break from Earth and Shadow War of season three, the huge conflicts of the fourth or even the fall of Centauri Prime from season five. But all those moments that fans love so much would not have been possible without the careful groundwork of season one.

The pace and tone of *Babylon 5* season one is very much a reflection of the station's commanding officer, Jeffrey Sinclair. Michael O'Hare brings a much more introspective performance than his season two replacement, Bruce Boxleitner's John Sheridan. He is patient and considered, a true diplomat and a man perfectly suited to navigating the day-to-day activity of the station, with its quarter-million inhabitants and all the negotiations and schemes that come with different alien races living together. He isn't the most exciting of lead characters—Boxleitner would nail that with his enthusiastic energy later on—but, like much of season one, there's plenty to enjoy from O'Hare's performance on repeated viewing.

The first season has a few clunkers. "Infection" is a ghastly OTT episode that sees an ancient alien weapon turn its victim into a killing machine. It's a standard science fiction trope with all the subtlety of a sledgehammer. That it was the first episode recorded after the pilot (though the fourth to be aired in season one) suggests that *Babylon 5* was still very much finding its feet. "TKO" has the cliched alien boxing ring storyline that would be repeated in everything from *Angel* to *Sanctuary*, while "The War Prayer" is a misjudged attempt to deal with a xenophobic and militant Earth group that comes across as terribly dull to watch.

And yet, even these "terrible" episodes of *Babylon 5* have something to offer. Sinclair's speech about humanity going to the stars in "Infection." Ivanova coming to terms with her father's death in "TKO." The setup of the xenophobic Earth that would infect humanity in later seasons first glimpsed in "The War Prayer." There are so many seeds planted in season one that it makes for a richly rewarding experience on rewatch. There is an incredible amount of world-building that makes everything that follows as believable as it is exciting.

It might be hard for season one episodes to make the "top 10" of any fan's *Babylon 5* list, but there are still strong episodes. After the clunky and slow pilot, *The Gathering*, which is a million miles from the *Babylon 5* fans would come to love, season one opener "Midnight on the Firing Line" is a superbly paced episode that immediately gets to the heart of the show's core selling point, Londo and G'Kar. "The Parliament of Dreams" is a fascinating meditation on spirituality and religion that does a tremendous amount of world-building for the different alien races while also exploring a side not seen in the humanity of *Star Trek*: the idea that different people can have different beliefs. "And the Sky Full of Stars" is the first "big" episode of the series, exploring the trauma of Sinclair's missing 24 hours from the Battle of the Line, while "Believers" is one of the best allegorical episodes of any science fiction season, with an absolutely harrowing ending.

And then comes "Signs and Portents," an episode that introduces Mr. Morden and the Shadows, sees Londo begin his dark path to power, and teases much greater things to come. The season's only two-parter, "A Voice in the Wilderness," establishes Draal and the Great Machine on Epsilon III, another key aspect of the show moving forward, while "Babylon Squared" taps into the mystery of the disappearance of Babylon 4. Finally, "Chrysalis" blows everything wide open, as Santiago is assassinated, the Shadows begin to move, Delenn starts her transformation, and the galaxy is forever changed.

While not as grand as later seasons, the first full year of *Babylon 5* is quite the journey, carefully and consideringly moving all the pieces into play, ready for J. Michael Straczynski to start ramping things up in season two.

13

Season Two
The Changing of the Guard

Season two of *Babylon 5* was perhaps the most important year in the show's history. With the tremendous groundwork laid in season one, it needed to start building toward the big events that would define its five-year arc. The rise of the Shadows, Londo's deal with the devil, an increasingly corrupt Earth, and the mystery of why the Minbari surrendered at the Battle of the Line.

There was one problem. The show lost its central star.

The departure of Michael O'Hare could have ended the show before it had even really begun. How does the long-form narrative stay on track when you have to introduce a new lead?

Straczynski envisioned Sinclair as a character that would command both Babylon 5 and its predecessor/successor, Babylon 4, in a subsequent five-year series, *Babylon Prime*. His connection to the Delenn and the Minbari was pivotal to the foundations of the show, and his investigation into what happened at the Battle of the Line would have carried through nine further years of storytelling.

As we discussed in chapter 4, most of those story ideas ultimately changed, and given the situation with PTEN, the chances of a *Babylon Prime* series materializing were virtually zero. Instead, the war with the Shadows and the formation of the Interstellar Alliance, all key elements of the spin-off series, would be massively condensed into seasons three, four and five of *Babylon 5*. Which meant elements like the fall of the Narn regime to the Centauri would also take place much sooner.

The result would be a far more thrilling *Babylon 5* than the slightly more sedate version hinted at in those early drafts. But how would Straczynski navigate the loss of Commander Jeffrey Sinclair?

Enter Bruce Boxleitner as Captain John Sheridan.

13. Season Two

Sinclair to Sheridan and Getting Back on Track

By the end of season two, the threat of the Shadows had been revealed and an army of light was preparing for war. Earth would take an insidious path following the assassination of President Santiago, with the formation of the Nightwatch and an increasingly xenophobic government that would oppose the very beliefs Babylon 5 stood for.

For Sinclair, learning about the Shadows, joining the good fight, and forming an underground movement against the increasingly corrupt President Clark would have been a natural progression of his path. He had already demonstrated that he was willing to break the rules to achieve peace, though his dealings with senators, Earthforce Internal Affairs and even the Psi Corps. Forming an underground movement would have been a completely natural extension of his character arc. His strong relationship with Delenn would have stood him in good stead with the revelations about the Shadows awakening at Z'ha'dum, and he would have used every diplomatic muscle in his arsenal to navigate the Centauri–Narn conflict.

If the original plan was to transform Sinclair into a disillusioned, rebellious warrior of light by the end of season two, Straczynski would need to perform some narrative acrobatics to get a new station commander to the same position. All the patient world-building of season one could come to naught if he didn't have someone who could fill the position vacated by Sinclair.

Casting Bruce Boxleitner was a masterstroke. He was a veteran TV actor: he had been the series lead in *Bring 'Em Back Alive* and spent four years as the co-lead in *Scarecrow and Mrs. King*. He had also starred in 1982's science fiction extravaganza *Tron* with future *Babylon 5* costar Peter Jurasik. He was more than up for the challenge of spearheading Straczynski's epic novel for television during the remainder of its run.

He also came with bags of charisma and was instantly likeable as Captain Sheridan, the by-the-book captain who would take over the running of Babylon 5. Where O'Hare's introverted performance was often seen as dull, Boxleitner was a much more engaging leading man. He was well placed to tackle the action and high drama that would follow, in a way that O'Hare might have struggled with. When Sinclair became the action hero, O'Hare's performance came across as wooden. When he was the diplomat, he was the encapsulation of everything the show needed.

Sheridan had a wealth of experience as the captain of the *Agamemnon*, and that skill and strength of character shines even in the earliest episodes of season two. As a war hero from the Earth–Minbari war, his presence shakes things up with Delenn's people, but there is instant chemistry between Mira Furlan and Boxleitner (arguably more so than with Furlan and O'Hare).

Straczynski had to create some narrative shortcuts. Audiences would soon learn that Sheridan, who was a conspiracy buff and an ally of anti-Clark rebel General Hague, had a side mission to spy on the senior staff and see who was loyal to Clark. He would also throw himself into the darker conspiracies surrounding Bureau 13 ("Spider in the Web") and the Psi Corps' obvious influence in the government ("A Race through Dark Places"). It would allow Sheridan to become disillusioned with Clark's regime quickly and with a surprising degree of believability.

In addition to the brilliant casting of Boxleitner to keep the show thriving, there was also a second advantage to switching from Sinclair to Sheridan. The former commander's backstory was tied to the Minbari and what happened to him at the Battle of the Line. However, Sheridan found himself more directly involved in the emerging Shadow threat. The grief over the loss of his wife Anna years earlier would inform much of his character, coming to the fore in the pivotal late season two episode "In the Shadow of Z'ha'dum." It would be revealed that Anna was part of the expedition that went to the Shadows' home world and alerted him to the growing threat in the galaxy. The emotional dilemma of seeking answers about Anna from her fellow survivor Morden, and risking the Vorlons exposing themselves to the Shadows, would be a significant step in Sheridan's heroic path.

Captain John Sheridan would become the central hero of *Babylon 5*. Season two had a lot to prove to get him to that disgruntled "it's the point that counts" speech in the season finale, "The Fall of Night." He begins as a decorated officer, fiercely loyal to Earthforce, and ends the season ready to rebel against everything he previously stood for. A station that started out as just the latest posting in his military career would become a place worth fighting for, above all else. That is quite the journey, and one that would have been much easier if O'Hare had been able to continue on the show as Sinclair.

That Straczynski and Boxleitner achieved this is perhaps season two's biggest achievement. The switch from Sinclair to Sheridan not only kept Straczynski's story arcs on track; in some ways they accelerated them and helped deliver a tremendous season of television—even if it would promptly be outdone by the epic events of seasons three and four. Few shows could survive the loss of their lead character after just one season. *Babylon 5* is an example of not just how to navigate such a change, but to actually make the show even better for it.

The Shadow Influence

Season two was where Straczynski would really kick the series arcs into the next gear. With the replacement for Sinclair in place, his goal was to build on the "signs and portents" hinted at during the first full year of *Babylon 5*. And that meant the threat of the Shadows.

This new enemy had only made a couple of appearances in season one, most dramatically in the finale, "Chrysalis," when Londo used his connections to new ally Mr. Modern to arrange for the attack on the Quadrant 37 outpost and the death of 10,000 Narns. It was a terrifying display of their strength and would set the stage for the coming conflicts.

The second season is permeated with a sense of dread as the galaxy slowly succumbs to the growing darkness of the Shadows emerging from the Outer Rim. G'Kar returns with the warning of an ancient enemy in the second episode, "Revelations," but no one will believe him. And yet this is just the first portent of doom. The departing techno-mages in the third episode, "The Geometry of Shadows," leave to avoid the growing darkness, while "A Distant Star" sees Starfury pilot Keffer spot one of the monstrous Shadow vessels during a rescue mission to save a stranded ship in hyperspace. The fifth episode, "The Long Dark," would continue to tease the growing threat with a sleeper ship drawn off course and heading toward the Outer Rim, while a Shadow-like menace is brought upon the station.

In the grand scheme of things, this four-episode run does not offer any huge dramatic moments or revelations concerning the Shadow threat. But they successively build on the Shadows' introductions in season one's "Signs and Portents" and "Chrysalis," making the threat of the unknown just as terrifying as a direct encounter with one of their vessels.

Once again, the Shadows would be shown in their full, terrifying might in "The Coming of Shadows," the episode of *Babylon 5* that won Straczynski his first Hugo Award in 1996 for Best Dramatic Presentation. At the behest of Londo, the Shadows would stage a devastating attack on Quadrant 14 that would ignite the Narn–Centauri war. It was also the episode that would first introduce the idea of Rangers, with Sinclair's surprise return in a video message to Garibaldi and Delenn (recorded by O'Hare just before he left *Babylon 5*).

By the time Delenn and Kosh revealed the Shadow threat to Sheridan in "In the Shadow of Z'ha'dum," audiences would understand the full dread and might of the enemy. Despite a sizeable chunk of the second season being devoted to other plot elements and stand-alone episodes, Straczynski had successfully established the story arc that would come to dominate *Babylon 5* and fans were ready for it.

Long-form storytelling was already starting to dominate, with Londo and G'Kar at the center of a devastating war between their peoples. "In the Shadow of Z'ha'dum" is a pivotal episode for the show (it also introduces the xenophobic Nightwatch), as it gives Sheridan a mission statement, using Babylon 5 as a center of operations in an upcoming war with truly stupendous odds. The Earth-Minbari and Narn-Centauri wars were just the tip of the iceberg. Suddenly, every civilization is at stake.

The last four episodes of season two are dominated by story arcs. Talia's betrayal as a sleeper agent in "Divided Loyalties" would deliver on the Control storyline Straczynski had envisioned for Takashima and reintroduce Lyta to the fold. "The Long, Twilight Struggle" would deliver a dramatic, brutal end to the Narn-Centauri war. Again, the Shadows would play a key role. The slaughter of the Narn fleet at Ragesh III sees the Shadows at their most powerful and terrifying yet. The battle of Ragesh III is by far the biggest battle in *Babylon 5* history at that point and would hint at the scale of war that audiences would see in seasons three and four.

The Shadow threat would continue to lurk in the background over the final episodes of season two. As well as aiding the Centauri in their victory over the Narn, the threat of war with them would see Sheridan and Delenn face the Inquisitor, known only as Jack in the penultimate episode. "Comes the Inquisitor" is another key episode, cementing Sheridan and Delenn's roles as leaders in the army of light that would be instrumental in the defeat of the Shadows—and the Vorlons—in season four.

While "The Fall of Night" is dominated by the fallout of the Narn defeat and Earth's rising xenophobia, the presence of the Shadows is still felt. Kosh revealing himself to save Sheridan is enough to announce to the Shadows who the Vorlons really are, while Keffer's quest to locate the Shadow vessel he saw in "A Distant Star" will see him meet a fiery end—and reveal the Shadows to the galaxy with the news clip of his final moments reaching the air waves for all to see.

> It was the end of the Earth year 2259, and the war was upon us. As anticipated, a few days after the Earth-Centauri treaty was announced, the Centauri widened their war to include many of the Non-Aligned Worlds. And there was another war brewing closer to home. A personal one whose cost would be higher than any of us could imagine. We came to this place because Babylon 5 was our last, best hope for peace. By the end of 2259, we knew that it had failed. But in so doing, it became something greater. As the war expanded, it became our last, best hope for victory. Because sometimes peace is another word for surrender, and because secrets have a way of getting out.

Ivanova's ominous closing monologue in "The Fall of Night" would reflect how far *Babylon 5* had already been affected by the events of season two. Earth's xenophobia, the increased Centauri aggression, and failure of Babylon 5 as a place of peace are all the result of the Shadow influence. Never had an enemy been so effectively built up as this one. And fans had only seen the tip of the iceberg when it came to seeing just what the Shadows could really do.

The Tragic Rivalry of Londo and G'Kar

From the very beginning Londo and G'Kar were a force to be reckoned with. Of all the castings on *Babylon 5*, the magic of Peter Jurasik and Andreas Katsulas on screen was like no other. They went through quite the journey over five seasons, from rivals, to bitter enemies, to firm friends and allies. Their stories are on the level of great Greek or Shakespearean tragedies, filled with joy and anguish. An episode, or even a scene, focusing on Londo and G'Kar together was always a joy to watch.

In the first season, their roles were distinctly reversed. This was all part of Straczynski's plan to create characters that were wholly transformed by their experiences. No character on *Babylon 5* was the same by the end as they were when they made their debut, and this was true for Londo and G'Kar most of all. They were always rivals, but in the beginning it was G'Kar who was the true villain of the show, having a hand in the criminal underground lurking within the station and seeking to undermine Babylon 5's mantra for peace with his own ruthless schemes of revenge.

The Narn were quickly established as the former slaves of the Centauri, now fueled by a desire to seek terrible retribution against their former aggressors. G'Kar embodied this to his core. But things changed. As early as season one's "Mind War," G'Kar showed that he wasn't wholly a villain, rescuing Sinclair's lover Catherine Sakai from certain death at Sigma 957. "No one here is quite what they seem," he exclaims. It's a comment that rang true for every inhabitant of Babylon 5.

But something more profound happened to change the status quo between Londo and G'Kar. Londo chose to form an alliance with Mr. Morden and the Shadows. Season one ended with Londo's new allies launching a devastating attack on the Quadrant 37 outpost, putting the aggressive Narn on the back foot. Suddenly we felt sympathy for G'Kar and his people; as season two began, that sympathy would only grow.

The second episode, "Revelations," is a disturbing precursor to the big event of season two—the Narn–Centauri war. While G'Kar's attempts to warn the station of an ancient enemy returned falls on deaf ears, Londo jokes to Morden about eliminating the entire Narn home world. "Not yet," muses Morden, teasing the devastating events of "The Long, Twilight Struggle."

Londo's dark path is teased through several key episodes, most notably the prophetic warning of techno-mage Eldric in "The Geometry of Shadows":

> "As I look at you, Ambassador Mollari, I see a great hand reaching out of the stars. The hand is your hand. And I hear sound; the sounds of billions of people calling your name."
> "My followers?"
> "Your victims."

While G'Kar has not yet crossed the line from villain to hero, Londo is quickly becoming corrupted by his alliance with the Shadows, and there is no turning back. By the time we reach "The Coming of Shadows," Londo and G'Kar are faced with a crossroads—peace or war—and their choices will have ramifications for the rest of their journeys across *Babylon 5*.

The arrival of the aging Emperor Turhan provides G'Kar the chance to exact his revenge in the most public way possible. But his assassination attempt fails and instead creates an olive branch for peace as G'Kar receives a personal message from Turhan; an apology for the Centauri occupation of Narn. For the first time in his entire life, G'Kar's thoughts are not consumed by revenge, but the very foreign concept of peace between his people and the Centauri.

However, given the tragic nature of their relationship, peace was not to be. Londo's new alliance awakens the aggressive, expansionist tendencies of the Centauri court, most notably in Lord Refa, who makes his first appearance in season two. Eager to curry favor and secure his rise in status, Londo uses the Shadows to attack and slaughter thousands of Narns, resulting in a devastating war. G'Kar's offer of a handshake just as Londo has committed to his actions makes for one of the series' most devastating moments, conveyed masterfully by Jurasik's silent facial expression. The onset of war and G'Kar's subsequent rage at Londo's betrayal will send their rivalry spiraling to new depths.

While season two overall is concerned with the rise of the Shadows and an increasingly xenophobic Earth, Londo and G'Kar are at the heart of this run. G'Kar fails in his attempts to secure allies in a war his people are losing, while Londo faces his own personal losses as his good friend Urza Jaddo is eliminated for his opposing views on the Centauri's aggressive stance. Personal happiness is trumped by a position of power and influence. It is a cost Londo will continue to face all the way up to his ascension to emperor in season five.

"The Long, Twilight Struggle" is the devastating climax to a terrible war that should never have happened. With Londo's alliance with the Shadows leading to the destruction of the only Narn force able to make a

13. Season Two

difference, G'Kar faces loss at every stage. His uncle dies in battle and his home world is bombed into the Stone Age with the Centauri's illegal use of mass drivers. Humiliated at every stage, he is forced to seek sanctuary and finds himself on his own, stripped of his position and forced to hide on Babylon 5 while his people are enslaved.

> No dictator, no invader can hold an imprisoned population by force of arms forever. There is no greater power in the universe than the need for freedom. Against that power tyrants and dictators cannot stand. The Centauri learned that lesson once. We will teach it to them again. Though it may take a thousand years, we will be free.

G'Kar's words in that fateful council chamber, delivered with such haunting pathos by Andreas Katsulas, are as evocative in the real world as they are on *Babylon 5*. While the Narn are horribly beaten, he will not give up. It speaks to the strength of G'Kar and the Narn people that the Centauri cannot truly defeat them. While Londo has become *the* villain of the show, there is still something heartbreaking about his situation. From watching the bombarding of Narn from the Centauri warship to being forced to go against everyone he knows on Babylon 5, he is completely and utterly alone.

The end of season two sees Londo and G'Kar's journeys at their darkest. Londo is unable to break free of either the shackles of his alliance with the Shadows or his new position of power in the Centauri royal court. He would attempt to shed himself of both in season three, only to fail. For Citizen G'Kar, he has lost his home, his people, and his position, but is not yet in a place to act on it. His attempts at revenge in season three would lead to his spiritual awakening—courtesy of Kosh—but at this point he has quite a mountain to climb before he becomes the enlightened, heroic figure fans would fall in love with.

The sad tale of Londo and G'Kar is one of *Babylon 5*'s greatest triumphs. In season two, they take center stage, forced into a war neither of them wants and losing themselves in the process. There would be moments of greatness to come, but the second season is where we recognize just how important they were to Straczynski's grand novel for television.

A Note on Viewing Orders

We've covered the differing viewing orders in season one. The differences between the broadcast order and the JMS Viewing Order and *Babylon 5 Historical Database* are less notable in season two.

The JMS Viewing Order for Season Two:

- "Points of Departure"
- "Revelations"
- "The Geometry of Shadows"
- "A Distant Star"
- "The Long Dark"
- "Spider in the Web"
- "A Race through Dark Places"
- "Soul Mates"
- "The Coming of Shadows"
- "GROPOS"
- "All Alone in the Night"
- "Acts of Sacrifice"
- "Hunter, Prey"
- "There All the Honor Lies"
- "And Now for a Word"
- "Knives"
- "In the Shadow of Z'ha'dum"
- "Confessions and Lamentations"
- "Divided Loyalties"
- "The Long, Twilight Struggle"
- "Comes the Inquisitor"
- "The Fall of Night"

The Straczynski-approved *Babylon 5* Historical Database Viewing Order for Season One (with chronological dates):

- "Points of Departure"—Sunday, January 8, 2259
- "Revelations"—Thursday, January 12–Thursday, January 19, 2259
- "The Geometry of Shadows"—Wednesday, January 25–Sunday, February 5, 2259
- "A Distant Star"—Monday, January 30–Thursday, February 2, 2259
- "Spider in the Web"—March 2259
- "A Race through Dark Places"—Tuesday, March 14–Friday, March 17, 2259
- "Soul Mates"—May 2259
- "The Long Dark"—June 2259
- "The Coming of Shadows"—Tuesday, June 13–Saturday, June 17, 2259
- "GROPOS"—Tuesday, June 20–Friday, June 23, 2259
- "All Alone in the Night"—July 2259
- "Acts of Sacrifice"—July 2259
- "Hunter, Prey"—July 2259
- "Knives"—August 2259
- "There All the Honor Lies"—August 2259
- "And Now for a Word"—Saturday, September 16, 2259
- "In the Shadow of Z'ha'dum"—Sunday, September 24, 2259
- "Confessions and Lamentations"—November 2259
- "Divided Loyalties"—November 2259–Saturday, December 2, 2259
- "The Long, Twilight Struggle"—Sunday, December 3–Sunday, December 10, 2259.
- "The Fall of Night"—Monday, December 18, 2259 (start of story)
- "Comes the Inquisitor"—Tuesday, December 19–Wednesday, December 20, 2259
- "The Fall of Night"—Sunday, December 24, 2259 (end of story)

The JMS Viewing Order is almost identical, with "Soul Mates" and "Knives" the only minor tweaks to the run. However, the *Babylon 5* Historical Database Viewing Order also breaks up the two-week run of "A Distant Star" and "The Long Dark," interrupting the buildup of the Shadows across the first chunk of the season, before we get to "The Coming of Shadows." It certainly makes Ivanova's concerns about the rumors from the edge of the Rim feel more ominous, given the Shadow attack of Quadrant 14 next episode.

There is little lost by watching season two in the original broadcast order. The double bill of "A Distant Star" and "The Long Dark" arguably make more of an impact coming together after "The Geometry of Shadows," as originally aired. "Knives" works better before "In the Shadow of Z'ha'dum," making the final six-episode run of season two a true heavy hitter.

The Unmade Episodes of Season Two

As with season one, there were a number of episodes that got as far as the concept stage but were never fully realized. David Gerrold, a veteran *Star Trek* writer who penned season one's "Believers," also worked on three additional scripts for *Babylon 5* that failed to make it onto the show. While little is known about the details of these stories, we do know that the scripts for both "Target: Unknown" and "Metaphors and Body Counts" were both originally planned for season one and pushed to season two before being dropped altogether. Gerrold also worked on a third script entitled "Expectations," plus an outline for an episode called "Laser-Mirror-Starweb."

Another *Star Trek* icon and contributor to *Babylon 5*'s first season with "The War Prayer" and "Legacies," DC Fontana would go on to pen season two's "A Distant Star." However, she had a fourth story planned, entitled either "All Our Songs Forgotten" or "Unnatural Selection." The primary plot of this episode would have focused on a new leader rising up in Down-Below while the secondary plot had Keffer taking a Starfury out on personal leave for his friend's memorial.

There were also a number of planned scripts by Straczynski, some of which would have their ideas woven into other key episodes from the season. "The Very Long Night of Susan Ivanova" would have been the episode that dealt with the breakout of the Narn–Centauri war, the arrival of Babylon 5's founder at the station, and Ivanova being forced by Sheridan to take some time off. While the events leading to the war would move into "The Coming of Shadows," the idea of a visiting Babylon 5 founder would be pushed to season three's opening episode "Matters of Honor" before being dropped altogether.

Another element brought into "The Coming of Shadows" was the visit of Centauri emperor Turhan. This became the B plot of another planned episode, "Rites of Passage," which would focus primarily on Keffer being sentenced to death for being a spy as he is caught in a war between two alien governments, and Talia being forced to breed with another telepath by the Psi Corps—an idea that would find its way into season two's "Soul Mates."

Little is known about "The Commander's Hour," other than Straczynski eventually using elements of the story in *Crusade*'s "The Path of Sorrows" years later. "The Customer is Always Right" would focus on a holo-brothel on the station—an idea that would eventually find its way into the TV movie, *The River of Souls*. The B plot focused on Delenn being kicked off the Grey Council, an event that made its way into season two's "All Alone in the Night" instead.

While season two would introduce more experimental ideas like the ISB special broadcast on "And Now for a Word," Straczynski had an even more wacky concept for "Dream Within a Dream."

> *"He is Captain Jack Carr of the Earth Alliance; his female Russian second in command is Commander Dylan (a human version of Delenn, played by Mira without makeup), and his security chief is Len (the human version of Londo, played by Peter without makeup). They don't believe his story that this is a dream ... neither do the various ambassadors, Minbari ambassador Sherdinn, Narn ambassador S'san, or Centauri ambassador Garabaldo.... The only constant in the real world and the dream world is Kosh, who may hold the secret G'Kar needs to heal himself and break out of his dream existence."*

Ultimately, "Dream Within a Dream" never came much more than a concept, due to the network's instance that it would be confusing. Like Straczynski's other planned episode, "The Mysterious Mr. Jones," a story about a mysterious recurring character of unknown origin, it's unclear whether this was a story planned for season two or later.

After season two, Straczynski wrote every episode of *Babylon 5*, aside from Neil Gaiman's "Day of the Dead" in season five, so there are no other planned episodes from other writers that never made it to production, with one exception. "Gut Reactions" was written by Peter David and Lennier himself, Bill Mumy, for season five, but was ultimately rejected.

Supplemental: A Season Two Review

The second season of *Babylon 5* really kicks the five-year arc into gear. After a season of patient world-building in a largely episodic format,

13. Season Two

J. Michael Straczynski started to weave even greater use of story arcs and long-form storytelling to build on the twin threats of the Shadows and Earth.

The replacement of Sinclair with Sheridan is deftly done, with Bruce Boxleitner bringing instant charm and charisma as the new lead character on *Babylon 5*. He fits into the crew dynamic, initially butting heads with Garibaldi before earning his respect and building a strong bond with the newly promoted Commander Ivanova. He is passionate, intelligent and the perfect focal point for the show.

While the opening episode works to wrap up the loose ends surrounding Sinclair and Sheridan's own past with the Minbari, the next four episodes all turn their attention to the big new threat: the Shadows. There is a real sense of darkness and dread permeating these early season two stories, which lead into the ninth episode, the season two titular episode (and Hugo Award–winning) "The Coming of Shadows." It is a momentous episode, focusing on the bitter cold-war conflict between the Narn and the Centauri and plunging them into open warfare.

The Narn–Centauri war is the axis point of season two; aided by his new allies, the Shadows, Londo continues his ascent to power. After acting as a largely sympathetic, tragic figure in the early days of season one, the second season sees him become one of the central villains of *Babylon 5*, albeit an unwilling one. Peter Jurasik commands every scene, eager to regain past glories and soon finding his attempts to do so spinning out of control. By the time he watches the bombardment of Narn in "The Long, Twilight Struggle," he has crossed a line from which he cannot return, even if he wanted to.

Season two is equally G'Kar's season. Andreas Katsulas does tremendous work as the Narn ambassador. His desperate attempts to warn the station of the returning Shadows quickly fall on deaf ears and he goes from villain to tragic figure—a reverse Londo, so to speak. His desire for revenge and then peace in "The Coming of Shadows" is met by betrayal at the hands of Londo, and as season two progresses, he begins to lose everything he has fought for. This culminates in his request for sanctuary as his people are slaughtered back home. Stripped of his status and freedom, he remains, nonetheless, a character of strength and conviction, as demonstrated by his powerful speech in the council chamber of Babylon 5 as his people lose the war.

"The Coming of Shadows" and "The Long, Twilight Struggle" are not just some of the best episodes of the season, they are some of the best *Babylon 5* ever produced. But there are other all-time classics in this second season run. "And Now for A Word" is a tremendous piece of satire that explores *Babylon 5*'s uneasy relationship with the media, while also building on the seeds of Earth's growing xenophobia. "In the Shadow of Z'ha'dum" is another great episode, tying Sheridan directly to the rising Shadow threat as the enemy's true intentions are revealed, while also introducing the terrifyingly insidious Nightwatch, a xenophobic organization that will only grow in power.

"Confessions and Lamentations" is another powerful episode, exploring the nature of disease and spiritual purity as the Markab race slowly succumbs to a fatal disease. It's a tense, harrowing episode that doesn't play to convention. There is no last-minute cure, no chance to save the Markab from their own destruction. The sight of Delenn and Lennier alone among the dead Markab is one of the saddest, most horrifying moments in *Babylon 5* history.

That final run of episodes, starting with "And Now for A Word," is spectacular. *Babylon 5* could have rested on its laurels with the culmination of the Narn–Centauri war and the revelations about the Shadows. But it continued to deliver one great episode after another. When Andrea Thompson decided to leave the show, Straczynski wrote a thrilling climax to Talia's journey, which sees her revealed to have a latent traitorous personality that wipes the original telepath's mind—and with it all hope of a romantic relationship with Ivanova. It also sets up the return of original telepath Lyta Alexander to replace her. "Comes the Inquisitor" is another striking episode that sees Sheridan and Delenn tortured by Jack the Ripper—at the behest of the Vorlons—to prove they are the right people to lead the fight against the Shadows.

By the time "The Fall of Night" brings season two to a close, viewers have been on quite the journey. Delenn has transformed into a half-human, half–Minbari leader in a coming galactic war and Sheridan has not only joined her side but begun a secret revolution against the increasingly corrupt regime of President Clark. G'Kar has lost everything and Londo has gained everything, at the cost of his soul. It's a grim ending that sees Earth side with the Centauri and Kosh being forced to reveal himself to save Sheridan's life. As Ivanova notes in the season's closing moments, the Babylon 5 project had failed. Now, they had to prepare for the wars to come.

While not as arc-driven as later seasons, the second season of *Babylon 5* is that transition from episodic to long-form storytelling. It overcomes the hurdle of losing its lead character and weaves an even more complex world, one where empires rise and fall and an even greater enemy waits in the shadows. It set *Babylon 5* up perfectly for the even bigger events to come.

14

Season Three
Tearing Up the Television Rule Book

The third season of *Babylon 5* is when everything changed. After two years of impressive world-building, J. Michael Straczynski would pull the trigger on several plot threads that had been building since the pilot episode. Captain Sheridan and the crew of Babylon 5 would rebel against President Clark as Earth itself became increasingly corrupt. The Shadow War would break out, plunging the galaxy into darkness. Characters would go through pivotal changes, and life on the station would never be the same again.

The threat of cancellation would force Straczynski to wrap up these big plot threads by the end of the fourth year, ending some storylines prematurely. But as *Babylon 5* entered its third season, it was hitting the midpoint of the planned five-year story arc. The foundations had been built and now it was time for the showrunner to start tearing it all down. It was a gamble: if the show didn't get a fourth year, the arc would be left in tatters, but now was the chance to deliver on everything the show had been teasing.

And more.

The events that followed resulted in a truly epic season of television. Every episode was written by Straczynski himself—a television first. There were tumultuous narrative changes and stories were rarely resolved by the end of the credits. Characters had to deal with the ramifications of what had happened to them, week after week. This was genre television truly embracing long-form storytelling and proving that it was unlike any of its sci-fi contemporaries.

Season three was J. Michael Straczynski's vision of *Babylon 5* incarnate.

Making History, JMS-Style

It's amusing to think that Straczynski "accidentally" broke records by writing an entire 22-episode season of an hour-long drama series single-handedly. It had not been attempted before, and it wasn't Straczynski's intention to be the first to achieve that distinction. As he describes in *Becoming Superman*, he was aiming to assign a number of scripts to freelance writers, until Warners failed to give the show an advance script order. Coupled with a late pick-up (the threat of cancellation always hanging high), Straczynski was immediately on the back foot and wrote the first five scripts.[1]

After that, there was no time to stop and regroup. So he just kept writing.

It's also remarkable to think that the standard of storytelling was as high as it was. In the eyes of the show's fans, there are no duds, though the late season three episode, "Grey 17 Is Missing," comes close. While the first handful of episodes suggest a more episodic tone, there is an immense amount of setup for the two big conflicts about to come, from the Shadows ("Matters of Honor") to Earth's growing xenophobia ("Voices of Authority"). The fallout of season two is explored in episodes like "Convictions" and "Dust to Dust," reminding us that Londo and G'Kar's story is far from over. And even singular episodes like "Passing through Gethsemane" offer plenty of twists and turns that still resonate long after the credits have rolled.

Audiences thinking that they were going to see only subtle changes in the status quo of *Babylon 5* were surely not expecting the epic trilogy that was "Messages from Earth," "Point of No Return," and "Severed Dreams." In the space of three 45-minute installments, Straczynski tore up the rule book as Delenn broke the Grey Council of Minbar, the Shadows began to move more openly, President Clark plunged Earth into a dictatorship, and Sheridan went up against his own people and forced Babylon 5 to declare independence. We would never see Sheridan in an Earthforce uniform again for the duration of the show.

Any lesser writer would probably struggle to keep the momentum going. Instead, Straczynski would plunge the galaxy into a war with the Shadows just four episodes later. In the space of another three episodes, he would kill off Kosh, bring back Commander Sinclair, deal with the mystery of what happened to Babylon 4, and reveal the identity of Valen. These were huge events, leading to a thrilling final run of episodes that saw the biggest battle the show had ever delivered and sacrificed its lead character in the season's closing moments.

Season three was not only one of the finest years of *Babylon 5*'s run, but one of the finest seasons of television—science fiction or otherwise. "Severed Dreams" won Straczynski a Hugo Award for Best Dramatic Presentation, his second in two years. The same year, *Dreamwatch* magazine awarded *Babylon 5* the Best SF Television Series of All Time.

He was doing something right. In fact, his attempts to write every episode was so successful that Warners asked him to do the same thing all over again for season four.

Of course, such greatness came with a cost. Straczynski describes the experience of 18 to 20-hour days that destroyed his immune system, gave him carpal tunnel syndrome, and turned his hair white. It even led to the (amicable) collapse of his marriage.

This didn't go unnoticed, with *Newsweek* infamously publishing an article, "Master and Slave of 'Babylon 5,'" in 1997,[2] something Straczynski himself noted in his autobiography.

> IN THE LAST FOUR YEARS, J. MICHAEL Straczynski's full head of brown hair has gone to thinning gray. Before he bought an ergonomic keyboard about a year ago, he had to stop typing every 20 minutes to ice down his aching wrists. He's made it to two movies in the last year and a half. Straczynski lives for his creation, the cult sci-fi TV show "Babylon 5." He has written more than 50 consecutive episodes of the syndicated weekly series, as well as working on the special effects, editing, set and costume design, even "B5" merchandise and toys. And he spends a couple hours a night answering e-mail from fans.

The award-winning third season made history and would continue the trend with season four. But it came at a cost, one that Straczynski, it seemed, was willing to buy into.

The Problem with Earth

Babylon 5 has always been a show with immense rewatch value. Snippets of information seeded in the first season have huge relevance on rewatch, to events taking place sometimes three or four seasons later. Watching the character journeys—G'Kar from villain to religious leader, Vir from bumbling fool to courageous diplomat—makes for an immensely satisfying second or third—or tenth—viewing experience.

One of the most fascinating aspects of *Babylon 5* on rewatch, and in particular its third season, is the exploration of an increasingly xenophobic Earth. In the '90s, it was clear that Straczynski was drawing on parallels from the rise of Nazism in the 20th century, with the Nightwatch and Ministry of Peace as nightmarish allusions to World War II and George Orwell's *1984*. But on rewatch, what seemed fantastical now seems scarily relatable.

The Nightwatch made their debut late in the second season: officers recruited to keep a watchful eye on people who might be disloyal to Earth for the price of 50 credits a week. Zack Allan is eager to sign up and wear an armband. After all, what does encouraging people to think about peace really mean? The seeds of this dark Earth were sown in seasons one and two but really come to fruition in the third, in all its frightening glory. This is most apparent in the episode "Voices of Authority."

Enter Julie Musante, assigned to Babylon 5 as a political officer by the Nightwatch and Ministry of Peace to "advise" Captain Sheridan on governmental policy. The insidious nature of Earth as it has become is revealed in a truly chilling scene where she talks about the reframing of crime and homelessness as the purview of the mentally insane and lazy, disloyal to the government and seeking only to criticize and sow discontent. Very quickly it becomes clear that Earth is stamping out cultural freedoms like free speech and association, while the media is forced to present stories that reflect the corrupt government's own agenda. Her words in "Voices of Authority" are as chilling as anything we have heard in twenty-first-century media.

> Why embarrass our leaders by pointing out flaws in society that they're aware of and dealing with in their own time, in their own way? Some people enjoy finding fault with our leaders: they're anarchists, troublemakers, or simply unpatriotic.

Unpatriotic troublemakers. It's a phrase bandied around about those who might voice their frustrations at increasingly right-wing, authoritarian policies enacted by the Conservative and Republican governments in the U.K. and U.S. respectively. In a 2020 article, *The Independent* called Remainers (those who voted to stay in the EU during the 2016 Brexit referendum) the silenced people of Britain.[3] There is a "contemptible trope casting Remainers as unpatriotic quislings and traitors" who are "considered profane and perfidious to point out that nasty and illiberal messages helped deliver victory to the Leave side." Musante would be right up there with Farage, Johnson, and Gove, flying the patriotic flag of Britishness and dismissing those who wanted anything else as traitors to the greater good.

The growing xenophobia is explored more heavily in "Point of No Return" and "Severed Dreams," forcing Sheridan's hand, and causing him to break away from Earth. The fall of ISN, the independent news broadcaster presented in the show from day one, the enacting of martial law, and the arresting of the president's political opponents turns Earthforce into the military arm of a corrupt dictatorship.

In season three, the rhetoric spouted by the likes of the Nightwatch and Julie Musante is frighteningly relatable to modern audiences. While the "us and them" divide draws chilling parallels with the fallout of Brexit and the objections of dissenters who criticize governmental policy, there are other disturbing mirrors to modern society too. The idea of a "better age," enshrined by the Nightwatch, is eerily evocative of the "Blitz spirit" invoked by those telling the public to toughen up as Brexit takes its toll on the country. In her 2021 article for *The Times*, Clare Foges famously wrote, "We have got used to a degree of chaos during the pandemic and many secretly enjoy the chance to show some Blitz spirit" in response to the thousands of drivers queuing at Dover in the wake of Brexit.[4] The fantasy of world war to bring people together is a sickening but sadly realistic facet of the "us and them" debate, which Straczynski eerily taps into though this insidious organization.

Equally, the misinformation of the press and the fall of ISN draw scary parallels with the increasingly right-wing monopoly on free speech in the U.K. media, while the Nightwatch's attempt to take control of Babylon 5 is eerily similar to Trump's January 6, 2021, Capitol attack in the U.S.

These parallels to own lives make Straczynski's work strangely prophetic.

The Shadows, Time Travel and Delivering on Babylon 5's *Promises*

If "Severed Dreams" shakes the foundations of the show, then the Shadow War tears up the rule book completely. The buildup of Shadow forces on the edge of the galaxy runs across the first half of season three. "Ship of Dreams" kick-starts that conflict, plunging *Babylon 5* into a war that will run throughout the final eight episodes of the season and the first six of season four.

"Ship of Tears" is arguably the point at which *Babylon 5* really started to show what long-form storytelling on science fiction television would look like. Every episode had a purpose and contributed to the ongoing storyline. The war wasn't wrapped up by the 45-minute mark. It took its toll on the characters, with Sheridan growing more ravaged in his appearance with each episode. The war room became a prominent setting on the show, and the White Star was joined by a fleet of vessels, ready to lead the fight against the Shadows. The scale was bigger than ever before.

It's the sort of storytelling that's now taken for granted in science fiction and fantasy shows like *Battlestar Galactica* and *Lost*. A narrative that spans years, growing more complex and pushing its characters to their limits. *Babylon 5* paved the way for those shows, not only making multi-year arcs accessible to audiences, but helping to bridge the gap between genre and traditional mainstream television. Straczynski noted this when reflecting back on *Babylon 5* during the show's 25th anniversary in an interview with Newsorama:

> Those two shows further crystallized the five-year arc structure, and within fellow geek circles, that really made a huge impact even though initially you didn't initially see it happening in the mainstream shows.[5]

With *Babylon 5*, Straczynski led the way for these genre giants to come and demonstrated that science fiction could be far more than the adventure-of-the-week trope so familiar from *Star Trek*. Interestingly, *Babylon 5*'s use of an ongoing war spanning multiple episodes would be attempted a year later with *Deep Space Nine*.

In addition to finally realizing long-form storytelling in science fiction, Straczynski also used the Shadow War as a platform for some truly grandiose stories that delivered on the promise of the last three years. After pulling the strings since day one, the mysterious Vorlons unleashed their full might against the Shadows, going to war at the behest of Sheridan. The scale of the conflict with the Shadows was immense, and the battle in the penultimate season three episode, "Shadow Dancing," delivered a stupendously epic spectacle for viewers. The events of the Shadow War keep the audience on their toes, with the unexpected death of Kosh pulling the rug from under Sheridan and his army of light. If a Vorlon could die, so could anyone.

Still reeling from those events, the epic two-parter "War Without End" saw the payoff of the mystery of Babylon 4 and the return of Michael O'Hare as Sinclair in a thrilling and unexpected time travel adventure. From the deaths of Londo and G'Kar in the future (and the tease of Centauri Prime's fate) to the revelation that Sinclair is Valen, the scope of the show became astonishingly huge and showed that Straczynski was able to deliver. By the time Sheridan flew the White Star into Z'ha'dum, killing himself in the finale to defeat the Shadows, there really was a sense that there is nothing *Babylon 5* wouldn't do.

It's also notable that the third season also serves to pay off several character arcs amid all the high drama and stakes of the Earth and Shadow conflicts. In addition to the return of Sinclair, Londo and Refa's rivalry was elevated to another level, with Refa poisoning Londo's true love Adira before falling into a trap and dying at the hands of the Narn. Lyta finally became the enhanced Vorlon telepath superweapon in "Walkabout," building on the story arcs set up by her debut in *The Gathering*. G'Kar would have a religious awakening and become a keen ally of the army of light as he began his path to becoming a religious prophet. Franklin's stim addiction from season two saw him face a personal crisis in his career, while Sheridan and Delenn would cement their romance—only for it to fall apart with the sudden arrival of his dead wife Anna.

Season three was a staggeringly epic year of television. Straczynski single-handedly wrote the entire season, winning a prestigious award and delivering on the promise of what the show could be. Amid all the spectacle, audiences were treated to transformational story arcs, a galactic war that was as good as they had hoped for, and the return of the show's original commander. Most significantly, it proved that long-form storytelling in science fiction could be successful.

Season three of *Babylon 5* might, then, be one of the most influential years not just for science fiction, but for television as a whole.

A Note on Viewing Orders

In season three, the differences from the broadcast order are far subtler, given the season's full push to long-form storytelling from "Messages from Earth" onwards.

The JMS Viewing Order for Season Three:

- "Matters of Honor"
- "Convictions"
- "A Day in the Strife"
- "Passing through Gethsemane"
- "Voices of Authority"
- "Dust to Dust"
- "Exogenesis"
- "Messages from Earth"
- "Point of No Return"
- "Severed Dreams"
- "Ceremonies of Light and Dark"
- "A Late Delivery from Avalon"
- "Sic Transit Vir"
- "Ship of Tears"
- "Interludes and Examinations"
- "Walkabout"
- "War Without End, Part One"
- "War Without End, Part Two"
- "Grey 17 Is Missing"
- "And the Rock Cried Out, No Hiding Place"
- "Shadow Dancing"
- "Z'ha'dum"

The Straczynski-approved *Babylon 5* Historical Database Viewing Order for Season One (with chronological dates):

- "Matters of Honor"—Wednesday, December 27, 2259–Tuesday, January 9, 2260
- "Convictions"—Saturday, January 13–Sunday, January 14, 2260
- "A Day in the Strife"—Monday, January 15–Tuesday, January 16, 2260

- "Passing through Gethsemane"—Thursday, January 18–Sunday, February 4, 2260
- "Voices of Authority"—Monday, February 5–Wednesday, February 7, 2260
- "Dust to Dust"—Wednesday, February 28–Friday, March 1, 2260
- "Exogenesis"—Sunday, March 10–Wednesday, March 13, 2260
- "Messages from Earth"—Monday, March 18–Monday, April 8, 2260
- "Point of No Return"—Monday, April 8–Wednesday, April 10, 2260
- "Severed Dreams"—Sunday, April 14–Monday, April 15, 2260
- "Ceremonies of Light and Dark"—Tuesday, April 16–Thursday, April 18, 2260
- "Sic Transit Vir"—Sunday, June 30–Friday, July 5, 2260
- "A Late Delivery from Avalon"—Thursday, July 11–Friday, July 12, 2260
- "Ship of Tears"—Wednesday, July 24, 2260
- "Interludes and Examinations"—Saturday, August 3–Monday, August 5, 2260
- "War Without End, Parts One and Two"—Friday, August 9–Monday, August 12, 2260 (This story takes place over four time periods 2260, 2254, 2258 and 1260)
- "Walkabout"—August 2260
- "Grey 17 Is Missing"—Tuesday, November 26–Sunday, November 30, 2260
- "And the Rock Cried Out, No Hiding Place"—Saturday, December 7–Wednesday, December 11, 2260 (Z minus 14 days–Z minus 10 days)
- "Shadow Dancing"—Saturday, December 14–Thursday, December 19, 2260 (Z minus 7 days–Z minus 2 days)
- "Z'ha'dum"—Thursday, December 19–Wednesday, December 25, 2260 (Z minus 2 days to Z day, Sunday, December 21 when Sheridan leaves for Z'ha'dum, A four-day jump from B5)

Both viewing orders place "A Late Delivery from Avalon" before "Sic Transit Vir"; however, the JMS viewing order also places "Walkabout" before "War Without End," which makes more sense thematically as it deals with the immediate repercussions of Kosh's death.

Overall, though, there is little to distinguish from the production order. The serialized nature of season three means that almost everything that aired went exactly according to Straczynski's vision.

Supplemental: A Season Three Review

There is a confidence going into the third season of *Babylon 5*. Ivanova's voiceover in the dramatic title sequence hints that this is no longer a show about peace; the audience is entering the war room and the mood of the show is darker and more ominous as it builds toward two major events in the show's history.

The arrival of Jason Carter as Ranger Marcus Cole shakes up the other very military-driven human cast, and his relationship with Claudia Christian's Susan Ivanova is electric from the start. His swagger and charm is incredibly endearing, and he's as close to Aragorn as we get when it comes to the show's homage to all things *The Lord of the Rings*.

But Marcus isn't the only star in those early episodes. The fallout of the Narn–Centauri conflict allows for two Londo and G'Kar gems. Trapped in the elevator after an explosion in "Convictions," G'Kar's delight at watching Londo die is hilarious and satisfying, while "Dust to Dust" (which also features fan favorite Bester), is hugely transformative as G'Kar's vision at the hands of Kosh sets him on a path to becoming a hero and prophet. Andreas Katsulas is offered the chance to deliver a new side of G'Kar's character this season, and his transformation into a benevolent warrior of light is a joy to watch.

Of the few stand-alone episodes of the season, "Passing through Gethsemane" is a real gem. *Babylon 5*, never afraid to examine religion and spirituality, introduces an order of monks to the station, with a dark and haunting mystery surrounding genre favorite Brad Dourif's Brother Edward. The ending is powerful stuff, examining what it means to be truly able to forgive someone for their crimes. Equally as haunting is "Voices of Authority," which sees Shari Shattuck as a terrifying Earth political officer spouting the rhetoric of an increasingly xenophobic Earth government.

This paves the way for a magnificent trilogy of episodes and one of *Babylon 5*'s all-time greats. "Messages from Earth" features a tense *Wrath of Khan*-style battle between Sheridan's new warship, the *White Star*, and a Shadow vessel in the atmosphere of Jupiter, setting the stage for Earth to stage martial law as President Clark's dictatorship is exposed. "Point of No Return" builds on two years of immense world-building, shattering the illusion of humanity as a force for good, while also offering some delightful hints of Londo and Vir's future in the arrival of Majel Barrett's seer, the Lady Morella.

But nothing prepares you for the almighty "Severed Dreams," an episode that packs plenty of punch in more ways than one. Not only does it feature a tense standoff between ships loyal to Clark and the station, but it also gives us Delenn's greatest moment. Coming off the shattering of the Grey Council, her last-minute arrival and speech to the enemy is phenomenal. It is moments like this that cement her as one of science fiction's greatest female leads.

There is calm between storms after "Severed Dreams," but the pace rarely falters and the show still gives the audience plenty to enjoy, from the cruel twist around Vir's chilling fiancée Lyndisty in "Sic Transit Vir," to the joy of Marcus and G'Kar on a quest with Michael York's King Arthur in "A Late Delivery from Avalon." But it is the return of Bester, played by the scene-stealing Walter Koenig, and the revelations of "Ship of Tears" that really turns the show on its head as the Shadow War breaks out. "Severed Dreams" could have been the big moment of the season, but the shocking death of Kosh in "Interludes and Examinations" is equally game changing.

While Londo and G'Kar take a back seat after the events of season two, they are still afforded one of the most satisfying sequences in the entirety of the season. The rivalry between Londo and Lord Refa reaches new levels with the death of Adira. William Forward continues to play one of the vilest villains on *Babylon 5*, making his death in "And the Rock Cried Out, No Hiding Place," backed by an amazing gospel choir, a truly satisfying moment.

"Severed Dreams" might be arguably the most thrilling episode of the season, but in terms of epic scale, the "War Without End" two-parter is the true gem in season three's crown. Playing off the events of season one's "Babylon Squared," this episode offers a satisfying conclusion to the Babylon 4 mystery. The return of Michael O'Hare as Sinclair is the icing on the cake; it's fun to see him play off Boxleitner's Sheridan, and the resolution to his story arc is a surprising and fulfilling reward for fans of this all-too-brief character. It is a story that teases so much, from the fate of Londo and G'Kar to Sheridan and Delenn's future, and Tim Choate's return as Zathras is truly delightful.

Not everything works. Jerry Doyle's Garibaldi gets one of the worst episodes in "Grey 17 Is Missing," but even this story features a fantastic rivalry between Marcus and recurring Minbari antagonist Neroon. Richard Biggs plays Franklin's addiction and journey to find himself well, though the decision to focus on his doomed love affair with a singer in "Walkabout," when the episode should have been centered on Lyta taking on a Shadow vessel, was far from satisfying.

Still, the season ends strong with a spectacular battle with the Shadows in "Shadow Dancing" and some huge revelations in the finale with the ominous return of Sheridan's wife, the arrival of the Shadow fleet at Babylon 5, and a showdown at Z'ha'dum that shakes things up in truly epic style.

14. Season Three

Epic is the word for season three. There is a scale and grandeur to the storytelling, with the buildup of the Earth and Shadow conflicts paying off in spectacular fashion. This feels like the story Straczynski had been waiting to get to from the start. Fortunately, it does not disappoint.

15

Season Four
The Race to the Finish Line

Season four of *Babylon 5* is another epic run of episodes. Having plunged the station—and the galaxy—into chaos in season three, J. Michael Straczynski would spend the fourth season bringing multiple plotlines to a head that had been running since the pilot episode. Not all of this was planned, of course. Straczynski had planned to tell his story over five years, and yet by the end of the fourth, all the main threads were resolved.

The collapse of the Prime Time Entertainment Network (PTEN) was a huge factor in the shaping of *Babylon 5*'s penultimate season. The success of PTEN as a network was in doubt as early as 1993, with the creation of United Paramount Network (UPN) by one of its parent companies, Warner Bros. Entertainment Division. One of the co-owners of PTEN, Chris-Craft Industries, switched their attention to UPN, leaving PTEN to struggle to work with local partner stations on selling PTEN content.

Several PTEN-affiliated stations objected to the forced split of advertising between PTEN and UPN, which left very little room to sell programs locally. PTEN was forced to let stations out of their back-end commitments for several series and became a syndication service for its remaining shows. It ceased operations altogether in 1997, when it was sold off to MCA, Comcast, and Raycom Media.

All of which left *Babylon 5* adrift in the water. Without a network to house the show, the chances of a fifth season seemed unlikely, and there was a good chance the show would be canceled on a cliff-hanger.

Most science fiction shows might have a few loose threads or unanswered questions if it was canceled. But the serialized nature of *Babylon 5* meant that huge plot threads might be left unresolved. It was a risk Straczynski had taken when he pitched *Babylon 5* as a five-year novel for television, and now it looked like that risk might materialize. *Babylon 5* deserved to end on its own terms, which meant Straczynski needed to finish the story in four years, rather than five.

The Hangman's Noose and the Need for Closure

Babylon 5 had evolved significantly since the early days of Straczynski's original plans for the show. The loss of Michael O'Hare and other key cast members moved the story arcs in interesting new directions, and by the time season four arrived, the show was in a very different place. Most notably, many of the elements of the proposed sequel series *Babylon Prime*, such as the open Shadow War, had also been integrated into *Babylon 5*'s run.

This made sense. The original premise suggested a more sedate *Babylon 5*, perhaps mirroring Sinclair's reserved nature, while the sequel series was more action-packed and grander in scale. Merging these concepts together made for a richer, more engaging television series. Given the struggles with PTEN, the idea of a second five-year show was increasingly unlikely to happen. By merging the ideas, Straczynski would be able to tell at least a version of the epic 10-year tale he had devised.

Babylon 5 had risen to the challenge of creating a science fiction show like no other, challenging studio and audience perceptions of what genre television could be. It didn't have the legacy of a franchise like *Star Trek* to help shield it from cancellation. But the impending collapse of PTEN was the biggest threat to the show yet. Going into that fourth season, it became the hangman's noose around the show.

All those epic moments, teased in the first two seasons and then expanded massively in the third, deserved closure. At the start of the fourth season, the galaxy was in the grip of a titanic war with the Shadows. Sheridan had sacrificed himself at Z'ha'dum. Garibaldi had been kidnapped by the Shadows. President Clark ruled over a dictatorship on Earth, and Babylon 5 was a rogue state. Even the smaller threads, such as Londo's rise to emperor of a doomed Centauri Prime, the enslavement of the Narn, the broken Grey Council of the Minbari and the divide between the Warrior and Religious Castes—all needed to be resolved sooner than planned.

The fourth season of *Babylon 5* was, again, wholly written by Straczynski, who took on the ambitious task of bringing *everything* to a head. And it delivered the closure the show needed. The Shadow War went to grandiose levels before it was resolved. The Earth civil war delivered some of *Babylon 5*'s most intense moments, from Sheridan's capture and Garibaldi's betrayal to the final fight to save Earth from Clark himself. It was a grand space opera of the highest order, and season four became the highlight for many fans.

Against the odds, Straczynski was able to tell his story in breathtaking fashion.

It is likely that the Shadow War would always have ended in the fourth season. In the book *Babylon 5 Season by Season #4: No Surrender, No Retreat*,[1] Straczynski suggested that the conflict would have been resolved closer to the mid-season point. The climax, "Into the Fire," was reduced from two and a half episodes to just one, in order to make room for events coming up later in the season.

Other storylines were given short shrift to allow for closure. The Minbari civil war was condensed into what amounted to a single episode, "Moments of Transition," a week before the Earth civil war kicked off in "No Surrender, No Retreat." Londo's eventual ascension to emperor was announced by the end of the fourth season, though the events would only play out in season five.

The Earth civil war was also condensed and Straczynski explained how he moved several episodes from season five into the fourth, in order to wrap up the civil war arc:

> Season Four would have ended with 418 ["Intersections in Real Time"] because that's a good cliffhanger. You've got Sheridan sitting in the box. You've got him sitting there until the next season begins and you get him out of the box, and you then begin the process of starting the movement that gets the Earth thread going.[2]

The season four cliff-hanger was moved up, allowing for episode 21, "Rising Star," to serve as a de facto conclusion to the main storyline. "Sleeping in Light" was filmed at the end of season four and was always intended as the finale; it was pushed into season five when TNT picked up the show and replaced with "The Deconstruction of Falling Stars," filmed prior to beginning work on season five.

Had "Sleeping in Light" followed "Rising Star," ending *Babylon 5* at four seasons, rather than five, Straczynski would have navigated the fall of PTEN to deliver a satisfying end to the show. The condensed changes would have a somewhat detrimental impact on season five, with the drop in momentum turning off some fans. But that was a challenge for later. With season four, *Babylon 5* got the ending it deserved.

Giants in a Playground

In the space of just six episodes, *Babylon 5* would be changed forever. The Shadow conflict had been building since mid-season one, resulting in

15. Season Four

the eruption of a grand, galactic war in season three. The Vorlons had also been a key component of the show since *The Gathering*. The mysterious race had conditioned the younger races to see them as their saviors, preparing for the war against the Shadows, and then lost Kosh in the struggle that followed.

By episode six, "Into the Fire," the Shadows and Vorlons would be gone from *Babylon 5* forever.

The opening six-episode arc of season four was a staggering feat of narrative engineering, weaving in several threads. Sheridan's death and resurrection at Z'ha'dum, Garibaldi's disappearance and return, Vir and Londo dealing with the insane Centauri emperor Cartagia and his plans for godhood, the end of the Centauri occupation of Narn, the removal of the Vorlon ambassador, and the final showdown between the Vorlons and Shadows at Coriana VI.

The first three episodes are concerned with moving all the chess pieces into position. "The Hour of the Wolf" deals with the aftermath of the events of season three, revealing that Sheridan died, only for him to be reintroduced in the second episode, brought back by *the* First One, Lorien. G'Kar's search for Garibaldi finds him in the clutches of the Centauri, leading to horrific torture in "The Summoning" and the strange alliance with Londo to kill Cartagia and free his people. Marcus and Ivanova attempt to recruit the First Ones, while Garibaldi's return sets up events that will play into the Earth arc later in the season. Sheridan's messianic appearance at the end of "The Summoning" is a call to arms for the second half of season four's Shadow War arc.

With the key players in place, the fourth to sixth episodes of season four are as epic as *Babylon 5* ever got. The emergence of Shadow and Vorlon planet-killers makes the stakes impossibly high. Whole worlds and civilizations, allied to the Shadows and Vorlons, face utter destruction—including Centauri Prime. The decision to turn the Vorlons into the enemy may have felt a little left field (perhaps the casualty of a condensed arc), but it makes for a thrilling showdown as a colder, more ruthless Sheridan races to eliminate the new Vorlon ambassador Ulkesh, leading to the battle for the fate of the station as the last remnant of Kosh battles its successor.

"Falling toward Apotheosis" and "The Long Night" are huge episodes of *Babylon 5*. Whole worlds are eliminated, refugees flood the station and there is a rising panic. But Straczynski still puts the characters at the heart of these events, from Londo and Vir's attempts to rid their people of Cartagia to G'Kar's suffering, and Sheridan and Delenn's bittersweet reunion and the reveal that he has just 20 years to live.

These small moments matter, and even as the Shadow—and now Vorlon—War heads toward its climax, audiences are reminded that it is the "little people" that matter. The final showdown at Coriana VI sees the White Star fleet, the Minbari and the League of Non-Aligned Worlds position themselves between the two giants in a playground, risking the lives of thousands to save billions. While the arrival of the last of the First Ones plays a part, it is ultimately Sheridan and Delenn's actions, forcing a dialogue and exposing the hypocrisy and rivalry of the Vorlons and Shadows, that forces them to leave and go beyond the Rim.

The Shadow conflict was ultimately always about ideology. Order versus chaos. Vorlons or Shadows. The younger races rise above centuries of indoctrination to follow their own path, without the influence of the First Ones. "Who are you?" "What do you want?" These were questions asked of humans and Minbari, Centauri and Narn since the beginning of *Babylon 5*. In "Into the Fire," the younger races, under the leadership of Sheridan and Delenn, reject those questions and choose their own path.

While there is certainly a huge momentum to those final episodes of the Shadow War, they follow a different path than the episodes that ran through the back half of season three. Gone are the battles and threats to the station in favor of something more cerebral. Whether it was always Straczynski's intention to the end the Shadow War this way will probably never be fully answered. But given that he only cut the story short by a couple of episodes, it suggests that season four was always going to treat the final stages of the Shadow War in a very different way from the season preceding it.

What would those extra couple of episodes have given audiences? More time might have been spent rallying the other races to put themselves on the line for freedom. Perhaps we would have had more time with the mad Emperor Cartagia. Would the Vorlons' true, ruthless nature have evolved more naturally?

Perhaps we would have had more time with the telepaths. This does seem to be the one casualty of season four in general. While it was never realized on screen, the Byron arc of season five was always the first major step in the subsequent Telepath War on Earth. With the virtual reset of season five, Byron and his followers had to be set up from the word go. But if there had been more time to flesh out the Shadow and Earth conflicts of season four, their roles might have been seeded earlier.

The telepaths were weapons, created by the Vorlons to fight the Shadows and then corrupted by the Shadows, as seen in season three's "Ship of Tears." We glimpsed moments of Lyta holding off other Shadow ships in seasons three and four. Would other telepaths have joined the fight? Telepaths who might have gone on to join Byron's cause in the final season? The absence of these human weapons may have been the biggest casualty of a condensed fourth season.

Was the resolution of the Shadow War rushed? Perhaps, but not by much. *Babylon 5* was always heading toward that final high-stakes debate at Coriana VI, even if it got there a little sooner than intended.

The Fight Against Earth

While the Shadow War was the central conflict at the heart of *Babylon 5*, there were two significant narratives that spun out of the influence of the Shadows on other races: the corruption of the Centauri and the rise of a xenophobic Earth. The Narns were freed from Centauri occupation as the Shadow War ended, but the conflict against the corrupt President Clark was the key storyline that needed resolution. With season four looking to be the show's last, the Earth civil war needed to take place and end in the space of a single year.

Earth makes its move before the dust is even settled on the Shadow War, putting a stranglehold on Babylon 5 in the seventh episode, "Epiphanies," and running a propaganda machine against Sheridan and his people in episodes like "The Illusion of Truth." This leads to Franklin and Marcus's mission to link up with the Underground movement on Mars. For several episodes, there is a cold-war dynamic between Earth and Babylon 5 before open warfare erupts in "No Surrender, No Retreat."

The attack on a transport convoy carrying thousands of civilians prompts Sheridan to act and attack Earth ships blockading Proxima III. It's the biggest development in the Earth conflict since Babylon 5 broke away from Earth a whole season earlier, and it kick-starts an intense sequence of episodes that propels *Babylon 5* to its literal endgame.

Like the Shadow War, the Earth civil conflict is a battle of ideologies. Clark and his people aren't looking to conquer; they are looking to sow the seeds of hatred, pushing their xenophobic views on humanity and portraying aliens as a corruption of human beliefs. Those who stand up to Clark are crushed. Civilians are bombed, ostracized, and painted as villains, out to destroy humanity. As covered in the last chapter, the ideas Straczynski was playing with in the Earth storyline have become increasingly, disturbingly uncomfortable in light of more recent cultural events.

Sheridan taking a stand against the hatred, xenophobia, and bloodshed makes his actions seem even more heroic, but *Babylon 5* was never a show that dealt with absolute blacks and whites. Sheridan is a changed man after his return from Z'ha'dum, and that is no clearer than in his desperate actions to rid humanity of Clark's regime. His intentions might be good, but his actions compromise him.

Up to this point, the treatment of human telepaths has been portrayed through the good—innocent telepaths who are forced to go underground—and the bad—the militant Psi Corps with its own twisted ideologies. Good people, good telepaths have been mistreated by the likes of Bester and his kin. Franklin, Lyta and Ivanova have represented the good guys, opposing the Psi Corps and everything it stands for.

Sheridan, however, crosses the line. He uses innocent telepaths as cannon fodder to take down Earth ships in the final stand against Clark's forces. Sure, he selects those who don't have loved ones that will miss them, but he uses people for his own ends, even if it comes out of a place of good—preventing further fighting and bloodshed. It reflects the more ruthless nature of Sheridan that was borne out of his resurrection at the hands of Lorien, which never fully dissipates—as his treatment of Lyta at the end of season five proves.

But of course, Sheridan is also the hero of the story, compromised as he might be. Mirroring Sheridan's actions is Bester, who gets a greater agency in season four through his manipulation of Garibaldi. Over the course of season four, we see Garibaldi hand in his badge as security officer, set up a shady business and get into bed with businessman and criminal William Edgars. With the Earth civil war at its height, he betrays Sheridan to Clark's forces before the horrible truth is revealed: Bester reprogrammed Garibaldi after his capture by the Shadows, to use him to destroy both Sheridan and Edgars—who has been developing a biological weapon to use against telepaths.

From Bester's point of view, he acted for good reasons, to remain loyal to Clark and save his people. It is an interesting mirror to Sheridan's own actions.

Babylon 5 doesn't deal in broad-stroke heroes and villains. While there are certain characters that gravitate toward one end of the spectrum or the other, Straczynski's writing offers nuanced characters that follow very human paths. They can do bad things for good causes and vice versa. Sheridan and Bester are examples of that.

The Earth civil war provided plenty of tremendous, often action-packed moments: from Ivanova's fury as she faces off Clark's Shadow–Earth hybrid ships, to the desperate stakes of Scorched Earth and the last-minute arrival of the *Agamemnon*. But again, it is rooted in human drama. Marcus sacrificing himself for Ivanova. Sheridan's interrogation. Garibaldi's desperate search for Lise. Again, the high stakes boil down to the preservation of innocent lives and a battle of ideologies.

Which makes the emergence of the Interstellar Alliance in "Rising Star" so important. In season four, everyone puts themselves on the line for freedom. Against the Shadows and Vorlons. Against Clark and the Psi Corps. The dream of something greater in such adversity was always the true mission mantra of *Babylon 5*. In "Rising Star," the show finally gets there.

The Minbari and Other Loose Threads

While the Shadow and Earth conflicts got the lion's share of the season four screen time, Straczynski also had to ensure that other long-running plot threads were addressed. Some of these were accomplished with seeds that could be drawn upon should the show continue in some form, whether season five or future spin-offs.

The Psi Corps get their biggest focus yet in season four, with Bester's manipulation of Garibaldi and the virus created by Edgars Industries. Moments like this show just how powerful Psi Corps are and the growing distrust for mundanes. While season five would continue this with the Byron arc, there is enough here to show that the Telepath War is coming sooner, rather than later.

After the defeat of Clark, Delenn's voiceover refers to the Telepath and Drakh Wars to follow. Again, season five would set up the evolution of this conflict with the manipulation of the Interstellar Alliance and the fall of Centauri Prime. But Straczynski plants enough seeds here with the appearance of the Regent's Keeper after Narn is freed, and the first proper appearance of the Shadow allies in "Lines of Communication." Similarly, Londo's eventual rise to the position of emperor is confirmed in season four, setting up his fall in the final season.

But there was one long-running arc that needed to be addressed if season four of *Babylon 5* was to be the last. The Minbari civil war ended up being something of a footnote in the fourth season, but it had just as much importance as the stand against Clark. Ever since the debut of Neroon in season one, there had been a growing divide between the Warrior and Religious Castes. The Grey Council had been in place to stop this rivalry from intensifying, but Delenn's actions in breaking the Grey Council to bring the Minbari into the fight against the Shadows left the Warrior Caste unopposed in their might. Just as the corrupt Earth and growing Drakh influence were the fallout of the Shadow War, so was the breaking of the once mighty Minbari.

There are three key episodes in the fourth season. "Atonement" sees Delenn confront her past actions that led her to cast the deciding vote on the Earth–Minbari war, while "Rumors, Bargains and Lies" would see Neroon betray Delenn for his own agenda. The civil war lasts just a single episode, but "Moments of Transition" is an important one.

The aggression of the Warrior Caste sees Minbari cities in flames and

Delenn and the Religious Caste on the losing side. The consequences of Delenn's actions to fight the Shadow War again come back to bite her. For the second time that season, she finds herself the driving force in a conflict that leads to the death of her own people. Her willing sacrifice is what is required to end the war, but she is saved by the actions of her rival Neroon, who dies as a member of the Religious Caste.

The Minbari civil war is handled extremely quickly and would likely have had more room to breathe if elements of the Earth civil war had been resolved, as planned, in season five. But Straczynski was able to deftly bring this plotline to a close with surprising finesse; Delenn rebuilds the Grey Council with the long-forgotten Worker Caste given greater power over the Warrior and Religious. It is a balance that will seemingly last beyond the confines of the show.

A Note on Viewing Orders

Given the heavily serialized nature of the fourth season, neither the JMS viewing order nor the *Babylon 5 Historical Database* Viewing Order differ from the broadcast order. The only story up for conjecture is *Thirdspace*, the second *Babylon 5* TV movie, produced by TNT and set during the events of 2261.

The JMS Viewing Order for Season Four:

- "The Hour of the Wolf"
- "Whatever Happened to Mr. Garibaldi?"
- "The Summoning"
- "Falling toward Apotheosis"
- "The Long Night"
- "Into the Fire"
- "Epiphanies"
- "The Illusion of Truth"
- *Thirdspace* (TNT TV movie)
- "Atonement"
- "Racing Mars"
- "Lines of Communication"
- "Conflicts of Interest"
- "Rumors, Bargains and Lies"
- "Moments of Transition"
- "No Surrender, No Retreat"
- "The Exercise of Vital Powers"
- "The Face of the Enemy"
- "Intersections in Real Time"
- "Between the Darkness and the Light"
- "Endgame"
- "Rising Star"
- "The Deconstruction of Falling Stars," which technically takes places centuries after Babylon 5

The Straczynski-approved *Babylon 5 Historical Database* Viewing Order for Season Four (with chronological dates):

15. Season Four

- "The Hour of the Wolf"—Saturday, December 28, 2260–Monday, January 6, 2261.
- "Whatever Happened to Mr. Garibaldi?"—Wednesday, January 8–Tuesday, January 14, 2261
- "The Summoning"—Saturday, January 11–Saturday, January 18, 2261
- "Falling toward Apotheosis"—Sunday, January 19–Monday, January 20, 2261
- "The Long Night"—Wednesday, January 22–Friday, January 24, 2261
- "Into the Fire"—Thursday, January 23–Thursday, January 30, 2261
- "Epiphanies"—Saturday, February 1–Saturday, February 15, 2261
- "The Illusion of Truth"—Thursday, April 3–Saturday, April 12, 2261
- "Atonement"—Saturday, April 26–Monday, May 5, 2261
- "Racing Mars"—Sunday, May 11–Tuesday, May 13, 2261
- "Lines of Communication"—Tuesday, May 13–Friday, May 16, 2261
- "Conflicts of Interest"—Saturday, May 17–Monday, May 19, 2261
- "Rumors, Bargains and Lies"—Monday, May 19–Wednesday, May 21, 2261
- "Moments of Transition"—Tuesday, May 20–Monday, September 1, 2261 (This story takes place over four months. The events of *Thirdspace* take place in June 2261 during this story.)
- *Thirdspace*—June 2261 (The story takes place in the middle of 2261, during the events of "Moments of Transition" after Delenn returns to Babylon 5 from Minbar, Franklin is back from Mars and Lyta has not been coerced to rejoin Psi Corps.)
- "No Surrender, No Retreat"—Tuesday, September 2–Thursday, September 4, 2261
- "Exercise of Vital Powers"—Saturday, September 6–Monday, September 8, 2261
- "The Face of the Enemy"—Friday, October 17–Wednesday, October 22, 2261
- "Intersections in Real Time"—Thursday, October 23–Monday, October 27, 2261
- "Between the Darkness and the Light"—Monday, October 27–Friday, October 31, 2261
- "Endgame"—Saturday, November 1–Tuesday, November 4, 2261
- "Rising Star"—Monday, November 3–Wednesday, December 31, 2261
- "The Deconstruction of Falling Stars"—Friday, January 2, 2262–3262 (1000 years after Babylon 5)

There are a number of challenges around the placement of the TV movie *Thirdspace*. It definitely takes place after episode 8, "The Illusion of Truth," as Zack Allan is wearing the new black uniform, but there are inconsistencies that prevent it from being given an accurate placement, such as the presence or absence of Delenn and Franklin—neither of them were on the station together from "Atonement" until the breakout of the war with Earth in "No Surrender, No Retreat."

However, *Thirdspace*, which we'll cover in more detail in a later chapter, is best watched after season four and as such has little bearing on the viewing order of season four itself.

Supplemental: A Season Four Review

"It was the year everything changed."

The fourth season of *Babylon 5* is most thrilling year of the show's run—and one of the most epic seasons of television ever made. While the threat of cancellation forced J. Michael Straczynski to wrap everything up early, it gave *Babylon 5* an urgent pace that propelled the audience from the heights of the Shadow conflict to a race to save Earth from the machinations of ruthless President Clark. The pace of season four was simply breathtaking.

The Shadow War dominates the opening six episodes. It is a game-changing narrative; Sheridan returns from the dead and rallies the League of Non-Aligned Worlds and his army of light to stand up against the dueling powers of the Shadows and the Vorlons. The stakes are impossibly high, with planet-destroying vessels putting billions of lives at risk. If the kickoff of the conflict in season three showed the Shadows at their most terrifying and mighty, then season four ups the ante by making the Vorlons the villains of the story too.

With Rangers, Lost Ones and even the flaming eye of Z'ha'dum, *Babylon 5* wears its *Lord of the Rings* influences on its sleeves. Coriana VI is *Babylon 5*'s Battle of the Pelennor Fields and the last stand at the Black Gate of Mordor, with the heroes of the story putting themselves on the line to save the lives of everyone in the galaxy. Sheridan's return from the dead is positively messianic, a hero of the light who will do what needs to be done to win the war against the darkness.

But these opening episodes offer more than grand battles and heroic last stands. There is some rich character drama in the bittersweet nature of Sheridan's return, Ivanova carrying on in his place, and Garibaldi's sudden return after his capture by the Shadows at the end of season three.

The debut of Wortham Krimmer's insane Centauri Emperor Cartagia almost steals the show. Londo and Vir find themselves caught up in his delusion vision of godhood, while a captured G'Kar finds himself tortured mercilessly at Cartagia's every whim. Andreas Katsulas, Peter Jurasik and Stephen Furst all do magnificent work in these episodes. From G'Kar refusing to scream as he is repeatedly tortured by the electro whip in "The Summoning," to Cartagia's shocking death at Vir's hands in "The Long Night," these are some of *Babylon 5*'s most jaw-dropping moments.

The pace barely falters as *Babylon 5* pivots from the fallout of the Shadow War to the breakout of the Earth civil war. New threats like the Drakh are carefully seeded into the show, setting up their actions in season five, the TV movie *A Call to Arms*, and *Crusade*. While undeniably rushed, the conflict between the Warrior and Religious Castes of the Minbari gives Mira Furlan plenty to work with as she is faced with the revelation that she cast the deciding vote on the Earth–Minbari war, while also dealing with the fallout of her actions in breaking the Grey Council. The brilliant John Vickery makes his final appearance as Neroon; his fate after going against Delenn in the Minbari civil war is a thrilling moment of redemption from one of the show's best recurring characters.

Another fan favorite, Walter Koenig's Psi Cop Bester, also gets plenty to do this season, as his fragile alliance with Sheridan comes to an end through his manipulation of Garibaldi. It is not an easy season for fans of the station's chief of security; Jerry Doyle plays up Garibaldi's aggressive paranoia as he quits his position and sets himself up working for shady businessman William Edgars. His hostility toward Sheridan is often uncomfortable to watch, but his betrayal at the height of the Earth civil war is genuinely shocking. Bester revealing his role in Garibaldi's manipulation is a particularly cruel twist as season four races toward the end.

There is a key difference between the Shadow and Earth conflicts this season; the war against Clark feels far more personal and intense, and the breakout of war offers plenty of "greatest moments" for *Babylon 5*. The fight against the Earthforce blockade in "No Surrender, No Retreat" and of course Ivanova's fury as she faces off against the Shadow-hybrid vessels in "Between the Darkness and the Light." The Operation Scorched Earth sequence in "Endgame" is a nail-biter, with a triumphant last-minute save from Sheridan's former ship.

Again, there are some rich character moments interlaced between the high stakes of the Earth civil war. Marcus sacrificing himself to save Ivanova is genuinely heartbreaking—and somewhat frustrating given that Claudia Christian would shortly leave the show. Londo and G'Kar finding a common cause in Sheridan's new Interstellar Alliance is genuinely a joy to watch. And one of *Babylon 5*'s most innovative episodes, "Intersections in Real Time," is a rich character study between Sheridan and Bruce Gray's cold, collected Interrogator.

There are moments when the high quality of season four falters. "The Illusion of Truth" feels like a flawed attempt to recapture the brilliance of season two's "And Now for a Word," while the mystery of Garibaldi's new boss Edgars seems to drag on for far too many episodes. The end of the Shadow and Minbari wars—as dramatic as they are—feel somewhat rushed, the casualty of wrapping up *Babylon 5* early. And with "Sleeping in Light" pushed to season five following the last-minute TNT renewal, the intriguing "Deconstruction of Falling Stars" feels like a cheap, experimental footnote, though it improves on repeated viewing.

But these are small gripes. Season four of *Babylon 5* is staggeringly epic. For this author, season three edges four by a hairbreadth, but there is no denying the jaw-dropping grand conflicts and rich character work that dominate the show's penultimate season.

16

Season Five

Epilogues and Opportunities

Had PTEN not collapsed, and had J. Michael Straczynski been able to stick to his five-year plan (based, at least, on the Sheridan-led show from season two onwards), then season five might have looked very different.

Like the fourth season, the fifth would have begun at a turning point in the war. Sheridan would have been captured by Earthforce, thanks to Garibaldi's betrayal, and Ivanova would have taken up command of the White Star fleet in his stead.

The events that took place in "Between the Darkness and the Light" through to "Rising Star" would likely have dominated the early episodes of season five's run, presumably wrapping up before the midyear point. What would have happened after? Ivanova would likely have taken command of Babylon 5, as Sheridan and Delenn moved to head up the newly formed Interstellar Alliance. The plan had always been to seed in the anti–Psi Corps telepaths earlier, making Byron's actions presumably even more tragic. The fall of Centauri Prime might have still occurred as it did, as the first catastrophic event in the Alliance's infancy.

Presumably there would have been no need for contract negotiations, and Claudia Christian would have remained on the show. What would her role have been, dealing with Byron's telepaths as captain of Babylon 5 and navigating her own hatred of the Psi Corps? Would Ivanova have taken on elements of Lyta's season-five arc? What about her own latent telepathic genes? It is likely that Ivanova would have been more closely entwined with the Byron arc than Lochley ever was; an arc that would surely have been more condensed than the one we eventually got on screen.

But PTEN did collapse, and *Babylon 5* wrapped up its main story arcs at the end of the fourth year. It seemed as if the end was nigh.

And then came TNT to the rescue. TNT was an American basic cable television channel, owned by Warner Bros., who picked up *Babylon 5* for a fifth season, giving Straczynski the option to finish the story on his terms. In addition to the season five pick-up, TNT also bought the rights to cablecast all four previous seasons of the show in syndication, and ordered two two-hour made-for-TV movies—one a prequel to the series and the other a wrap-up.[1]

Those two-hour TV movies would become four—*In the Beginning*, *Thirdspace*, *The River of Souls* and *A Call to Arms*—which would set up spin-off series *Crusade*. But first, the cast and crew would need to sign new contracts as production ramped up under TNT.

There has been a lot of debate as to why Claudia Christian chose not to return for the fifth season. On *The Lurker's Guide* at Midwinter.com, there are comments from both Christian and Straczynski, detailing both sides of the debate.[2]

In early June 1997, Warner Bros. asked for, and received, one-month extensions on their contract options from all cast members except Christian, to give Warner Bros. the time to work out the co-financing deal with TNT for the final season of *Babylon 5*. While she repeatedly confirmed that she was on board for a fifth season of the show, Christian chose not to accept the extension. Straczynski notes that the cast and himself received news through the press that Christian would not be returning to *Babylon 5* during the Wolf 359 event in July 1997 at Blackpool. With TNT and Warner Bros. both upset by this news, Straczynski claims that Christian, despite her assurances, did nothing to assure Warner Bros. of her commitment to the show.

Straczynski also noted that several cast members, including Bruce Boxleitner and Jeff Conaway, tried to convince Christian to stay on *Babylon 5*. Instead, she left the convention early and passed on the offer for season five.

Christian, however, provided a different story to the fans a day after Straczynski's comments on the *Lurker's Guide*. She contacted the *Babylon 5* office to confirm the fate of the show and hesitated to sign a new contract because she wanted four episodes off to work on a film. She was even involved in the promos for TNT. She was just as surprised by the gossip surrounding her departure from the show in Variety[3] and was then told her request for time off had been denied. She even noted that Ken Parks from Warner Bros. had told her agent to tell her to "find another job, we'll replace her."

Claudia Christian attended Wolf 359 and was told by Straczynski that she could have the time off. However, she was worried that this was not official and was told that TNT was insisting she be in all 22 episodes. She had to take the deal or leave it. Furthermore, her agent was never told of the deadline to sign the contract. The deadline passed, and she was written out of the show.

We'll likely never know the full story. In response to Christian's update, Straczynski noted that they were up against it. She had to choose to be in, or out. She chose out. It was no longer their responsibility, and it was flatly too late to bring her back. The door was closed on season five. With scripts already in production, a new station commander had to be created at the eleventh hour.

Enter Tracy Scoggins as Captain Elizabeth Lochley.

With a new captain incoming, Sheridan about to be inaugurated as the president of the Interstellar Alliance, and the galaxy in relative peace, season five was open for business.

What Next?

What do you do when the story you wanted to tell has been resolved? The original plan for season five was to open with Sheridan as a prisoner of Earthforce and the civil war in full swing. Instead, the final season would operate as something of an extended epilogue, telling the first year of the Interstellar Alliance, with all its triumphs and failures. For the first time since the beginning of season one, *Babylon 5* was starting fresh.

It was a luxury few epic stories ever got. We saw very little of the world of Middle Earth after the destruction of the One Ring in *The Lord of the Rings*. *Childhood's End* doesn't explore the fates of Karellen and the Overlords after Earth's destruction. When the story reaches its end, the closing chapters are just a brief goodbye to the characters that have survived these epic journeys.

Babylon 5 was in an interesting place. We technically didn't need to see what happened to Sheridan and Delenn after their victories and the reunification of humanity and the Minbari. The Shadows and the Vorlons were gone. There were certainly more trials to come—the Drakh, which would be explored more fully in *A Call to Arms* and spin-off series *Crusade*, and of course the impending Telepath War—but there was very little that could be incorporated into a single season of storytelling without feeling rushed.

Instead, *Babylon 5* season five operates in a period of relative peace. The Byron arc has little impact outside the station. The Drakh are already pulling the strings, setting the Centauri up for their great fall, but the open warfare lasts a matter of days. Despite the tragedy of the soon to be emperor Londo Mollari and his people, the fifth season—the year 2262—ends with a period of stability.

As with much of *Babylon 5*, there are rumors of abandoned plans that never saw the light of day, including one where Sheridan and Delenn's son David turned up from the future, where Ivanova ran the station with Franklin as her second in command, fell in love with Byron and the Drakh threatened to destabilize the new alliance in revenge against the defeat of their masters, the Shadows. The same rumors suggest these plans were abandoned when a hotel cleaner accidentally threw out Straczynski's notes in the trash.

But this is all just supposition. While Straczynski would undoubtedly have had to change his original plans in light of the original Earth arc being wrapped up and Christian's departure, it's hard to know if there were any significant changes between TNT picking up the show and the one that was broadcast.

Ultimately, season five of *Babylon 5* is dominated by two key plot threads: Byron and his colony of rogue telepaths and the fall of Centauri Prime, both of which were seeded by earlier events in the show. One delivered more successfully than the other.

A *Tragedy of Telepaths*

Telepaths had been on the run from the Psi Corps since the debut of Bester and the evil telepathic police force in season one's "Mind War." Season two introduced audiences to the telepath underground, a railroad of refugees seeking to escape the clutches of the Corps. Throughout the first four seasons of *Babylon 5*, audiences had witnessed their persecution and the corruption of the Psi Corps, meddling in the affairs of Earth, while becoming weapons in the war with the Shadows and Earth.

In the final season, the telepaths take center stage, setting up the off-screen Telepath War to come. Byron and his people came to the station, seeking sanctuary under President Sheridan, while the often used and neglected Lyta would find a community to call her own. In the first chunk of the season, *Babylon 5* explored a hopeful future for telepaths, finding safe shelter in the new Interstellar Alliance.

While there are some interesting ideas at play in these early episodes—the nature of free will, freedom of speech and personal security—the reaction to this narrative was less forgiving. Both Patricia Tallman and Robin Atkin Downes provide nuanced performances as doomed lovers Lyta and Byron, but the pacing becomes somewhat glacial, particularly in relation to the high stakes of seasons three and four. Coupled with the loss of Ivanova and the return to episodic adventures, there was the sense that *Babylon 5* had lost its way.

The arrival of the always wonderful Walter Koenig as Bester certainly spices things up as the season hits its midpoint and the aspirations of a telepath home world come crashing down. The telepath colony arc, as short-lived as it is, ends in a tragic note, with the death of Byron and his closest followers, forcing Lyta to pick up his quest for freedom. The event audiences were really looking forward to—the Telepath War—never materializes.

There was never any plan for a sixth or seventh season that would explore this conflict fully. Even the in-canon novels only dealt with events prior to—and after—the Telepath War. Straczynski had some plans for a big-screen movie adaptation of the Telepath War, but these never came to fruition either. We'll explore these in greater depth later in this book.

In season five, there is simply too much talking—and singing—and not enough action. Even the revelation that the Vorlons created telepaths as weapons fails to hit the shocking notes it was aiming for. Season five is often regarded as disposable and lackluster after the previous few years and that is somewhat unfair, given what takes place in the second half. But the real tragedy of the telepath arc is that it forced some fans to turn off before they got to the real meat of the final season.

Londo's Fate and the New Big Bad in the Galaxy

Londo was doomed from the start. In the very first episode of season one, "Midnight on the Firing Lane," audiences witnessed his prophetic dream: Emperor Londo Mollari dying at the hands of his rival G'Kar. Across the four seasons, we would see his rise to power—and descent into darkness—as his alliance with the Shadows had catastrophic consequences for the Narn and the rest of the galaxy.

In the fourth season, he would find redemption by removing the insane Emperor Cartagia and ridding the Shadows from his home world, helping to free Narn, and then eventually working to forge the beginnings of the Interstellar Alliance.

But as we saw in season three's "War Without End," no amount of redemption would ever be enough. He might become emperor, but his Centauri Prime was always heading for a fiery end.

Season five is perhaps Londo's strongest season since the second, dealing with the consequences of his actions. In the second episode, "The Very Long Night of Londo Mollari," his hearts would give out; his very body weakened by his actions as he sought redemption for his very soul. While he would survive this night, a greater trial would await him as the Drakh, the Shadows' closest allies, sought revenge.

The events leading up to "The Fall of Centauri Prime" are as strong as anything that came in previous seasons. It's sad that audiences had switched off after the Byron arc, unfairly dismissing the whole season for a handful of episodes. The cracks begin to appear in the Interstellar Alliance as member worlds face unwarranted attacks by unknown ships, later to be revealed as the Centauri.

A secret force of unmanned vessels, controlled by the Drakh at the behest of the Centauri Regent, would force the Alliance into open warfare against one of its founding members. The Narn and the Drazi, two races that faced the worst of the Centauri aggression, open fire on the Centauri home world, crippling it. With the defenses on Centauri Prime shut down at the behest of the Regent, a pawn in the Drakh's game, the Centauri face the same bloody Armageddon they had inflicted on the Narn home world three years earlier. "The Wheel of Fire," the episode that follows and also the of season five, is truly an apt one. Events come full circle as the Centauri face judgment for their actions by having those actions inflicted upon them.

With the lives of those closest to him at stake and his people facing annihilation, Londo is forced to accept the Drakh Keeper, condemning himself to a life of isolation and servitude to a race utterly consumed with hatred and revenge. As heartbreaking as G'Kar's offer of forgiveness is, it is Londo's lonely coronation march that stands as one of *Babylon 5*'s most haunting moments.

The actions of "The Fall of Centauri Prime" also cement the Drakh as the new big bad in the galaxy. Having crippled the Centauri in a total act of revenge, they force Londo to "gift" Sheridan and Delenn's unborn child with a Keeper. These events would not take place on screen, though a line from season three's "War Without End" suggests he is ultimately saved from servitude to the Drakh.

After their strong setup in season five (having briefly appeared in the fourth), the Drakh would continue to wreak havoc in the *Babylon 5* universe with the dual attacks on Earth in *A Call to Arms* and the open warfare that begins in *Crusade*. Sadly, the cancellation of that *Babylon 5* spin-off meant the Drakh never had a chance to be explored fully on screen—or be defeated—but they certainly made their mark late into the *Babylon 5* legacy.

Fond Farewells

Given the epilogue nature of the final season, *Babylon 5* is afforded plenty of moments of reflection—be it Londo's long night or the encounters

16. Season Five   145

with lost souls in "Day of the Dead." After the fall of Centauri Prime, the final four episodes concern themselves with goodbyes as characters prepare to leave the station for good.

There is a bittersweet quality to these final episodes. G'Kar finds that his new status as a religious prophet prevents him from remaining on the station, while Lyta, in her zealous attempts to continue Byron's legacy, finds that she is now considered a terrorist by her own former allies. Sheridan and Delenn prepare to move to the new Interstellar headquarters on Minbar, with Garibaldi prepares for life with Lyse on Mars, having faced his own return to the bottle following the events with Bester in season four. Even Franklin departs, taking up the role of his predecessor Benjamin Kyle on Earth, another full circle moment.

These episodes wrap up last-minute threads and establish new legacies: Ta'Lon and Vir take up the mantles of G'Kar and Londo; Lennier, now a Ranger, finds himself falling afoul of his unrequited love for Delenn and fleeing. Number One (the Mars Resistance leader, played by Marjorie Monaghan) takes up Garibaldi's position in the Alliance and as Sheridan and Delenn leave, the new crew of *Babylon 5* is in place, with Captain Lochley leading. "Objects in Motion" and "Objects at Rest" are episodes that would never have taken place if *Babylon 5* had stuck to its original plan for the five-year arc, but become some of the most emotionally driven, cathartic installments of the show's run.

Set 19 years later, "Sleeping in Light" is a beautifully haunting episode that offers a final look at the world of *Babylon 5*. Filmed at the end of season four, when that run looked to be the show's last, it features the "return" of Ivanova, still haunted by the death of Marcus, and a bittersweet reunion before Sheridan passes beyond the Rim. While the final goodbye of Sheridan and Delenn remains another incredibly sad moment in *Babylon 5* lore, it is the destruction of the station itself that really pulls on the heartstrings.

"Objects in Motion" through to "Sleeping in Light" might be akin to *The Lord of the Rings*' many endings, but like that book (and film), they are deserved and not overly indulgent. In the space of five seasons (and a pilot episode), Straczynski crafted a grand and epic tale of ancient races, epic conflicts and powerful tragedies and triumphs. He achieved the grand novel for television, and it absolutely deserved to end on its own terms.

A Note on Viewing Orders

Despite the return to stand-alone episodes for part of the season, the different viewing orders for *Babylon 5* season are largely the same as the broadcast order, with one exception: "Day of the Dead." It was the only episode not penned by Straczynski; this honor went to Neil Gaiman, the first additional writer for *Babylon 5* since season two.

The JMS Viewing Order for Season Five:

- "No Compromises"
- "The Very Long Night of Londo Mollari"
- "The Paragon of Animals"
- "A View from the Gallery"
- "Learning Curve"
- "Strange Relations"
- "Secrets of the Soul"
- "In the Kingdom of the Blind"
- "A Tragedy of Telepaths"
- "Phoenix Rising"
- "The Ragged Edge"
- "Day of the Dead"
- "The Corps Is Mother, the Corps Is Father"
- "Meditations on the Abyss"
- "Darkness Ascending"
- "And All My Dreams, Torn Asunder"
- "Movements of Fire and Shadow"
- "The Fall of Centauri Prime"
- "Wheel of Fire"
- "Objects in Motion"
- "Objects at Rest"
- "Sleeping in Light" (takes place 19 years later, after the events of *Crusade* and the TV movies)

The Straczynski-approved *Babylon 5* Historical Database Viewing Order for Season Five (with chronological dates):

- "No Compromises"—Tuesday, January 13–Saturday, January 17, 2262
- "The Very Long Night of Londo Mollari"—Tuesday, January 20–Wednesday, January 21, 2262
- "The Paragon of Animals"—Friday, January 30–Saturday, January 31, 2262
- "A View from the Gallery"—Thursday, February 12–Friday, February 13, 2262
- "The Day of the Dead"—February 2262
- "Learning Curve"—Sunday, May 17–Friday, May 22, 2262
- "Strange Relations"—Saturday, May 23–Sunday, May 24, 2262
- "Secrets of the Soul"—Monday, May 25–Thursday, May 28, 2262
- "In the Kingdom of the Blind"—Wednesday, May 27–Sunday, May 31, 2262
- "A Tragedy of Telepaths"—Tuesday, June 16–Thursday, June 18, 2262
- "Phoenix Rising"—Friday, June 19, 2262
- "The Ragged Edge"—Saturday, June 20–Tuesday, June 23, 2262
- "The Corps Is Mother, the Corps Is Father"—Wednesday, June 24–Monday, June 29, 2262

- "Meditations on the Abyss"—Monday, July 13–Wednesday, July 15, 2262
- "Darkness Ascending"—Thursday, July 23–Thursday, July 30, 2262
- "And All My Dreams, Torn Asunder"—Friday, July 31–Thursday, August 6 2262
- "Movement of Fire and Shadow"—Sunday, August 9–Friday, August 14, 2262
- "The Fall of Centauri Prime"—Friday, August 14–Tuesday, August 18, 2262
- "The Wheel of Fire"—Wednesday, August 19–Friday, August 21, 2262
- "Objects in Motion"—Tuesday, September 1–Saturday, September 5, 2262
- "Objects at Rest"—Sunday, September 6–Friday, September 11, 2262
- "Sleeping in Light"—Wednesday, December 28, 2280–Friday, January 20, 2281

Both viewing orders agree that the placement of "Day of the Dead," broadcast smack bang in the middle of the escalating telepath arc, doesn't work. The JMS viewing order makes far more sense. It is something of a reflective palate cleanser after "Phoenix Rising" (the episode even makes reference to the drama of recent weeks) before the season moves into the Centauri-dominated events that culminate in Londo's doomed coronation as emperor.

However, the chronological order is a curiosity in itself. Coming just five episodes into the season, "Day of the Dead" becomes less a reflective and more a character-building piece, particularly for Lochley. Arguably the JMS viewing order makes the most sense, narratively speaking; as an episode not penned by Straczynski, it has a unique flavor and works most effectively as a transition point from one arc to the next.

Supplemental: A Season Five Review

The final season of *Babylon 5* is the one looked upon most unfavorably by fans. While there are arguably greater highs this year than in season one, it also suffers from coming off the back of one of the most intense years of television. The pace feels almost glacial in the first half of the season, by comparison.

The final season also suffers from the loss of the fiery, charismatic Susan Ivanova. Claudia Christian's departure is keenly felt, and while

Tracey Scoggins does an excellent job of bringing her replacement, Captain Elizabeth Lochley, to life, she never quite gets the deeper character work she deserves.

Bringing in a brand-new character for a final season is always an uphill challenge. *Babylon 5*'s rival, *Star Trek: Deep Space Nine*, struggled to give Nicole DeBoer's Ezri Dax the depth of her predecessor Jadzia following Terry Farrell's departure. While he had a great introduction in season eight of *The X-Files*, Robert Patrick's John Doggett never quite got the attention he deserved after David Duchovny left the show.

Given Claudia Christian's last-minute departure, Lochley became something of a last-minute script addition. Her by-the-book style is refreshing and her relationship to Sheridan is an intriguing narrative hook, but by the end of the season, we know very little about the new captain that we didn't know at the start. Interestingly, she would be fleshed out as a character during her recurring role in *Crusade*, but that show's cancellation cut short her development too.

The other issue with season five is the telepath arc. The rushed resolution of many series arcs in season four meant that Byron and his people could not be seeded earlier in the show. When they do appear, they aren't that interesting a group of people; outside of Robin Atkin Downes's Byron and his relationship to Lyta (Patricia Tallman gets a meaty role this season), it is hard to remember any of the supporting characters beside their glorious hair and affinity for singing. The story concept is interesting, built on years of world-building with the Psi Corps and telepath undergrounds, but it's often flat and unengaging when it makes it to the screen. The arc ends strongly with Byron's tragic sacrifice and the always welcome return of Walter Koenig's Bester (who gets plenty to do this year too), but there's an almost palpable relief when the story is over.

Season five of *Babylon 5* certainly finds its feet again in the wake of the telepath arc. The scope of storytelling returns to the galactic scale, with Alliance members attacked by mysterious ships and Sheridan's fragile peace in jeopardy. The renewed focus on Londo and G'Kar, who are truly the heart of *Babylon 5*, is a welcome one. After an early episode, "The Long Night of Londo Mollari," gives Peter Jurasik his first real focus since the end of the Shadow War, the mystery of what is happening on Centauri Prime, entwined with Ranger Lennier's own investigation into the shipping attacks, culminates spectacularly with the reveal that the Centauri are behind the new threat.

Of course, the biggest curveball Straczynski throws audiences is the revelation behind the Drakh and their long game, using the Centauri in a cruel act of revenge to sabotage the Alliance and seek retribution for the defeat of the Shadows. While they get limited screen time, the Drakh are an effective late-stage villain. Wayne Alexander, who also brought the mysterious Lorien to life in season four, and Inquisitor Sebastian in season two, gives a deliciously cruel performance as the Drakh who destroys Londo's life completely.

Some of Peter Jurasik's best work is done in the final season. Londo's hard choice to subject himself to a life of servitude and isolation in order to save his people—and the lonely march to his coronation—are absolutely heartbreaking. Equally as powerful are G'Kar's words of forgiveness to Londo as Centauri Prime burns around them. It is the kind of high Shakespearean-level tragedy that has come to encapsulate their relationship, and "The Fall of Centauri Prime" in particular ranks as one of the show's greatest episodes.

Fans who dismissed *Babylon 5* season five after the telepaths missed out on a superb story arc; the nature of Centauri Prime's attack by the Narn and Drazi is a twisted full-circle moment that raises the stakes and threatens everything that was won in the previous season. It is a tremendous piece of storytelling.

And then come the emotional goodbyes. *Babylon 5* had earned these episodes. G'Kar and Lyta leave the station, neither able to continue in their roles; G'Kar becomes a revered, religious prophet, unable to have a normal life, while Lyta is now a dangerous weapon and terrorist in the war against the Psi Corps. There is a bittersweet note to their endings on the show. Others are more hopeful: Sheridan and Delenn welcome the birth of their child as they leave for Minbar, Garibaldi and Franklin are able to start new lives on Mars and Earth, and a new group is assembled to take their place.

Only Londo suffers cruelly, alone and imprisoned on the Imperial Throne he so desperately sought. "When we first met, I had no power and all the choices I could ever want. And now I have all the power I could ever want and no choices at all. No choice at all." Those lines are some of the most powerful—and most tragic—words ever spoken on the show.

Finally, "Sleeping in Light" ranks as one of the greatest TV finales of all time. Filmed in season four, it gives a haunted Ivanova a chance for a new life as head of the Rangers, while Sheridan prepares to meet his end at Coriana VI as his 20 years runs out. It is a beautiful, haunting, majestic piece of character work, from that lovely reunion on Minbar with old friends to Sheridan and Delenn's Sunday-morning farewell. But, somewhat ironically, it is the destruction of the station itself that pulls the heartstrings the most, with Christopher Franke's majestic score making for a goosebump-inducing sequence.

The fifth season of *Babylon 5* is flawed. The virtual reset, the introduction of a new commanding officer and the somewhat dull telepath arc drag the momentum of the show down. But it certainly finds its feet again in the second half. From an epic conflict that threatens the hard-won peace, a final tragic journey for Londo and G'Kar, and a series of emotional finales, it ends on a majestic scale that cements its worthiness alongside the seasons that came before it.

17

A Chat with Patricia Tallman

In early 2022, I chatted to Patricia Tallman about her time as Lyta Alexander on *Babylon 5* for my podcast, *A Dream Given Form*.[1]

An actor and stunt performer, Patricia was of course best known for her role as Lyta on *Babylon 5* but has had acting roles in films such as *Army of Darkness* and *Austin Powers: International Man of Mystery* as well as TV appearances in *Castle*, *Criminal Minds* and more. And of course, she had a long-running relationship with the *Star Trek* franchise. While she would make brief on-screen appearances in *The Next Generation* and *Deep Space Nine*, she spent a great deal of time as a stunt double. Her film stunt work is extensive, from *Jurassic Park* to *Speed*, *The Long Kiss Goodnight* and *Godzilla*.

Patricia is passionate about her experience of being on the show, its legacy, and its fans. It was more than just a job. It allowed her to form lifelong friendships with the cast and crew, and she loves talking about *Babylon 5* as much now as she did back when the show aired, something that was clearly apparent when I chatted to her.

She continues to be a strong advocate for the show and founded B5 Events[2] in 2020 as a way to connect with fans. Described as a mix of *Inside the Actors Studio* and Master Class, online, members of the cast have shared their own experiences as actors, both as part of the show and beyond. B5 Events include a shop, providing signed memorabilia and other gifts. It is an experience, curated by Patricia, reflecting her passion for *Babylon 5*.

This interview took place before the announcement of the 30th anniversary event, the animated movie *The Road Home* involving the surviving members of the *Babylon 5* cast.

BAZ: *Thank you for taking the time to talk about the show.*

PATRICIA: I love hearing that people are still interested in *Babylon 5*. And, you know, it's really an honor to continue the conversation around a show that meant so much to us. It was the little show that could.

In the beginning, nobody could find us. We were on this little network. And then then it started to spread. And now, you know, it was on HBO, for crying out loud! That's pretty incredible!

B: *It's always finding new fans.* **Babylon 5** *is a show that people continue to discover and explore, which is wonderful.*

    P: I know, I find that amazing that it's over 25 years old now or something, and I still have—I've got people, young people who weren't even born when the show was on, coming up and saying how much they're loving the show. I just think that's incredible.

B: *It's 30 years old next year!*

    P: Thirty! Right. How did that happen? I didn't get any older. So, that's crazy!

B: *It is crazy how old the show is. So, my first question, then. What is your fondest memory of working on the show?*

    P: Well, you know, I think we all say this, too, it was the camaraderie that we had. We had such a beautiful group of loving souls working on that show. Not just the cast. The crew were just wonderful people. I looked forward to seeing everybody every day. When you're on a show like that, that's a regular series, you spend a *lot* more time with the cast and crew than you do with your own family at home. Because you're working so hard, and long hours. And then you're doing publicity and stuff in your off time.

    So it was important to have a good relationship with the people that you're working with, and it was it was effortless with this group. They were so fun. The crew was amazing. I keep reflecting on John Flynn, who was our director of photography—we call him a DP in the U.S.—and he was such a joy. Such good energy, so professional and even-keeled and fun. He understood the need for the work-life balance. We had to have fun but needed to get the job done. We never worked any overtime because there was no budget for overtime. So that was it. Whatever you got, you got. But his crew were all the same kind of vibe, you know. That professional yet fun group of guys. Very supportive.

    And then the cast: super fun, sweet people. I just had iced tea with Bruce Boxleitner, the day before yesterday. We just hung out for a couple hours, just having an iced tea and catching up, because he'd been in in Arizona shooting a film. And Claudia [Christian] is one of my best friends. And Bill Mumy and his wife. We're all still in touch and care about each other after almost 30 years later, as you pointed out!

    So that, to me, is what stands out, head and shoulders above everything else.

17. A Chat with Patricia Tallman

I've worked on all the *Star Trek* shows, back in the day. I haven't worked on the new ones, but I worked on *The Next Generation*, *Voyager* and *Deep Space Nine*. And those were super fun shows too. But the vibe was *completely* different. You're on a studio lot. The suits are walking through all the time. There's a certain stiffness when you were there.

We were out shooting, in what was called the orange bang building. It was a hot tub factory that we converted into soundstages next to a recycling dump, up in Sunland, which is 45 minutes away from any other studio. So we didn't have suits dropping by for lunch. They didn't want to come out there for lunch! And we were so lucky to have our autonomy. So, there was relaxation. There was a certain freedom. We were the little show that could!

We just kept going. We never knew, season to season, if we had another season. Every time we wrapped that season, we didn't know if we were ever going to hang out again, together. And we didn't know until maybe midsummer, when we got the next series order, and we knew we were back. So, it was it was just this appreciation for the fact that we had the time that we had.

And the fans. Extraordinary! The fandom, that was what kept it going. That's why PTEN ran the show, and that's why, eventually, TNT picked up the show. Because the *fans* wanted to see it. Because people were calling into their local television stations and saying, "Where's *Babylon 5*?" "When do we see *Babylon 5*?" So the local networks were pulling us in and that made that made the studio go oh, somebody really does want to see this show? That's crazy! It was a cool little section of life. We were a microorganism that kept going and growing!

B: *What the show was doing was groundbreaking. What JMS was doing with the show, and the kind of long form of storytelling, was amazing to watch.*

P: Exactly!

B: *What was it like then when it came to the fifth season, and you knew this was the end of the story?*

P: Well, of course, it was very emotional. The vibe that was going around was, why? Why are we ending? Because everyone wants it. TNT wants it, the fans want it. We could keep going. Why are we ending it? There was a lot of confusion around why Joe was making that decision. Joe wanted to move on and go to do *Crusade*. He had said, "*Babylon 5* is a five-year arc and that's all we're doing." So, he was sticking by that.

I remember walking through the hallway, past Joe's office, and Jeff Conaway comes out. And he's shaking his head. And I'm like, what, what's going on? And he said, I just had to tell Joe, it's so rare to have a show go for five seasons. They want another season. It's crazy to stop this! He had been on *Taxi*. He'd been on shows, he had been on TV in the old days and knew how rare it was to have a show keep going the way our little show did.

So yeah, that was one vibe going on. It was like, why? Why are we quitting when we're just really hitting a certain stride?

And the other thing that was going on was that *Crusade* was being kept such a big secret. A secret from us. There were rumors that, oh, some of the *Babylon 5* actors will be on *Crusade*. But there weren't any specifics. So we're like, what does that mean? Who's going? Who's not going? It was that close of a spin-off that these characters would still be alive. We really didn't know what was going on. And there was a certain amount of discomfort. Like, why aren't we allowed to know anything? This is affecting our future. Are we invited in or not?

It was confusing. It didn't feel good. Let's just put it that way. It didn't feel good. I'm not saying that Joe didn't have his reasons. That's his business. Our business was, well, why can't we know? Why can't we have some sense of what's going on? That was very frustrating.

But of course, as we were wrapping up the season, moment by moment, people were getting what we call "wrapped." When you're being released for the final time. Our producers didn't actually visit the set. But we had John Flynn, our director of photography, going, "Yay everybody! Hey, this is a wrap for Bruce! This is a wrap for Patricia!" And we're all kind of stunned by that. Like, wow. Okay. This is it?

B: *It was your family. Your family was breaking up.*

P: Yes, that's it! Yeah. We're suddenly selling the family house, you know what I mean? And we're all being kicked out into the cold! Obviously, everyone had work, and it wasn't drastic. But it was weird that it didn't end on a on a completed note. It ended in this weird way. What's happening? What's not happening? Bye, I guess. Yeah, come over for a barbecue? I mean, it was so odd!

B: *Did you know that you would be coming back to the* **Babylon 5** *universe in* **Crusade***, at all?*

P: I didn't know at first. Lyta got written into one episode. I think they were already up and running by this time. And whoever were the producers at the time offered me a ridiculous amount of money. Like $1,000 or something. A one-off for my character, you're paid for your popularity on the show, the character's history. It's important, you know, all of this stuff.

Lyta was going to come in for one day, and then she's gonna die.

And I just said, no, I don't think that my character deserves that kind of write off in a one-day episode. Boom, she's dead. I saw what was written, and it was ridiculous. So I just said no. I wasn't going to participate in that indignity for Lyta. That's what it felt like. And it was also just handled disrespectfully. So, the whole thing felt terrible. I just said, yeah, I don't want to do that to Lyta. I'm not gonna do it.

B: *I know there are in-canon books, which deal with Lyta's story. But where do you imagine Lyta's storyline went, after she left with to go traveling with G'Kar in season five?*

P: I just I hope that Lyta and G'Kar would just go off and have outrageous adventures! Both of them had superpowers. Lyta [was] obviously dealing with being Vorlon-enhanced. But G'Kar had these amazing powers of perspective, and soul and experience. I think he was the only person that could have handled Lyta, or that Lyta could have responded to in such a positive way. So I loved that they went off together.

I know that there's all these storylines—I haven't read them—about Lyta dying, or this and that. I'm like, well, okay. But, for me, Lyta never dies.

B: *She goes off on wonderful adventures!*

P: That's it! Yeah! Adventure! Adventure! Adventure! Adventure! Right?

B: *So, what was it like working with the likes Andreas Katsulas, or Mira Furlan? These actors who are sadly not with us anymore.*

P: All of them were incredible. I had the best time. Loved them all. Mira was one of my best friends, too. Claudia, Mira, and I.

It's kind of inconceivable. I can't wrap my head around it. I don't get it. I deal with our photos all the time. Because we have an online store. So I've been gathering autographs from my friends, and then we put it up in the store. We talk about what we want to put in the store. So I'm seeing pictures of Mira every day. All the time. I don't think of her as being gone. It just doesn't make any sense. Right? It doesn't make any sense. Because we were high into the pandemic, we weren't allowed to see her. There's been no memorial. Again, it's just so odd. I've had my own memorial for her online, with the fans. It makes no sense. I don't get it.

I don't get it. I've been sending some things to Rick Biggs's widow. As I'm packing up my house and moving things out, I'm finding little things. She's asked for some things, so I've been sending things, pictures of Rick. And again, I still see him as alive. I still see him every day in my head, you know. I think we all do that with people that we love. They never leave. I see them in the world. I see them in the fans.

I meet fans at conventions, and they talk about Rick, or they talk about Andreas, they talk about Jeff, and they talk about Mira. And I see my friends in them, in the fans that talk to me.

So, I don't know. I don't know. It's an eternal thing. And then, you know, I really bristle when people want to say something negative about the fact that so many people have passed away. Do you think we don't know that? Of course we know that! We're very aware of it. It's like someone's saying to you, oh too bad your mom and your dad and your sister and your brother and your uncle died. How do you feel about that? Everybody? How do you feel? It's like, you guys, these people are my family! Let's not start beating me down.

Let's just say how much joy they give us. And how much they're still alive every time you watch the show. I think that's partly why they don't they don't feel gone to me, in a certain way. Because they aren't!

B: *They live through the fans. Having seen these characters for years and years, it has been a joy watching them and seeing these staggering, phenomenal performances.*

P: Such good actors and such beautiful voices. You know, I can hear Mira's voice all the time.

B: *She had such a rich voice.*

P: Yeah, exactly.

B: *So, going back to Lyta. What was your favorite episode or storyline from the show?*

P: I had a blast in a lot of the different scenes but there was a storyline where Rick Biggs and were together. I worked with Rick a lot! Franklin and Lyta kind of ended up on a few missions, you know, and one of my favorite ones was when we went to Drazi. That was hilarious to shoot. John Flynn, our director of photography, was the director on that episode. And he's a joy to work with. I would go to Rick's condo—he had a condo he was sharing with his fiancée, Laurie, before they got married. And I'd bring my little baby boy, and Laurie would watch Julian, while I would rehearse with Rick. We'd play doctor and telepath in space! We'd work on our scenes and come up with ideas, and then we when we went to shoot it, we would present our ideas to the director, in this case, John Flynn.

And so, at that beginning, Lyta and Franklin are walking through Drazi, and Rick is all cool as a cucumber and handsome, and he's lost. You know, he won't look at the map. You can't read the map! I'm carrying all the luggage. I'm sweating. My hair is sticking to me. And I'm like, why don't you just ask? That was just improvised. That was something we came up with, and John Flynn loved it. That's sort of based on truth, because I would go to the makeup trailer, and it would take them two hours to make me look presentable. Rick would walk in, sit down. They powder him, and off he goes. He was just as beautiful when he arrived, after having woken up 10 minutes before, as when he left the makeup trailer ready for the camera. You know, he was always fucking gorgeous! And I was like, you bastard!

So, I thought he's got to be perfect. On Drazi, everyone else is a sweaty mess. He's very cool. Cool. Calm. Gorgeous. We had a great time. There was some fun stuff we did with it on that episode.

B: *You were in the pilot,* **The Gathering.** *And then you came back in season two and three and were a main character season four onwards. When you did* The Gathering, *did you think you would return to the show, later on?*

P: Yes, we were all told that we were part of the series. I didn't end up in season one because there was a producer at Warner Bros. who I wouldn't sleep with—I talk about this now—and he got me off the show.

B: *Oh, that's horrible.*

P: Yeah. He even confronted me later, I think it was season three when I was back on, at a holiday party. And he said, "how did you get back on this show?" I just sat there and smiled.

Then how Joe did it, he brought me back when Andrea Thompson wanted to leave the show. He saw this as an opportunity for Lyta to start coming back, and he didn't need studio approval for a guest star. So, he just brought me back as a guest star. By the time I was back listed as a regular, that was simply a contract negotiation point to keep this particular suit at Warner Bros. from being able to turn down my contract.

B: *Lyta was such a badass character. When those Vorlon abilities kicked in, it was amazing to watch, so it's great that you were able to return.*

P: Thank you.

B: *Are there any kind of missed opportunities with Lyta that you would have liked to see explored on the show?*

Lyta: Well, besides having adventures with G'Kar? Yeah, um, I think Lyta served a very specific purpose for the story arc, for Joe. He had a large cast of regulars if you will. So, not all of us could have these amazing storylines all the time. There was a lot of information to move the show forward, so I just felt like Lyta didn't serve the bigger story enough to warrant much more of a storyline than she got.

I didn't feel bad about it or anything like that. But sure, I would think of things all the time, that a telepath could participate in a little more, you know. Or the interpersonal struggles with her and the command staff. Because they treated her *very* badly! And a lot of that wasn't explained. Like, oh, we need you, we need you, we need you, and we're kicking you out of your quarters. Or we need you, we need you, we need you, and now we're going to ignore you after you've just saved our ass. It kind of happened over and over again. It would have been interesting to see Lyta's point of view on all that. Like, why was she so willing to help after she'd been treated so badly? I don't know.

B: *I think she was very much on her own, as a telepath. Babylon 5 was a place for refugees to come together and fight a common cause, but she was treated so badly. After her help with the Shadow War, she was kicked out of quarters, forced to rejoin the Psi Corps and then, in the end, Sheridan put a gun to your head!*

P: Right!

B: *I think what was pretty interesting was that Lyta wasn't part of the big, happy ensemble. She was out on her own and had to fight her own corner, a lot of the time.*

P: It's funny you should say that because when we were shooting that whole telepath thing with Byron, my friend Robin Atkin Downes, who's a wonderful actor—I'm so grateful that he was he was my partner for that storyline—I realized I had never smiled! I mean, for five years later, she didn't smile, until she got her storyline with Byron.

B: *Wow.*

P: Yeah, she was a tough head to be in, you know, to put on my Lyta head to perform her. To be her, it was a tough place to be. So, people have asked me, do you wish *Babylon 5* had gone on? And while obviously I would never have said no, I also was okay with stepping away. Because it was a hard place to be.

The cast and crew were a blast, they were amazing, but the storylines for Lyta were sad and tough. It was way more fun when she started to go out of control at the end of season five and start to mess with people, and not give a flying you know what!

B: *Well, she'd had enough.*

P: She'd had enough! She was a nuclear weapon! I love that she wore that straitjacket. I call it the sexy straitjacket, the cleavage happening in the straitjacket. She wore it to make other people feel comfortable. Because she could get out of it any time she wanted! I love that. That for me was pretty much Lyta. She wanted everyone else to be okay.

B: *One of my favorite subplots I always liked was Zack's unrequited love for Lyta. Do you think Lyta ever really knew what was going on with him?*

P: I had to play it as if she did not. Because it would have been so mean, had she known what was going on with him, and ignored him. So I had to believe that she was just clueless. She didn't get it. He's bringing her pizza because he really likes her.

Jeff was so funny because we would talk about this strange thing between Lyta and Zack. Why doesn't she get it? And he's like, "I'm bringing you some sausage on this pizza! Come on! You know what I'm saying?" He was such a goofball. I guess she was just really inexperienced. She just didn't know. And you think, oh, she's a telepath. But I think that that proves her integrity. She would never scan somebody without permission. She just would never do that.

B: *Maybe it was that lack of human connection. When Lyta was the Vorlon attaché, she was very much separate from everyone else going on. And then she was abandoned. I think with Franklin maybe, you at least got a kind of buddy cop kind of a type of interplay, which really lovely to watch. When they were on Mars as well, you got to see Lyta have bit of fun. Not smiling but having fun.*

P: Being in a relationship, where you're talking and working things out together, she didn't have a lot of that. So yeah, you're right. Franklin was one of those people that wasn't afraid of her. You know what I mean? He wasn't afraid of her. We talked about that, that as a doctor who worked with a lot of different alien forms, he wasn't afraid or disgusted by her. So I think that's part of why the command staff put him with her. He was one of the only people that wanted to be around her on a regular basis.

B: *So, you mentioned that you worked on all the* Star Trek *shows of the TNG era. What did you enjoy most about that time?*

P: I love doubling [for] Nana [Visitor]. I did a lot of stunt doubling for Nana. She's a dancer and so she was really good in fight scenes. I had fun when I was doubling Terry [Farrell] because we created all that Klingon fighting style on *Deep Space Nine*. But I think my favorite show was *The Next Generation*, because I'm a huge Patrick Stewart fan. And I came to love everybody a lot. I'm in touch with Gates [McFadden] still.

And, oh, Jonathan Frakes! So I was in Hawaii, doing a convention there. And I was running all the excursions because I've started this travel business.[3] That was one of my first times thinking, hey, I could do this! And Jonathan came along for it. And he's like, Patricia, what are you doing here? I love this! He said Questers! [That's what] I call my business, Quest Retreats. He's like Questers! Every time he saw us all over the weekend and on the island. We had so much fun. What an amazing guy, Jonathan Frakes.

So, that was another set with some great vibes. Like I said, you were on the Paramount lot, so you have a different level of scrutiny. It's a corporation, the *Star Trek* franchise. On *Babylon 5*, we were our own little family. Off in the corner we lived in, we were kind of the white trash over there. Literally, next to a trash dump! But *Star Trek* was just a pleasure to be on.

I was so proud that I had a uniform in every color in wardrobe because I doubled everybody. I had everybody's. My wardrobe was a rainbow and was just amazing. Very cool. Yeah. Very cool.

B: *You were on screen a few times in small roles, but it was mainly stunt work that you were doing?*

P: Yeah, I doubled just about any guest star female that came on all three of those shows, as long as I was about the right size. I am five nine. I was about a size six at the time. Six or eight. So I was a really good size to double a lot of the actresses that came through. And then occasionally they would just put makeup on me and then kill me! If you recognized me, something bad was going to happen!

B: *Of all the stunt work you've done, what was the craziest stunt you've worked on?*

P: *The Long Kiss Goodnight.* I was doubling Geena Davis. That was a grueling shoot. It was the opposite of my experiences on *Star Trek* and *Babylon 5*, in that it was a miserable group of people! It was in Toronto. A lot of nights, in winter. There wasn't a lot of warmth or camaraderie. I think the Americans and the Canadians had some tension going on? I don't know.

I got along great with everybody, but there was this weird hierarchy. You've got these stars, up here. And then you've got the little people and they're down here. And I'm in between. I'm doubling for Geena, but I'm down here with the little people, you know? I'm seeing both worlds, which is something that happens as a stunt person. You see both worlds. I wasn't impressed. I thought these people are kind of assholes.

But I did some of the gnarliest stunts on that film. A lot of it was experimental. We weren't sure how to pull off the effect.

I loved working on *Jurassic Park*. That was hard, but a completely different vibe. I was doubling Laura Dern, who was the sweetest person on the planet. She still says hello to me when she sees me. She always remembers me, which is amazing to me. She's a huge star!

I had a lot of fun on *Jurassic Park*. We had no idea what we were shooting. We didn't know. We had never seen effects like that. It's like when they were making *Star Wars*, they didn't know. They didn't know that they were going to have these incredible effects, because they had never seen it. The incredible effects came years later! It took two years to put it all together, and the soundtrack. They didn't know!

So, we're on *Jurassic Park* and our stunt coordinator has this little bag, and in this bag, he pulls out a Hot Wheels jeep and pulls out these little plastic dinosaurs. And he says, "okay Pat, you're in the jeep." And the jeep goes rrrrrrr and here goes the dinosaur. Grrrrrrr. Argh! He's acting it out. And then we get on our feet to go and do it and there's no dinosaurs? Right? There are no dinosaurs. We're just going "ahhhhh!" We're running away from nothing.

In the case of the jeep, they had this massive stick, about 15, 20 feet long. And it's black, white, black, white, all the way along. And at the top of the stick is a three-foot round diameter, white cardboard circle nailed to the top. And somebody had taken a Sharpie and drawn a happy face with teeth. And that was the T. rex!

And so, they would position it, so I would have an eyeline of where the T. rex was when it breaks out of the forest. I'm looking way up high because it's tall. Now it's bending its head down, so my eyeline is here, about six or seven feet off the ground. And then it hits the jeep with its head, so my head is down here, by my knees, looking down the side of the jeep and I have all that action to do.

But we go to the movie theater, to see it for the first time, and no one can talk. We're like WHHHHAAAAAATTTT?! I mean gosh!

B: *It's an actual T. rex!*

P: It was so real. It was unbelievable. It looked amazing!

B: *It still holds up today.*

P: When we were doing the rotunda scenes at the end of *Jurassic Park*, where the raptors are chasing them down the scaffolding. The scaffolding is going back and forth. On the set, there were these raptor puppets, that were life-size, that were built on these men that were inside the suits, so their heads were where the shoulders of the raptors are. And then there were these long necks extending above their heads; the neck is all animatronic. Its eyes and its teeth and its neck move, and these little raptor hands and the body and the long tails. The guys didn't have raptor legs. That's all CGI'd later. They had blue pants on and Nikes!

That kind of wrecks the illusion, right? We still don't get it. But when you see it on film, you see this amazing creature and it's seamless. You don't see a guy in a suit with a puppet, wearing Nikes. Each one had maybe six puppeteers, working on one animal. It was insane! So yeah, we forget that all that stuff isn't in there. The guys making *The Lord of the Rings*. The guys making *Harry Potter*. They're working in front of green screens, most of the time. There's nothing there. So that acting is even more amazing when you think about it.

B: *That's amazing. It sounds like a great experience.*

P: A great experience, sure.

B: *So, let's come back to* Babylon 5. *There's a reboot that JMS is working on now. Would you return to play a new character, if asked?*

P: Oh, sure. Joe's been pretty transparent, talking to us about it. We're all game. We're all game. Let's see what happens. Joe created such a remarkable show. It's *so* remarkable, so why wouldn't we trust him to make something else remarkable? He's had 30 years to think about how he would want to do *Babylon 5*, but better. Why wouldn't we want to see that? We should trust him!

B: *What kind of character would you like to play?*

P: A character that smiles. I would love that. A character that smiles. A character that is warm and likeable. And I don't mind badass too. But I don't know if you would cast me as that now. I would trust Joe.

B: *Final question then. What does* **Babylon 5** *mean to you?*

P: *Babylon 5* means family. *Babylon 5* was such a gift; it was a treasure. I am so blessed to have had that in my life, and it's been the gift that keeps giving. It's giving me the fandom, who show up and watch me, what I'm doing now, or wanna buy my book, or see me at a convention, or join me online. I'm very grateful for that.

18

The TNT Movies

Looking Back Before Moving On

The TNT deal to save *Babylon 5* brought with it not just a concluding fifth season, but also two TV movies. After years of struggling to stay on the air, there was hope for the *Babylon 5* franchise. Those two movies became four, and a spin-off series, *Crusade*, was announced. J. Michael Straczynski's world was growing once more.

It's surprising to think that the end of *Babylon 5* was also the most exciting time for the franchise. Straczynski now had the resources to explore stories beyond the scope of the five-year arc, while also fleshing out existing narratives. At the end of season four—and before the cast contracts for season five were even signed—production was underway on prequel story *In the Beginning*, which told the story of the epic Earth–Minbari war, and *Thirdspace*, an alien invasion horror story set during the events of season four (hence the involvement of Claudia Christian as Ivanova).

A new version of *The Gathering* was also produced, which made subtle changes in line with the series that followed. While no new footage was shot, 14 minutes of existing scenes were restored. Kosh makes a reference to Sinclair as "Entil'zha" (Valen), foreshadowing his ultimate destiny as the revered Minbari leader in season three's "War Without End." Kosh's hands also glowed, in keeping with the revelation at the end of season two.

Tamlyn Tomita's original dialogue was reinstated after being deemed too harsh by PTEN, Londo's reference to Sinclair being the last station commander was removed, and Sinclair and Lyta's trip through the alien zoo was removed for being too hokey—as was the overly dramatic "privacy moment." A couple of moments with Carolyn and Sinclair's confrontation with a Dust smuggler were also reinstated, while *Babylon 5* composer Christopher Franke replaced the electronic score of original composition by Stewart Copeland.

The special edition of *The Gathering* and *In the Beginning* aired in

January 1998, shortly before the fifth season of *Babylon 5* commenced. *Thirdspace*, which was set during early post–Shadow War season four, would then air in the break between season five's "Movements of Fire and Shadow" and the final five episodes of the show later that year.

Two more TV movies were produced. *The River of Souls* is set after the events of "Objects at Rest," acting as a pseudo-season six story of *Babylon 5*, which aired simultaneously with the end of the show. Finally, *A Call to Arms* aired on TNT at the beginning of 1999, acting as a launchpad for spin-off series *Crusade*, which debuted in June of that year.

The Legend of the Rangers and *The Lost Tales* would follow, two attempts to resurrect the *Babylon 5* franchise after the deal with TNT collapsed and *Crusade* was canceled. Like the doomed TV spin-off, we'll cover these in a later chapter.

> We've finished the producers' cuts of the two TNT movies and have come through without notes. Everyone loves 'em, and agrees that while *Thirdspace* is very cool, *In the Beginning* is the best thing we've ever done. On every level: acting, writing, the directing, sets, costumes … everything. This one's got Hugo written all over it.[1]

The special edition of *The Gathering*, *In the Beginning*, *Thirdspace*, *The River of Souls* and *A Call to Arms* marked a resurgence in the *Babylon 5* franchise under TNT. The cable network, which had saved *Babylon 5* and pumped $3 million into the production of new TV movies, loved what Straczynski was doing. The ratings only cemented the success of this new venture. Along with the final season, the future looked bright.

Sadly, it wasn't to be.

In the Beginning

Before moving forward, *Babylon 5* had to look back. TNT had secured the rerun rights to the show and wanted to attract new viewers. While a remastering of *The Gathering* in line with series continuity made sense, *In the Beginning* was the spectacle TNT was looking for.

Filming of *In the Beginning* took place at the end of season four. While it was the first new TV movie released, it was produced second after *Thirdspace*, allowing for the use of existing sets on the primarily Babylon 5 station–based second TV movie.

Telling the story of the Earth–Minbari war, *In the Beginning* was a fusion of new sequences recounting the story of Sheridan, Delenn, Franklin, Londo and G'Kar's involvement in the conflict, while also blending in existing scenes—Delenn's revelations in season four's "Atonement" and of course Sinclair's desperate actions from season one's "And the Sky Full of Stars." Peter Jurasik reprised his role as the aging Emperor Londo Mollari, telling the story of humanity's struggles against the Minbari shortly prior to his own death as witnessed in season three's "War Without End." This tied thematically to Londo's opening narration from *The Gathering*.

For the second time since season one, Mira Furlan filmed in her original season one makeup as Delenn, as her journey from acolyte and pupil of Dukhat to vengeful member of the Grey Council charted her perspective on the conflict. On the other side was Bruce Boxleitner's Sheridan, the first officer of the *Lexington*, who scored the first victory against the Minbari and became a war hero. Franklin's refusal to create a genetic weapon sees him and Sheridan work with arms dealer G'Kar to try to change the course of the war.

In the Beginning was a truly epic installment in the *Babylon 5* franchise. From the misunderstanding with the *Prometheus* that led to a disastrous first contact situation and started the war, to the president's desperate speech and humanity's final stand at the Battle of the Line, this TV movie was an enriching experience for fans, while also adding plenty of context to the early episodes of the show, particularly Sinclair's arc. While Michael O'Hare did not film new scenes for the TV movie, his flashbacks from season one were enough to grant him a special guest star credit.

It also provides new context to the wider series arcs. The Grey Council are journeying to Z'ha'dum to see if the Shadows have awoken when they encounter the *Prometheus*. Lenonn is a principal character, acting as the head of the Rangers. The fact that the war allows the Shadows to expand only adds to the high tragedy of the events that unfold. Moments like this—and the reveal of Sinclair's heritage—do lessen the impact of the revelations that took place on the show, but in writing *In the Beginning*, Straczynski looked at the long term.

> Would the hole in Sinclair's mind be the same mystery it was in season one, or would it be kind of known thereafter? If so, then do you want to play with the mystery, or set up what actually happened? I figured, okay, let's go for the latter ... let's let the audience know (which will mostly know by now anyway), and set up the background, with the characters not knowing the first season. I took basic Greek tragedy as my model, with ItB functioning more or less as a Greek chorus that sets things up.[2]

Greek tragedy plays a big part in the shaping of *In the Beginning*. By adding the context of the coming war with the Shadows, the deviation into a bloody war between two races destined to fight the enemy make the stakes even higher. Even the decision to call the ship that fires on the Minbari and kills Dukhat the EAS *Prometheus* adds another thematic call back to

Greek tragedy: Prometheus was the hero to protect humanity from the wrath of the gods—in this case, the Minbari.

In the Beginning is also a tour de force in its music and effects. Christopher Franke's score is some of the best work he did on *Babylon 5*, and sequences like the Battle of the Line and the sight of Minbari warships exterminating humanity are truly jaw-dropping.

The first TV movie produced under TNT was extremely well received by fans and wider audiences alike. As Straczynski noted, TNT were "dancing in the aisles" over the ratings. The broadcast of *In the Beginning* virtually tripled the regular audience and built on each quarter hour. It remains the highest-rated TV movie on IMDB, and while it didn't win Straczynski his third Hugo award, it did garner enough attention to receive an Emmy nomination in 1998.

In the Beginning was truly a success for everyone involved.

Thirdspace

The first TNT movie produced and the second to air, *Thirdspace* is another movie that looks backward in the *Babylon 5* timeline. Set during the events of season four, the exact positioning of *Thirdspace* is somewhat hard to pinpoint. After the Shadow War but before the Earth civil conflict, there are a few suggestions for its exact positioning (see Chapter 15); the biggest consensus is that it falls either between the first and second scenes of "Atonement" or just after "Moments of Transition."

Thirdspace sees the crew of Babylon 5 discover an ancient alien artifact in hyperspace, abandoned by the Vorlons for being too dangerous, that opens a gateway to another dimension. Attempts to open it create a terrifying telepathic link with the other side and an alien invasion even the Vorlons were hard put to stop previously.

As it was filmed in 1997, prior to the season five cast contracts, it marks the last time Claudia Christian would play Susan Ivanova (with the exception of a cameo in *In the Beginning*, recorded later). "Sleeping in Light" was filmed first but broadcast at the end of season five. Along with Christian's Ivanova, *Thirdspace* also features appearances from season four regulars Sheridan (Bruce Boxleitner), Delenn (Mira Furlan), Vir (Stephen Furst), Franklin (Richard Biggs), Lyta (Patricia Tallman) and Zack (Jeff Conaway). Alongside Boxleitner, Christian and Furlan, Shari Belafonte got top billing as Dr. Elizabeth Trent, sent by Interplanetary Expeditions to study the device.

Thirdspace is another effects-heavy spectacle; coproducer George Johnsen confirmed that the TV movie contained more new special effects shots than all of season one combined.³ Like *The River of Souls* after it, *Thirdspace* has no impact on the wider *Babylon 5* narrative, though its high-stakes adventure was well received by fans.

Thirdspace was originally planned for a November 1998 release, after the completion of season five. But it was pushed up to July 19, 1998, as a present to *Babylon 5* fans after having to wait for the NBA playoffs to finish.⁴ The broadcast was placed between season five episodes "Movements of Fire and Shadow" (which aired a month earlier) and "The Fall of Centauri Prime," which kicked off the final five-episode run of *Babylon 5* in October 1998.

While not as critically successful as *In the Beginning*, *Thirdspace* continued to reward fans with an ever-expanding *Babylon 5* universe. The next two movies would look forward in the timeline, as Straczynski prepared the groundwork for the next spin-off series *Crusade*.

River of Souls

> RIVER OF SOULS—The Next TNT Movie!
> An ancient vault filled with relics believed to hold the secret to eternal life is the centerpiece of the Turner Network Television (TNT) Original Film *BABYLON 5: The River of Souls*. Julie Weitz, executive vice president of original programming for TNT, today confirmed that series stars Tracy Scoggins, Jerry Doyle, Richard Biggs and Jeff Conaway will headline TNT's next BABYLON 5 full-length movie. Douglas Netter and series creator J. Michael Straczynski will executive-produce the two-hour film from the script by Straczynski. The film is a co-production of TNT and Babylonian Productions.⁵

Originally planned for broadcast on November 22, 1998, to coincide with the release of the *Babylon 5* finale "Sleeping in Light," *The River of Souls* was pushed up a couple of weeks into the time slot originally envisioned for *Thirdspace*. Set mid-2263, several months after Sheridan and Delenn's departure from the station, Tracy Scoggins takes center stage in another stand-alone story which acts as a sequel, of sorts, to *Babylon 5*'s season one episode "Soul Hunter."

With Straczynski looking to rotate the *Babylon 5* cast across the four planned movies, Scoggins was joined by Jerry Doyle's Garibaldi, Jeff Conaway's Zack, a brief cameo from Stephen Biggs as Franklin, and recurring *Babylon 5* actor Joshua Cox as Lieutenant David Corwin. Ian McShane joined the cast as archaeologist (and associate of Garibaldi) Dr. Robert

Bryson. Martin Sheen turned down the role of Bryson in favor of the movie's principal Soul Hunter; he would receive an ALMA Award nomination for Outstanding Individual Performance in a Made-for-Television Movie or Mini-Series in a Crossover Role.

While the return of Garibaldi was welcomed by fans and Lochley gets her time in the limelight, *The River of Souls* was received less favorably than the other TV movies. Some interesting moral drama concerning the treatment of stolen souls aside, it didn't have the spectacle of the other entries and the guest acting was somewhat derided, including—somewhat ironically—Martin Sheen's performance.

In a segment for *The Independent* in 2004, where he answered questions about his career from the public, McShane said he wished that he had turned down the role of Bryson. He struggled with the technical dialogue, even making up his own dialogue to compensate, displeasing the producers. When asked what the most embarrassing experience he'd had while acting was, McShane answered:

> I did a science-fiction special called *Babylon 5*, and I had to look at Martin Sheen, who had one eye in the middle of his head. I didn't know what to look at. Sheen was hunting for souls in space, and I was trying to stop him. A bit embarrassing now.[6]

The lowest rated of the TNT movies on IMDB, it seems that *The River of Souls* didn't connect as well with fans as the previous two entries. Fortunately, it would be followed by the grand spectacle of *A Call to Arms*, even if the cracks were already to starting to form in Straczynski's deal with TNT.

A Call to Arms

A Call to Arms was supposed to be the launchpad for another five-year novel for television. While not technically a pilot for *Crusade* in the same way *The Gathering* was for *Babylon 5*, it sets up the core theme of the spin-off: a search for a cure for the Drakh plague that is infecting Earth.

Set five years after *Babylon 5*, *A Call to Arms* finds Garibaldi and Sheridan returning to Babylon 5 as work is underway to unveil two new starships—the *Excalibur* and the *Victory*—built using human, Minbari and Vorlon technology. Meanwhile, techno-mage Galen warns of a great threat to the galaxy, as the Drakh unleash one of the deadly Shadow planet-killers against Earth as revenge for the defeat of their masters. With the help of Lochley, Zack and Dureena, the last survivor of her race from the Shadow War, the race to stop the Drakh results in the plague, which

18. The TNT Movies

plunges Earth into quarantine and kick-starts the Drakh War that has been building since the fall of Centauri Prime in season five of *Babylon 5*.

A Call to Arms has a lot of plates to spin and is the first of the TV movies to feel like it advances the ongoing narrative of the *Babylon 5* universe. Bruce Boxleitner, Jerry Doyle, Tracy Scoggins, and Jeff Conaway are joined by Peter Woodward and Carrie Dobro as Galen and Dureena respectively, two characters who will cross over into *Crusade*.

Crusade was planned to launch in January 1999, the same month that *A Call to Arms* aired, only to be pushed back to June. Unlike the other three TV movies, the publicity for *A Call to Arms* was almost nonexistent. In the *Lurker's Guide*, Straczynski noted that he was in total darkness when it came to understanding TNT's philosophy of promotion.[7] As a source of explanation, he suggested they were focused on publicizing their *Houdini* flick (starring Johnathon Schaech as Harry Houdini) instead. Ironically, *A Call to Arms* managed 2.8 million viewers, which was higher than TNT was expecting, and equal to *Houdini*.

In retrospect, the signs were clear that TNT was already looking to pull the plug on *Babylon 5*. They made money on *A Call to Arms* but were not looking to invest in another five-year novel for television. We'll explore those reasons more fully in the next chapter, but it was clear that something wasn't quite right at this point. *A Call to Arms* should have been marketed as the start of another grand adventure. The lack of publicity was deafening.

19

The *Crusade* to Save Earth— and *Babylon 5*

With the relative success of the *Babylon 5* franchise, Warner Bros. saw the potential in a possible franchise and asked J. Michael Straczynski to come up with a sequel series.[1] With a whole season of *Babylon 5* under its belt and four TV movies with decent ratings, TNT commissioned *Crusade*, a series set up by the events of *A Call to Arms*.

Crusade would feature the crew of the *Excalibur* heading out into the distant reaches of space to find a cure for the Drakh plague that had infected Earth. With Gary Cole's Captain Matthew Gideon at the helm, *Crusade* would be a very different series from the one that preceded it. While the idea of a starship-based series felt closer to the successful *Star Trek* model, Straczynski envisioned *Crusade* as a series where humans were at the bottom of the pecking order, exploring ancient, dangerous worlds that were alien in the truest sense of the word.

Joining Cole was Daniel Dae Kim as first officer John Matheson, a telepath who grew up in the Psi Corps, but was now free of the totalitarian regime following the Telepath War that took place between *Babylon 5* and *Crusade*. David Allen Brooks played Max Ellerson, an archaeologist and employee of Interplanetary Expeditions, who would help the crew explore these strange new worlds. Marjean Holden took on the role of Dr. Sarah Chambers, a medical doctor and the leading virologist in the Earth Alliance Health Organization, seeking to find the cure to the plague.

Joining the crew from *A Call to Arms* was techno-mage Galen, played by Peter Woodward, and Carrie Dobro as Dureena Nafeel, the last survivor of a race exterminated by the Shadows. Tracy Scoggins also featured in the opening credits as Babylon 5 Captain Elizabeth Lochley, though she would only appear in three episodes of the show's run.

Crusade was the start of another five-year arc, expanding the *Babylon*

5 universe in exciting new directions. However, its time was up before the first episode even aired.

The Next Five-Year Arc

Before we look at the cancellation of *Crusade*, let's look at the concept of the show and what Straczynski had planned for the next chapter in the *Babylon 5* universe. Having proven that he could revolutionize long-form storytelling for science fiction television, there was a baked-in mythos from the first episode.

The Drakh, who had been set up as the galaxy's big new villains in the final season of *Babylon 5* and *A Call to Arms*, would be a constant threat to the crew of the *Excalibur*. The Drakh War had been teased by Delenn as a future conflict going right back to the end of the Earth war. This war was finally being realized on-screen, though the Drakh would not be a constant presence each week.

However, given that the primary mission of the *Excalibur* was to find a cure for the Drakh plague, the enemy would stop at nothing to prevent that from happening. While they briefly feature in the show that aired, and despite the *Excalibur*'s mission likely being sheltered from the fighting with the Interstellar Alliance, the Drakh would probably have been a recurring presence if *Crusade* had continued.

The cure itself was the impetus for the show, though interestingly, a cure would have been found by the midpoint of the second season.[2] Given the five-year timetable established by *A Call to Arms*, wrapping up the main arc so early in the show's run suggested this was a red herring for the bigger stories Straczynski wanted to tell.

By using the plague as a starting point, *Crusade* offered an opportunity to explore worlds and alien races not seen in *Babylon 5*. Some alien cultures had been explored within the confines of the Babylon 5 station; fans had seen plenty of the "big three" that were the Minbari, Centauri and Narn. It took four and a half years to visit the Drazi home world, despite their having a major recurring presence on *Babylon 5*.

In a universe that had given us the Shadows, the Vorlons and the First Ones, what other wonders were out there? That, in many ways, was the most intriguing hook of *Crusade*. Were there seemingly dead civilizations harboring ancient dangers like Z'ha'dum? With *Babylon 5*'s strong focus on alien cultures and politics, what trouble might the crew of the *Excalibur* stumble into during their search for a cure?

Equally as interesting were the techno-mages, a race of "space wizards" that had featured heavily in Straczynski's early drafts for *Babylon 5*.

With a main techno-mage character onboard the *Excalibur* in the form of Galen, Straczynski would finally be able to explore their potential. Galen wasn't the only intriguing character on the show. In Matheson, there was a principal Earthforce officer who was also a telepath. That was unheard of in *Babylon 5*. Commercial telepaths like Lyta and Talia were largely ostracized from the rest of the human crew. What would a fully integrated telepath in Earthforce look like, particularly in light of the recent Telepath War?

So, what was the big arc of *Crusade* if it wasn't the search for the cure to the Drakh plague? A huge conspiracy involving Earth's experimentation with Shadow technology would have been set up in the next, un-filmed episode of the show. We'll explore the "what-ifs" of this later in the chapter, the clues to what *Crusade* might have really been about.

But at only 13 episodes, fans got barely a glimpse of Straczynski's next five-year plan. *Crusade* was already canceled before the first episode aired in June 1999. And that story is as interesting as anything we might have gotten on screen.

The Path to Cancellation

Crusade should have kick-started its five-year run in January 1999, coming off the back of the last TV movie, *A Call to Arms*. But it was pushed back several months. Straczynski had already commented on the surprise lack of marketing for *A Call to Arms*, but he first got wind of a problem with *Crusade* when TNT ordered production to halt during the filming of the third episode.

The official statement was that TNT wanted to reevaluate the look of the show, but unbeknownst to Straczynski, TNT had just received a study commissioned to determine how *Babylon 5* was doing on the network.[3] TNT's core content was wrestling and Westerns, and TNT viewers didn't really like science fiction. When anything *Babylon 5*–related was on air, TNT audiences switched off and were replaced by *Babylon 5* fans. When *Babylon 5* was over, *Babylon 5* fans left, and the TNT viewers returned. Quite simply, *Babylon 5* was not compatible with the cable channel.

So what did that mean for the next five years of a television show they had provisionally commissioned? Not renewing it for a second season was one option, but as Straczynski later discovered, TNT wanted out immediately. They needed to prove that *Crusade* was not the show they wanted. They needed to force Straczynski to quit. In *Becoming Superman*, Straczynski detailed the many ways in which TNT started to provide

19. The Crusade to Save Earth—and Babylon 5

incredibly toxic notes on the tone and style of the show. Production began again under uneasy circumstances and news of the changes quickly leaked out. Aint It Cool News broke a story about the suggested increase in sex and violence by TNT.[4]

What started with an insistence on new uniforms and an episode that immediately picked up from *A Call to Arms* turned to such suggestions as having Dureena have sex with aliens from every planet the *Excalibur* visited, to understand them further. Worse still was the suggestion that Gideon arrange for a crew member to be raped by the antagonist of the episode, "The Well of Forever," so the captain could catch him in the act and blackmail him.

Straczynski naturally refused every single one of the notes. TNT was able to cite "creative agreements" and "contractual differences" as a way of canceling *Crusade*. Worse still, post-production continued on the 13 episodes already produced. Straczynski took the blame, not realizing until years later the real reason for the show's cancellation.

Rumors of the show's cancellation broke at the end of January 1999, just weeks after the broadcast of *A Call to Arms*. Using his online army of fans, Straczynski urged them to contact the Sci-Fi Channel and plead for them to pick up *Crusade*. Despite negotiations with Warner Bros., the Sci-Fi Channel simply didn't have the budget to pick it up for a full series. Straczynski formally broke the news of the show's cancellation on the rec.arts.sf.tv.babylon5.moderated page on February 26, 1999.[5]

Crusade made its muted debut in June 1999. The 13 episodes produced were a mess. Original studio notes, like the change of uniforms, ruined any real sense of continuity, and the series arc was left unresolved. Straczynski even attempted, unsuccessfully, to get his writing credit removed. He registered the pseudonym "Eiben Scrood" with the WGA, but pressure from Warner Bros. led to WGA's refusal of the pseudonym.

After successfully bringing all the major story arcs of *Babylon 5* to a close despite the collapse of PTEN—and then giving fans a final season of the show—Straczynski was unable to fulfill his promise of a spin-off series. As he later learned, he never stood a chance. His refusal to toe the line with TNT was not his fault. A couple of years later, he learned that TNT were determined to get out of the deal and there was nothing he could have done to change it.

From a triumphant final season of *Babylon 5* and four epic TV movies to a twisted death for *Crusade*, nothing quite encapsulates the long twilight struggles and triumphs of *Babylon 5* quite like the franchise's association with TNT.

Crusade: *What Could Have Been*

Babylon 5 got the closure it needed; there were few unanswered questions by the time fans watched the emotional finale, "Sleeping in Light." In contrast, fans were left wanting by the cancellation of *Crusade*. What happened in the Drakh War? Was Earth saved from the plague? What about the fallout of the Telepath War? What was the techno-mages' plan? What was the Apocalypse Box that Captain Gideon held? Would fans see these characters—or older, beloved characters like Sheridan, Delenn and G'Kar—again?

There were further attempts to reignite the *Babylon 5* franchise in *The Legend of the Rangers* and *The Lost Tales*, both of which we'll explore more fully in subsequent chapters. But there is plenty we do know about *Crusade* and what would have followed in season one and beyond.

Four scripts were already written for the remainder of the first season: three by Straczynski, which included the season finale, and one by Fiona Avery, featuring the return of Walter Koenig's Alfred Bester. A fifth script by Peter Woodward was also written, and was planned for the second season.[6]

But what would these stories have been? Straczynski's 14th episode, "To the Ends of the Earth," would have seen the Apocalypse Box give Gideon a message about the ship that destroyed his previous vessel, the EAS *Cerberus*. Gideon and the *Excalibur* would have discovered an Earth-Shadow hybrid vessel. What would have followed was a submarine-movie style game of cat and mouse across the stars that would set up the show's primary arc of Earth's black ops use of Shadow technology. "To the Ends of the Earth" would also have set up the connection between the techno-mages and the Shadows. The revelatory nature of this episode might have made it *Crusade* season one's equivalent of *Babylon 5*'s "Signs and Portents."

Fiona Avery's "Value Judgements," the show's 15th episode, might have been another fan favorite as it featured the return of Bester, now on the run after the fallout of the Telepath War. The focus would have been the conflict between Matheson's telepath turned Earthforce officer struggling not to arrest Bester in order to use the villain's telepathic abilities to open an alien vault that might hold a cure for the Drakh plague. It is unlikely this would have been the last audiences would have seen of Bester, given that the script has him rescued by a (surprise!) Psi Corps mothership at the end of the episode. Rather than being eliminated, it would seem the Corps had become a black ops underground movement after the war.

The next episode, "Darkness of the Soul," was planned by Straczynski but never scripted. It would have seen Galen discover Gideon's Apocalypse Box, possibly setting up the conflict to come between them. However, the script for episode 17, "Tried and True," was a draft-scripted story from Straczynski that never got to production. It would have been a Dureena-centric tale, examining her loyalties to the crew of the *Excalibur* and the Thieves Guild, who put her on trial. There were hints of bigger things at play, with the Guild having access to advanced Centauri weaponry.

The 18th episode didn't get beyond the one-line synopsis of the *Excalibur* discovering a construction base. It would have been written by Straczynski. However, episodes 19 through 21 would have been three-part story featuring a major return of the Drakh. The first part, "War Story," would have been written by Richard Mueller and featured the *Excalibur* protecting a Martian vessel from a Drakh fleet after two Earthforce ships are destroyed, and the mysterious appearance of a strange alien vessel that would have forced the Drakh to flee and abduct Dureena. "The Walls of Hell" would have marked Larry DiTillio's first script for the *Babylon 5* universe since season two. In the pursuit of Dureena and the alien vessel, Matheson would have been controlled by the Apocalypse Box and taken control of the *Excalibur*, sending it into a variant of hyperspace called dark space. He would also have transported Gideon to another place, one that had a connection to his past. The final part of the trilogy would have been written by Straczynski and featured Dureena returning from the strange alien vessel with implants and a magical sword to help in the fight. Little more is known, given that these episodes existed as outlines only, but they hint at the rising stakes in the show.

The season one finale, "The End of the Line," fully scripted by Straczynski, would see the *Excalibur* track down the Earth-Shadow hybrid vessel from "To the Ends of the Earth" to a secret Earthforce "need-to-know" research and development facility working on weapons tech for the protection of Earth and her colonies. Gideon would come to realize that humans were using Shadow technology and discover a horrifying facility of human–Shadow hybrid people. Revelations would come to light regarding Galen's mission to spy on humanity's pursuit of Shadow tech, something which the techno-mages themselves would have utilized, and the season would end with Gideon's assassination.

As for season two and beyond, it is clear that "To the Ends of the Earth" and "The End of the Line" were *Crusade*'s equivalents of "Signs and Portents" and "Chrysalis." Details are vague about what would have happened in year two, but we do know that Gideon would have somehow been resurrected by the Apocalypse Box. The mystery of that device, and others like it, would have been a key element of the overall story. Earth's experimentation with Shadow tech would have forced the *Excalibur* to go on the run from its own people.

Forbidden technology is a theme that Straczynski alluded to in the script books released after the show's cancellation. This would likely have been the dominating aspect of the show. What would happen if Shadow, Vorlon, even First One technology got into the hands of the races left behind? The Drakh had already used Shadow weaponry in *A Call to Arms* and now Earthforce was following a similar path.

We would have learned a lot more about the techno-mages and how they used Shadow tech for their own ends. This would eventually be explored in the Techno-Mages Trilogy of books but would likely have been another recurring theme across the show.

As for season two, a trip to a First One planet in search of the cure was hinted at, possibly exploring that forbidden technology theme further. And the cure itself would be found—but at a great cost. The setup from *A Call to Arms* might have been resolved by season two's midpoint, but it is clear that it would not be a glorious, victorious moment. Perhaps Earth's complicit use of Shadow technology might have influenced that.

Finally, we have Woodward's script, "Little Bugs Have Lesser Bugs," which was bumped from season one in favor of the planned "Tried and True." In search of a cure, the crew finds a dead Drakh and thousands of dead bugs, which soon lead to an infestation of the ship. The realization that the Drakh experimented on the bug planet seems to offer some clues about the cure. Despite the arc-driven aspect of the story, the script suggests a more whimsical adventure. The fact that Straczynski also pushed the episode to the second season suggested that the *Excalibur* would return to the search for the cure and a resurrected Gideon would not face the consequences of his actions in "The End of the Line"—until at least after the cure was found.

It's hard to speculate what seasons three, four and five of *Crusade* would have been about, in the same way the first season of *Babylon 5* only hints at the bigger arcs to come. Thanks to the (admittedly hard to find) script books released and detailed online discourse from sites such as Grey Sector,[7] we have some clues about the bigger story—and it wasn't all about the search for the cure to the Drakh plague. One thing is certain: we never got to see the *Crusade* that Straczynski envisioned. Its 13-episode run was just the first step toward something quite special indeed.

When *Crusade* aired its final episode, "Each Night I Dream of Home," on September 1, 1999, it marked the end of a seven-year run of television and TV movies. The *Babylon 5* dream was over.

19. The Crusade to Save Earth—and Babylon 5

A Note on Viewing Orders

Perhaps more so than any of the *Babylon 5* seasons, *Crusade* had an incredibly muddled viewing order, thanks to the interference of TNT. The five episodes produced after the show's initial hiatus saw the creation of new uniforms and a refocus on the beginning of *Crusade* immediately after the events of *A Call to Arms*.

I've touched upon a couple of key "viewing orders" with *Babylon 5* in JMS's Viewing Order and the Chronological Viewing Order. But with *Crusade*, there are multiple options.

"JMS Sci-Fi Channel" Order:

In 2001, the Sci-Fi Channel picked up *Babylon 5*, the TV movies, and *Crusade* for broadcast. Straczynski created an alternate viewing order for the show, which was "best from a story point of view, even though it means some visual inconsistencies in terms of unexplained costume changes."[8]

- *A Call to Arms*
- "Racing the Night"
- "The Needs of Earth"
- "The Memory of War"
- "The Long Road"
- "Visitors from Down the Street"
- "The Well of Forever"
- "Each Night I Dream of Home"
- "Patterns of the Soul"
- "The Path of Sorrows"
- "Ruling from the Tomb"
- "The Rules of the Game"
- "War Zone"
- "Appearances and Other Deceits"

This is a slightly odd ordering for the show, particularly as the penultimate episode in this order, "War Zone," takes place immediately after the Drakh attack on Earth. Perhaps, as this was a TNT-mandated change, "War Zone" and "Appearances and Other Deceits" become something of an "alternate" set of *Crusade* stories, tagged onto a show that ends with "The Rules of the Game"—an episode that concludes almost every other viewing order out there.

The Straczynski-approved *Babylon 5* Historical Database Viewing Order for *A Call to Arms* and *Crusade* (with chronological dates):

- *A Call to Arms*—Tuesday, December 17–Monday, December 30, 2266
- "War Zone"—January 1–January 5, 2267
- "The Long Road"—February 27–March 2, 2267
- "Appearances and Other Deceits"—March 2267
- "The Memory of War"—March 30–April 1, 2267
- "The Needs of Earth"—April 2267

- "Racing the Night"—May 2267
- "Visitors from Down the Street"—May 13–May 14, 2267
- "Each Night I Dream of Home"—May 2267
- "The Path of Sorrows"—June 2267
- "Ruling from the Tomb"—June 15–June 16, 2267
- "Patterns of the Soul"—June 2267
- "The Well of Forever"—July 2267 (JMS confirmed that Mr. Jones saying Matheson had sensed the emotions of others was indeed referring to Durkani and Lyssa from "Visitors from Down the Street.")
- "Rules of the Game"—July 2267

The "Continuity Order":

- *A Call to Arms*
- "War Zone"
- "The Long Road"
- "The Path of Sorrows"
- "Ruling from the Tomb"
- "Appearances and Other Deceits"
- "Racing the Night"
- "The Needs of Earth"
- "The Memory of War"
- "Visitors from Down the Street"
- "Each Night I Dream of Home"
- "Patterns of the Soul"
- "The Well of Forever"
- "The Rules of the Game"

While the chronological order makes more sense, the Continuity Order, which can be found online,[9] flows better. It takes the pacing and characterization of the chronological order and makes some adjustments to make the overall narrative flow better, such as the meeting of Gideon and Lochley on Babylon 5 the first time before in "Ruling from the Tomb."

Regardless of which order you follow to watch *Crusade*, it is a bit of a narrative mess. Uniforms change color from one story to the next, just the first of many noticeable changes at the behest of TNT.

However, perhaps the Continuity Order, much like the JMS viewing orders for *Babylon 5*, is the best way to watch *Crusade*. We only get a small fragment of the bigger story Straczynski would have told. But it holds closer to his vision of what *Crusade* should have been.

20

To Live and Die in Starlight

After *Crusade*, J. Michael Straczynski turned his attention to other projects. On television, he would become the showrunner of Showtime's *Jeremiah*, a postapocalyptic drama based on a Belgian comic book of the same name. Unfortunately, it faced the same behind-the-scenes drama that he experienced on TNT—a situation he described as worse than his experiences on *Crusade* by "several orders of magnitude."[1] Filming began in early September 2001 and the show ran for two seasons.

But his real passion was comics. After *Crusade*, he set up his own company, Joe's Comics, working on *Midnight Nation* and *Rising Stars*, before being asked by Marvel Comics' Editor in Chief to take over *The Amazing Spider-Man*.[2]

But *Babylon 5* was never too far from his mind. After securing the broadcast rights to *Babylon 5*, the TV movies, and *Crusade* in April 2000, the Sci-Fi Channel noticed that these reruns would regularly outperform original content in the ratings. They approached Straczynski about developing a new project. They might not have had the budget to continue *Crusade*, but they still saw the potential in this franchise, just as TNT had back in 1997.

In the early drafts of potential *Babylon 5* spin-offs, Straczynski had considered a Rangers-centric storyline. In an alternate version of *Crusade*, it was the Rangers and not the *Excalibur* searching for a cure for the Drakh plague. TNT had turned that idea down in favor of a more human-centric show, but the Sci-Fi Channel was more than open to the possibility and commissioned the script based on Straczynski's outline.

Babylon 5: The Legend of the Rangers was designed to be another *Babylon 5* TV series spin-off. The TV movie *The Legend of the Rangers: To Live and Die in Starlight* was designed as much more of a pilot (like *The Gathering*) than *A Call to Arms* was for *Crusade*. Veteran *Babylon 5* director Mike Vejar came onboard to helm Straczynski's script, and Andreas Katsulas would reprise his role as the beloved G'Kar.

With a potential Screen Actors Guild writer's strike on its way, Straczynski quickly wrote the script, and production got underway in May 2001. Once again, there was hope for the *Babylon 5* franchise.

A Failed Pilot

The Legend of the Rangers: To Live and Die in Starlight made its debut on January 19, 2002, three years after the last TV movie, *A Call to Arms*. Audiences were introduced to Dylan Neal's disgraced Ranger David Martell, captain of "haunted" ship the *Liandra*, who is given a second chance by Citizen G'Kar.

Martell's crew reflected the broader alien races of the Interstellar Alliance that were now members of the Rangers. Myriam Sirois's Sarah Cantrell, Dean Marshall's Malcolm Bridges and Warren Takeuchi's Kitaro Sasaki make up the other three human characters on the show, while Martell's best friend Dulann (Alex Zahara), Firell (Enid-Raye Adams) and Tafeek (David Storch) were Minbari.

The "pilot" for *The Legend of the Rangers* also featured other races from the Alliance. Jennie Rebecca Hogan played Na'Feel, the first ever member of the Narn race in the Rangers, and Gus Lynch played Tirk, the first Ranger to come from the Drazi Freehold. Had the pilot gone to series, Tirk would have also been the first regular Drazi character in the *Babylon 5* universe. Katsulas's G'Kar would have also recurred on the show, had it made it to series. Sadly, this was his final appearance in the *Babylon 5* universe.

To Live and Die in Starlight sees Martell seeking redemption after breaking one of the key tenets of the Rangers and retreating from battle. At the behest of G'Kar, Martell and the crew of the *Liandra* accompany a Ranger vessel, the *Valen*, which is transporting alien ambassadors to a security briefing. The sudden appearance of an ancient race known only as the Hand sees the *Liandra* striving to save the lives of the ambassadors while also fighting off this new threat.

Unfortunately, *To Live and Die in Starlight* failed to get picked up as a series by the Sci-Fi Channel. While it wasn't as well received critically as its predecessors (the VR gun fight sequence took a huge amount of flak, for instance), it seems the problems with taking the pilot to series had nothing to do with whether it was any good.

Ratings were a key issue for the Sci-Fi Channel. *To Live and Die in Starlight* aired at the same time as the NFL playoffs. The Sci-Fi Channel had expected viewing figures in the realm of 2.5 million, but the TV movie averaged only 1.7 million.

The rights issues with Warner Bros. were another factor. One reason the Sci-Fi Channel had not picked up *Crusade* was because the rights were wholly owned by Warner Bros. When it came to the development of *The Legends of the Rangers*, the Sci-Fi Channel approached Warner Bros., as owners of the franchise, to license the series. Warner Bros.' price was deemed too high, and a solution had been for Sci-Fi to produce *The Legends of the Rangers* as a one-off TV movie, rather than a pilot, with the option to enter into good faith negotiations to acquire the series if they liked it.

Both factors led to *Babylon 5: The Legend of the Rangers* dying before it even had a chance to develop as a series. Once again, the franchise was dead, and this time it was unlikely that it would ever get off the ground again.

The Next, Next Five-Year Arc

If the ratings had been a winner for the Sci-Fi Channel, and it had been picked up for a full series, what would *Babylon 5: The Legend of the Rangers* have been like? Details are understandably scarce. No TV series was ever commissioned, and after being burned by TNT, it's understandable that Straczynski was less inclined to share his hopes for the series.

> It's set in the B5 universe just under 3 years after the events of "Objects at Rest." At this point there's one major character from the B5 universe in the script (a fan favorite). Where B5 was a heavy drama with some adventure/action elements, this one is a little more skewed toward adventure with underlying drama (which is about what you'd expect from the Anla-Shok).[3]

The fact that the show was set two years prior to *A Call to Arms* and *Crusade* might offer a hint about Straczynski's wider plans for the show. If *The Legend of the Rangers* were to become another five-year novel for television, then the second season would likely intersect with the Drakh attack on Earth and the conflict that followed. Straczynski might have been able to reintroduce the plot threads that never got off the ground in *Crusade* and follow them up. There might have even been the opportunity to reintroduce Gideon and the crew of the *Excalibur* and resolve the search for the cure.

While the Drakh War would almost certainly have been featured, it is unknown whether Earth's experimentation with Shadow technology or the techno-mages would have been as prominent. The Shadow tech angle was tied personally to Gideon and the fate of his former ship, and the crew of the *Liandra* would not have the same ties to Earthforce as the *Excalibur* did.

The emergence of the mysterious new Hand—or Hand of God—would likely have served as a primary antagonist in the show the same way that the Drakh presence hung over *Crusade*. Another ancient race, they could have played to the same strengths as the Shadows. However, the lack of mention outside of *The Legend of the Rangers* leaves them as little more than a footnote in the *Babylon 5* mythos.

Ultimately, we'll never know what the next five-year arc would have been. Straczynski would not attempt another spin-off series again, and the Hand, the Drakh plague, and all his other ideas for the continuing *Babylon 5* story would remain unrealized ideas. *The Legend of the Rangers* was the franchise's last attempt to continue the narrative as a full series.

But there was one more story still to tell.

21

The Lost Tales and What Could Have Been

After the Sci-Fi Channel failed to pick up *The Legend of the Rangers* to a full series, *Babylon 5* seemed truly dead in the water. Following his experiences on *Jeremiah*, J. Michael Straczynski stepped away from television altogether; he wouldn't return until *Sense8* in 2014. His career as a writer would continue in comics, on *Thor* and *Superman*. He also found success as a film screenwriter, writing scripts for *World War Z*, *Underworld: Awakening* and, most significantly, *Changeling*, for which he would receive a BAFTA nomination for best original screenplay.

Straczynski's expansion into writing for film almost resulted in a *Babylon 5* movie, which we'll explore in the next chapter. But the first hints of a theatrical *Babylon 5* story had emerged in 2006, when Warner Bros., continuing to see the potential in the *Babylon 5* franchise, approached Straczynski to write a film based on the show. At the time, Straczynski declined; the recent loss of regular actors Richard Biggs and Andreas Katsulas meant he could not see himself committing to a project on that scale.

As an alternative, Straczynski proposed a series of short films or episodes, in an anthology format, that would each focus on one character from the *Babylon 5* universe. It was an idea he had touted as far back as 1997[1] as an alternative to a sixth season of *Babylon 5*.

> The only other option would be to do a "Tales from Babylon 5" sixth season, which would be an anthology series, to all intents and purposes, using our characters almost like a repertory group.

The Twilight Zone was a huge influence on Straczynski, and he ranked Rod Serling as one of his icons; one of his proudest achievements was his adaptation of Serling's "Our Selena Is Dying" in the third season of the '90s *The Twilight Zone* reboot.[2] As such, Straczynski had a deep understanding of the potential of anthological storytelling and how this might provide the opportunity to write new stories of beloved *Babylon 5* characters without having to account for the absence of those who were no longer living.

The Lost Tales was not envisioned as a TV show. Instead, it would be a straight-to-DVD release from Warner Bros., with each release containing character-centric stories linked thematically across each disk. As Straczynski described the concept, each release would focus on different aspects of the *Babylon 5* universe: the issues of command with Sheridan, Psi Corps stories featuring Lyta and Bester, something with a strong Minbari theme, featuring Delenn, Lennier and Sheridan, or a Centauri sequence with Londo and Vir.[3]

While the first story envisioned would take place post–*Babylon 5* season five (between "Objects and Rest" and "Sleeping in Light"), the anthology approach would have allowed Straczynski to explore stories at any point in time. In the publicity for the first volume of *The Lost Tales*, he suggested other stories might move forward or backward in time, giving him the ability to do a Sinclair or Marcus story.

While it is unclear whether Michael O'Hare would have been able to commit to a new Sinclair-centric story (or a Valen one?), the possibilities were endless. Would a Bester and Lyta story have explored the never-seen Telepath War? Would Lennier's fate have finally been sealed on-screen? Would Claudia Christian have been open to reprising her role as Ivanova? Had *The Lost Tales* been a success, fans might have witnessed all of these things.

Once again, there was hope for a continuation of the *Babylon 5* franchise.

Babylon 5's Final Breath—The Lost Tales

Straczynski announced *The Lost Tales* at San Diego Comic-Con in July 2006,[4] less than two weeks after the project had been green-lit by Warner Bros. Production was planned for that September and Straczynski would also direct as well as write these stories. It would be his second directorial experience after helming the *Babylon 5* finale, "Sleeping in Light."

The initial concept was a set of three 30-minute stories, each focusing on a different character. Bruce Boxleitner would return as President John Sheridan, Jerry Doyle as Michael Garibaldi, and Tracy Scoggins as the now Colonel Elizabeth Lochley. With new CGI work to enhance the look and feel of the *Babylon 5* universe, Straczynski had envisioned himself as director of the first DVD release, with others to get involved as the scope of the stories expanded.

21. The Lost Tales *and What Could Have Been* 185

Unfortunately, the plans for volume one of *The Lost Tales* soon changed. The Garibaldi-centric storyline was deemed the most expensive—and the most complicated visually and technically—and was pushed to the planned second DVD. It would remain forever unproduced, and Jerry Doyle's last *Babylon 5* appearance ended up being *A Call to Arms* at the start of 1999.

Instead, Straczynski expanded the length of the Sheridan and Lochley stories to 40 minutes each. Due to cast availability, production was delayed until November 2006, and the DVD, *The Lost Tales: Voices in the Dark*, was finally released by Warner Home Video in the U.S. on July 31, 2007, and September 3, 2007, in the United Kingdom.

The press release for *Voices in the Dark* promised the most innovative filmmaking technology, which was unavailable during the original series.[5] Interestingly, it was marketed as an original made-for-video movie rather than a set of two stories in the *Babylon 5* franchise. It was also not sold as volume one of a planned series of movies, despite Straczynski's announcements or the extras pertaining to this on the release.

During the New York Comic Con in February 2007, Straczynski had already confirmed that if the *Lost Tales* release was successful, a follow-up could follow in "early 2008 at the earliest."[6] Critical reaction was mixed. IGN gave *Voices in the Dark* a 6/10, noting that "[Straczynski] clearly was facing budget limitations with this project, and one can only hope that if another installment is produced, the scope of the piece will be greatly expanded."[7] Aint It Cool News, who had spearheaded the buzz over *The Lost Tales* announcement a year earlier, noticed some flaws but also praised the production values.[8] They did not recommend it to non–*Babylon 5* fans, who wouldn't have a hope of figuring out what was going on, but believed that existing fans of the show would like it a lot.

However, it was not the critical reception but the Writer's Guild of America strike in late 2007 through to early 2008[9] that caused any plans for a follow-up to grind to a halt. With Warner Bros. impressed with the DVD sales for *The Lost Tales: Voices in the Dark*, Straczynski urged them to commission another DVD release. Believing the writer's strike would not go ahead, Warner Bros. refused to speed up the bureaucratic process. When the strike actually happened, more *Babylon 5* was simply put on hold.

Over Here and Over There

But what of the story itself? Set in 2271, nine years after "Objects at Rest," *Voices in the Dark* was a set of two episodes covering the same

72-hour timespan. "Over Here" focused on Colonel Elizabeth Lochley as Babylon 5 prepared for the arrival of President John Sheridan during the 10th anniversary celebrations of the Interstellar Alliance. A supernatural tale, "Over Here" sees Lochley summon a priest from Earth, Father Cassidy (Alan Scarfe), to deal with a seemingly possessed crewmember, Simon Burke (Bruce Ramsay). With claims that God had salted this region of space with fallen angels to keep mankind in check, Lochley must outwit the lies before Sheridan's arrival.

"Over Here" didn't quite receive the critical acclaim Straczynski might have been hoping for and is generally regarded as the weaker of the two stories. Despite the development of Lochley as a character and new, improved visual effects, it failed to resonate with fans who had waited for years to see new stories set on Babylon 5.

"Over There" was better received, perhaps because of the focus on Boxleitner's John Sheridan in his final *Babylon 5* appearance until 2023's *The Road Home*. En route to Babylon 5, he picks up a passenger, Prince Vintari (Keegan Macintosh), on the edge of Centauri space. A warning from returning techno-mage Galen (Woodward) tells of Vintari's ruthless ambitions and a danger to Earth 30 years in the future, not unlike the Drakh attack which Galen warned of previously. Taking Galen at his word, Sheridan must grapple with the decision to potentially murder Vintari—destroying one life to save billions.

This moral drama, while low key compared to other *Babylon 5* stories, reflected the more nuanced storytelling fans were used to. Galen was a big enough returning character to flesh out the *Babylon 5* universe and give "Over There" a grander scope that explored the future stakes of the *Babylon 5* universe.

Both Boxleitner and Scoggins do solid work in bringing these characters to life one final time. There is no huge setup like the Drakh War or the Hand this time around; Straczynski had been careful not to leave more unanswered questions for fans, should *The Lost Tales* fail to continue. As Aint It Cool News noted, this was a release fans would love.

However, as the final entry in the *Babylon 5* universe until 2023's *The Road Home*, it failed to give the franchise the send-off it deserved. *Voices in the Dark* became little more than a footnote.

The Untold Tales of Londo and Garibaldi

Like *Crusade* and *Legend of the Rangers*, there is plenty of conjecture and very little fact when it comes to plans for *The Lost Tales* beyond that first volume. The Garibaldi script was completed, but few details are

21. The Lost Tales *and What Could Have Been*

known about the story; online rumors suggest it would have involved Edgar Industries and an archaeological dig on Mars, but this may be little more than supposition from fans.

In an interview with *The Babylon Podcast* in November 2006,[10] Peter Jurasik confirmed that Straczynski had contacted him about a potential Londo Mollari story for volume two and he had already said yes to it. However, he later contradicted that, saying he had little interest in returning to the character (see part 2 of my interview with Peter for more details).

Beyond that, it looked likely that Straczynski would finally explore the Telepath War; at New York Comic Con in February 2007, he talked about a possible direct-to-DVD Telepath War story he had in mind that, given his earlier comments, would have seen Patricia Tallman and Walter Koenig return as Lyta and Bester—and potentially Bill Mumy as Lennier too, given his fate that would be explored, of sorts, in the in-canon novels.

None of this ever materialized. The writer's strike killed the momentum of *The Lost Tales*, and finally, in July 2008, Straczynski announced that he would not continue the project.[11] The biggest factor seemed to be the budget; Warner Bros. only wanted to commit to a similar budget as the first, and Straczynski felt that it was not sufficient to effectively tell the stories he wanted to tell.

Warner Bros. had expressed interest in a second installment of *The Lost Tales*, but in the time since the first release, Straczynski had come to the realization that he would no longer commit to low-budget DVDs, cable series, or computer games. *The Legend of the Rangers* and *The Lost Tales* had not been big enough to enrich the *Babylon 5* legacy, as he had first conceived. The five years of *Babylon 5* stood on their own, and he was only interested in projects with the budget to build on what had come before.

Quite simply, Straczynski was only interested if Warner Bros. wanted to do a big-budget cinematic release set in the *Babylon 5* universe. There were several drafts of possible film scripts and even a significant attempt to give the franchise the motion picture treatment, which we'll explore in more detail in the next chapter.

But small-screen *Babylon 5* was well and truly dead.

22

The Memory of Shadows
The Big-Screen Babylon 5s That Never Were

Science fiction has long had a history of bringing TV shows to the big screen, some more successfully than others. *Star Trek* (and *Star Trek: The Next Generation*) leapt into movies with varied success; while *Star Trek II: The Wrath of Khan* and *Star Trek: First Contact* might be considered great films, others like *Star Trek V: The Final Frontier* and *Star Trek: Nemesis* are regarded far less favorably by fans.

The '90s was a big period for big-screen cinematic versions of beloved TV shows. *The X-Files*, a cultural juggernaut of '90s sci-fi, brought Mulder and Scully to cinemas in 1998's *The X-Files: Fight the Future*, set between seasons five and six.[1] The '60s classic series *Lost in Space*[2] and *The Avengers*[3] (not to be confused with the later Marvel Cinematic Universe offerings) attempted flashy movie reboots. Even *Power Rangers* got in on the action.[4]

But with the exception of a couple of *Star Trek* entries, these big-screen adaptations didn't delight fans. While certainly fun, *Fight the Future* was not the jaw-dropping spectacle fans were hoping for—though it was met with far more enthusiasm than the second movie attempt in 2008. Very few people will talk about the *Lost in Space* and *Avengers* movies (well, not *that* Avengers, at least).

So any *Babylon 5* movie had to be special. It had to offer a grand spectacle for audiences *and* be rewarding for long-term fans of the show. J. Michael Straczynski had to write the best possible big-screen continuation to a story that he had wrapped up in his five-year novel for television.

Unlike the TV show, Straczynski held the rights to any potential *Babylon 5* movie; Warner Bros. believed that there would never be any interest in a cinematic version. And while TNT, the Sci-Fi Channel and Warner Bros. were able to support a number of TV and DVD projects, Straczynski developed a number of big-screen ideas too, some originating back when *Babylon 5* was still airing.

Telepaths and Vorlons

As far back as 1996, *The Telepath War* was one such option for a big-screen *Babylon 5* movie, an idea that was, presumably, different from the DVD-movie option he touted for *The Lost Tales*. During the fourth season of the show, he started to map out ideas for a film that sees a conflict arise between telepaths and normal humans *and* a civil war within the telepath community. The film would have likely featured Ivanova in a prominent role, as both a latent telepath and a fierce opponent of the Psi Corps. Details of the story are sketchy, contained within a single paragraph of notes in a previously released script book,[5] but suggested the war would put her at odds with Sheridan, as the anti–Psi Corps faction determines that to win their freedom, they must bring down the entire Earth government.

A couple of years later, Straczynski wrote a treatment for a *Babylon 5* movie that would follow the fifth season on TNT, set between "Objects at Rest" and "Sleeping in Light." The outline of the *Babylon 5: The Motion Picture Feature* premise would be released in the same script book as the original *Telepath War* premise, though at ten pages, the details were considerably more in depth.[6]

Babylon 5: The Motion Picture Feature centered on Sheridan's investigation into a missing Earthforce ship, known as the *Vesper*, recruiting Garibaldi to learn the truth about the *Vesper*'s classified mission and leading a team of himself, Delenn, Garibaldi, Lennier, Lochley and Vir to an ancient planet. There, they would discover a former Vorlon colony, millions of years old, and a lone Vorlon who had gone mad through experimentation. Sheridan and his team would try to reason with the Vorlon and the threat it posed to the galaxy, while dealing with the arrival of Earth and Centauri ships, intent on plundering the planet for its advanced alien technology.

With *The X-Files* about to release a feature film between seasons, rumors were afoot online that Straczynski and producer Doug Netter had reached out to Warner Bros. to see if they were interested. However, Straczynski later contradicted that rumor, stating that he had not spoken to Warner Bros. about any movie concept concerning the Vorlons' impact on Earth.[7] While there were some preliminary discussions about a possible storyline, he had decided to focus on getting *Crusade* right, developing the right technologies for a theatrical release—and not competing with the sci-fi juggernaut that was upcoming *Star Wars* prequel trilogy.[8]

The time, it seemed, was simply not right. *Babylon 5: The Motion Picture Feature* could not have hoped to come to close to the box-office takings that *Star Wars Episode 1: The Phantom Menace* could (and would) achieve, and in Straczynski's mind, *Crusade* was the start of another epic five years of television. This Vorlon-centric movie would remain one of *Babylon 5*'s many unrealized cinematic releases.

Straczynski's original idea of a Telepath War feature film would recur in *Wars of the Mind*, a *Babylon 5* feature film premise he started to develop in the early 2000s.[9] There are key similarities between this and the 1996 version, with Sheridan still front and center. Given her departure after the fourth season, Claudia Christian's Ivanova was absent, though Walter Koenig's Bester gets a mention. In the introduction of the treatment, contained within the TV movies script book, Straczynski noted that the film would feature the main *Babylon 5* cast in prominent roles and feature the explosive demises of Lyta and Lennier in the conflict.

Outside of the potential *The Lost Tales* straight-to-DVD idea, this was the last attempt to tell the story of the Telepath War in all its glory. The Psi Corps Trilogy, written by J. Gregory Keyes and considered canon in the *Babylon 5* universe, would explore the fallout of the conflict through the character of Bester. But much about the war that had been seeded throughout *Babylon 5*, and the fifth season in particular, would remain forever a mystery.

The Memory of Shadows

The closest Straczynski ever got to making a full *Babylon 5* feature film was *The Memory of Shadows*, a story that began development in 2003, two years after the failure to bring *The Legend of the Rangers* to a full series. An unnamed production company expressed interest in a *Babylon 5* movie and on November 30, 2003, Straczynski wrote on *The Lurker's Guide*, "On the B5 front, there has been something of rather substantial proportion that's finally gone from talk to money, such that I'm now working frantically to meet some deadlines."[10]

This was followed up by another statement on January 29, 2004, that "writing on B5:TMoS is complete, and as soon as the powers that be sign off on everything, it can be turned in and we can start moving. At that point, I can say more about this."

Fans correctly guessed the title, *The Memory of Shadows*, and while a film was never explicitly announced by Straczynski, the general assumption was that it was the big-screen outing that had been rumored for years. With Warner Bros. now involved and cast engaged, it seemed like *The Memory of Shadows* would actually see the light of day.

There were stumbling blocks along the way, including the unfortunate death of Richard Biggs. Straczynski was open about this online,

22. The Memory of Shadows

stating that it had delayed some of the progress on the movie and that rewrites would need to happen; Dr. Stephen Franklin would not be recast. There were also rumors that Warner Bros. wanted to recast some of the original *Babylon 5* characters with new actors.[11] While this was never confirmed or disputed, it was telling that Straczynski responded to a question on this rumor by stating, "I would like to be able to comment on this, but for the time being I am not able to do so."

> Oh, and for the first time in five years, there is an office somewhere in England with the words Babylon 5 on the door....[12]

Still, despite these challenges, the announcements kept coming. Straczynski confirmed to fans that *Babylon 5* was back in production again in November. On December 8, 2004, *Production Weekly* officially announced *The Memory of Shadows* to the world, with Steven Beck directing. Filming was scheduled to begin in the UK in April 2005, with a planned 2006 release date. There was also a synopsis:

> In "Shadows," the technology of the ancient and extinct Shadow race is being unleashed upon the galaxy by an unknown force, and Earthforce intelligence officer Diane Baker, whose brother was recently killed in a mysterious explosion, is out to find out who is behind the intergalactic conspiracy.
>
> Joining her is Galen, a techno-mage who has been charged with keeping the technology out of the hands of those who would abuse it.

This was soon followed by a casting call; interestingly, Galen was on the list, suggesting that there was at least some truth to the rumored recasting and Peter Woodward was not guaranteed to return as the techno-mage he had played in *A Call to Arms* and *Crusade*.

Alongside lead character Diane Baker, an intelligence officer in her late 20s or early 30s, and a friend of Captain Elizabeth Lochley, Galen was listed as a cloaked, mysterious figure, 30–45, supernaturally powerful, enigmatic and witty, who would ally with Diane. There was a lot of detail for what is essentially an established character in the *Babylon 5* universe.

Also on the casting call was Colonel Joss Morgan, a dashing and handsome officer in his late 20s or early 30s, with the Earthforce Marines and head of a security detachment sent to Babylon 5 to protect a contingent of intergalactic diplomats who are meeting there. Tyrell was a dark, enigmatic, striking and chilling techno-mage and Galen's old childhood rival.

But what was it about? Details on *The Memory of Shadows* are more widely available than the other rumored *Babylon 5* movies. Diane, Joss, Tyrell and possibly Galen would have been played by new and possibly recognizable—and bankable—actors for the *Babylon 5* movie. Tracy Scoggins would have presumably returned as Elizabeth Lochley, commander of the Babylon 5 station.

The details of the script provide more recognizable faces in President Sheridan, Delenn, Emperor Londo and G'Kar, who would arrive on Babylon 5 to mediate a dispute between four warring races. As the four of the most recognizable faces of *Babylon 5*, it would have seemed wrong to exclude Bruce Boxleitner, Mira Furlan, Peter Jurasik and Andreas Katsulas in the film; had it been made, it would been Katsulas's final on-screen performance before his death in 2006.

It is clear that the stars of *The Memory of Shadows* would have been Diane and Galen (hence the possible recasting at Warner Bros.' insistence). Diane's investigation into her brother's death would have unearthed a secret Earthforce cover-up in its use of Shadow technology, while Tyrell would have worked as a dark mirror for Galen, a corrupted techno-mage who has used Shadow technology for his own nefarious ends.

Diane could have worked as the audience surrogate for those viewers who were not fans of the show; a savvy bit of storytelling from Straczynski, to make *Babylon 5* accessible to those not familiar with the rich, arc-heavy nature of the show's narrative.

However, the *Babylon 5* regulars feel like second fiddles in their own big-screen outing. There is no mention of Garibaldi, Vir, Lennier, Lyta or Zack in *The Memory of Shadows*, though that doesn't mean they wouldn't have supporting roles. Sheridan, Delenn, G'Kar and Londo have no direct ties to Diane, like Lochley, and would simply have been caught up in the conflict that would likely arise in the film's final act.

Still, it is clear that Straczynski was keen to explore the same ideas he had planned for *Crusade*, the nefarious use of Shadow tech and the cover-up by Earth. Given that this was likely to be the core arc of the spin-off series, and that the Shadows remain one of the most visually striking, and terrifying, elements of *Babylon 5*, it would have made for a thrilling, original narrative hook.

So what happened? With the director in place and stages reserved at Elstree Studios, the home of the original *Star Wars* movies, the future for *Babylon 5* seemed bright. But no casting was ever announced. On January 30, 2005, Straczynski gave a quick update on JMS News to say that the next two weeks were going to be critical for the future of *The Memory of Shadows*.[13]

On February 25, 2005, Straczynski announced that attempts to finalize agreements with Warner Bros. and all other parties had failed. The option the unnamed production company had taken out had expired in December 2004, and a deal could not be finalized to allow the film to proceed to production. *The Memory of Shadows* had "dead ended."[14]

Straczynski also confirmed that it was unlikely that this movie would arise again at any point in the future. Like *Babylon 5: The Motion Picture*

Feature and *Wars of the Mind*, *The Memory of Shadows* was consigned to the list of abandoned *Babylon 5* film ideas. However, he also confirmed that a big-screen *Babylon 5* story was inevitable, and in 2014, a decade after the failure of *The Memory of Shadows* and seven years after the aborted attempts to continue the *Babylon 5* franchise through *The Lost Tales*, Straczynski took one more stab at a *Babylon 5* movie. But it would be very different to everything that had been mooted before.

A Big-Screen Reboot?

By 2014, the world of *Babylon 5* was in a very different place. Four members of the original cast—Richard Biggs, Andreas Katsulas, Jeff Conaway, and Michael O'Hare—had tragically passed, and fans had not seen anything of the *Babylon 5* franchise on screen for years. Straczynski had vowed never to recast any of the main roles, and it was harder to continue stories that had been so long out of the public consciousness. Despite his assertion that he would continue *Babylon 5* in a big-budget movie after the failure of *The Lost Tales* in 2007, fans believed the franchise was well and truly dead.

In many ways, it was. There were no further stories of Sheridan or Delenn, Lochley, Garibaldi, Londo et al. But at the 2014 San Diego Comic-Con, Straczynski surprised fans with the announcement that he was working on a new *Babylon 5* feature film, and it would be a reboot.[15]

> It would have to be a reboot because it's been twenty-plus years since we started that show and some of the age ranges wouldn't work with some of these characters, so we'd need to move a few people around. But what I want to do is use the original cast one way or another but we'd have to move some things around. I'd love to see [series star] Bruce [Boxleitner] as the President of the Earth Alliance; it would be the perfect role for him.

Recognizing that any *Babylon 5* with the original cast in original roles would no longer work, Straczynski's decision to reboot the franchise made sense. Any feature film would not be burdened by years of backstory that *The Memory of Shadows*—and those ideas before it—would have had. By putting *Babylon 5* cast members like Boxleitner with new roles, he would still be able to honor their original performances, something he would do again when it came to plans for a TV reboot on the CW network several years later.

He also recognized that this reboot would require a bigger budget of approximately $100 million to $200 million to do the film justice, a cost he was willing to burden through his own company, JMS Studios, should

Warner Bros. pass on the option. That level of control would also allow him to avoid the issues that derailed *The Memory of Shadows*.

Straczynski confirmed the plan to write the screenplay in 2015, get the film into production in 2016 and release in 2017.

Two years passed before any further announcement, at the 2016 San Diego Comic-Con, where he confirmed that the film had been pushed back.[16] The reason was clearly budgeting (presumably Warner Bros. had passed), and he could only muster up approximately $60 million of the $100 million needed to produce the film. JMS Studios needed more "street cred" (i.e., at least a couple of smaller TV projects under its belt) before he could fully commit to the movie.

Sadly, nothing ever came of this reboot. The next fans would hear of *Babylon 5* was the reboot TV series announcement on the CW network in September 2021, a project that would face its own hurdles.

The attempt to conceptualize *Babylon 5* on the big screen is another long, twilight struggle against the odds, one that spans the lifespan of the franchise. But Straczynski, in his wisdom, called a *Babylon 5* movie an inevitability. So perhaps it's just a matter of when and with who.

23

A Chat with Peter Jurasik (Part 2)

In the second half of my exclusive interview with Peter Jurasik, we talk about *Babylon 5*'s legacy, the fandom, his own experiences of the struggles with network television, and some favorite moments from the show.

BAZ: *When you signed on for the pilot episode of* **Babylon 5***, did you imagine that the show would last as long, and become as popular, as it did?*

PETER: I did not visualize the show going for full five seasons. So many people love it. It had a small audience, but also a really smart and faithful audience. I had no idea. The truth of the matter is when I did the pilot, I thought it was going to be a one-time TV movie. That's all. I could not imagine, with all the pilots that I had done, that this was a pilot that was going to go.

You don't just see them that way, you know? I had done two TV pilots for Steven Bochco, who had quite a record on TV, with Gary Goldberg from *Family Ties*. There were top-notch scripts that should have gone to series, that didn't. And I certainly didn't know that this was going to go to series.

When we got the first season, we got a sense of how Warner Bros. treated the show—and I'm saying that as diplomatically as I can; they didn't have much love for the show. Occasionally, they would show up and smile a bit. But actions speak louder than words. They stuck us out in an old hot tub factory, but they paid us well. I would never complain about my pay! It was great. By the time we got to the second and third season, when it started to wobble and it looked like every year it was going to go down, there was something kind of heartbreaking about that too.

As I said, when we did the pilot, I had no hope that it was going to go. In the first season, everyone was looking to get their feet under them, all the time, and we were just trying to establish ourselves. In the first season of a television program, you're just looking to get your balance on the wire, with the character. Just to see if you can get up and walk and talk, and I wasn't expecting much more than that. When we got the gift of a second season, and Joe was really getting to tell his story, I was excited, and I wanted it to keep going.

But it wobbled after the second, and it wobbled after the third. I had been around, and so had everybody else—we were a pretty experienced cast—everybody knew that we didn't go on, if they didn't want to us go on. It's all about the money!

I did a series, with Steve Bochco, called *Bay City Blues*. It was a big baseball series. And he had hand-picked people off of the *Hill Street Blues* cast. Dennis Franz was on it, and Sharon Stone. Michael Nouri was the head of the cast. All good people. Everyone assumed that no question, this drama was going to go for three or four seasons. So, we were delighted to be in it, being a Bochco show, and all that. The studio had invested in it. They had built a baseball stadium and it was a big cast. Go on IMDB and look up *Bay City Blues*. See who was in it.

But they just walked in, after eight episodes, around 11 in the morning, and said we're going to serve you all lunch and the suits are going to make an announcement. And of course, the announcement was that the show was over. They didn't even let us finish that day.

B: *Wow.*

P: They didn't even let us finish the episode. They said, no, you're done. It's over. At no point in *Babylon 5* did we kid ourselves, or I certainly didn't, that we weren't going down at any point. There was so much wobble.

B: *And of course, with the collapse of PTEN, Joe Straczynski was trying to wrap everything up in that fourth season. What was it like to get that fifth season on TNT and bring the story to an end on Joe—and the show's—terms?*

P: We try and spend our whole lives, trying not to look back and saying I wish I had done that differently. I'll take it as it was. It was great! I can say that 25 years later when the fans have such an interest in it too. I can't complain about how it ended up. But I wish we could have done it differently. I wish Joe didn't feel so rushed in the fourth season. He was pretty sure it was going away, and we weren't going to get a fifth. That forced him to tell the story in a different way.

So, it got screwed up. It was wonderful to get picked up for the fifth season, and the great thing about JMS is that he let us know there was no way we were going on beyond that. He said don't have dreams of jumping

23. A Chat with Peter Jurasik (Part 2)

the shark, as they say, with these characters. There's not going to be any Londo and G'Kar end up running a dry cleaners together episode! It just wasn't coming up. It was bittersweet, the fifth season. Because we knew it was the end. I wish we had known in the fourth season that we were going to do a fifth, for Joe's sake, and ours.

But that's not the way it was. So, some of it was a little bumpy again. All first seasons of a television series are bumpy. Go back to any series you like, that is a good one, and watch how the writers struggle to find the lines, and how the actors struggle to get their feet under them and get their characters standing in a real way. It's difficult. But once you get into it, the second, third and fourth years were really fun to do. So I was really excited that we got to go on.

B: *What have been some of your favorite experiences of the* **Babylon 5** *fandom over the years?*

P: I never had any experience of fan conventions before *Babylon 5*. I assumed they existed only for *Star Trek*. Now they are a part of our culture, of course. I studied as a theater actor and I was used to being able to walk out of the stage door, and there would be four people, or ten people, depending on how good the show was! People that would say we loved it, and it was impactful, or we laughed our asses off, or broke our hearts.

Television and film are not that way. You finish your work, and you give your comrades in arms a hug. And then you head home and see your family and study your lines for the next day. So, you don't see the fans at all.

This idea of arriving at a convention, and there are thousands of people watching the show, and, I guess, liking the show or they wouldn't be here. I never had anybody come up and say, "I hate you as Londo." It's all compliments. It's all back patting. What a treat that is, as an artist, to have that. The recognition of the work by fans in general is such a nice thing, and so unique. When you're on stage as a theater actor, you play to your audience every night. Here, you don't know what they are doing at home when they are watching. So that's a nice thing about meeting the fans.

Now, individually, all I can say is that I had a number of people who acted as my personal assistants, and some of those people have remained lifelong friends of mine. I treasure those relationships. We were thrown together; they have to relate to you, drive you around, interact with you under good and bad circumstances. So, they are *Babylon 5* fans that have become lifelong friends.

And I also have a few *Babylon 5* friends, who I have picked up on social media. I do these little cameos now. And I realized that Londo is a lot more exciting than Peter Jurasik! He's funnier, more interesting. I'm just an actor. He's ambassador, or emperor, of the Centauri Republic! People would rather meet him! But people do punch through that, and get past Londo, to me. And what a treat.

B: *So, do you have a favorite episode, or moment, from* Babylon 5?

P: I don't know that I have a favorite episode. I certainly have favorite moments. I think about the bombing of Narn, in "The Long, Twilight Struggle." I particularly liked what director John Flinn did with me. He was a cinematographer first. I remember him on *Hill Street Blues.*

I'm a social guy. I like to talk and jazz around. I've said before, Londo is a character that you sometimes want to get away from. You don't want to hang out with him all day long because he'll wear you down. He's a pretty dominant individual. But John put me up on a ten-foot platform, and separated me from everyone in the cast, and everyone in the crew, and just left me up there. It was a wonderful technique. I just stood there, alone, all made up in costume and ready to go. That scene was a favorite moment of mine.

There are so many scenes with Andreas and Stephen that I wish I could redo again. I think of flying by the seat of our pants, Vir and I, for the Centauri opera stuff, in the episode "Knives." That was so much fun to do.

The few moments I had—and I didn't have nearly enough—with Mira, I treasure all of those. She was a wonderful person, and what an actress! When you got close to her, and looked into her eyes, you could feel her spirit. She was a wonderful actress to work with.

I would say that about Andreas too. I probably looked into his eyes more than his wife did! When he was doing his work, he was an interesting guy to be around. I had a ball. He was a fun actor to work with. People would think of the elevator scene in "Convictions." People love that elevator scene! It was something he did, and I just followed his lead. Again, you can't take JMS out any of the equations. He was always at the center of it. As they say, if it ain't on the page, it ain't on the stage!

You can imagine how much fun it was for me to talk to Vir about my wives, in "Soul Mates." I loved Jane Carr, who played Timov.

B: *She was wonderful. I wish she had been in the show a bit more.*

P: Yeah, I really wish too. I had done a recurring part in a show called *Dear John*, that she was on, and so I knew her too. She's just a real pro, and that was so fun to do. But to play with Stephen was really fun too. I mean, all the things that the fans love. The cats go quack joke.

B: *Yes! I love that scene!*

P: Yes, that's a good one. We had lots of fun scenes together. I also very much loved the TV movie, *In the Beginning*, where I got to play the young Londo. I had a great time on that, and we had a wonderful director in Mike Vejar. It was nice to play the character young.

B: *And the old emperor too.*

P: And old! Young! That was a real treat. The old stuff I would probably redo, but that's just the actor in me. There was stuff in that that I wish I had the chance to redo, but I enjoyed it so much. I was lapping it up, and that's not good for an actor. You need someone to pull the reins a little tight. But I love the arrogance and stupidity scene. That was a great moment. I could watch that over and over because I loved the energy of the younger Mollari.

B: *Going back to that first moment, you mentioned "The Long, Twilight Struggle." Londo watching the bombing of Narn. Obviously, that would have been a lot of green screens and special effects. You weren't actually standing on a spaceship, watching a planet being bombarded! But that look you gave, that shot that was reused on the season three and four title sequences, it was such a powerful moment for Londo. Just that realization of what was going on. Your performance was so deeply haunting, because even though he's probably at [the] worst he's been, in terms of a villain, you still feel sympathy for him. Londo was so out of his depth. That was an amazing sequence. No words. Just that look you gave. Such a powerful scene.*

P: Thank you for saying that. What's great about it is that there's a moment with Londo, when his villainy turns to tragedy. He gets it. And *that's* the difference. A character becomes tragic once he understands the mess that he has put himself in. Until then, he's just villainous, you know?

But at that moment he gets it and understands it. Once it closed on Londo, he thought, in the name of God, what have I done? It's a great moment for what it means and what was coming after it. And he knew it. When you realize what you have done and realize that you have to suffer the consequences: that's hard to get up from. It's hard to put on a good face, right?

B: *You see that in the following scene with G'Kar in the council chamber. Andreas delivers that wonderful speech about freedom, and Londo is so cold, and shut off, because he's trapped now in this situation. You get from that scene—and the scene where he looks out over the bombing of Narn—that he's as lost as anyone.*

P: It's so nice to hear you talk about it. I love it when fans talk about it. I tell fans all the time, when I get a chance to write to, or speak to them, that we did the show for you guys. But it's beautiful to hear people who got the script and take the power of it. Because it's true. In that scene, when I look back at it, I'm reminded of how fascists have been played in the news. I was conjuring up Benito Mussolini, I was going for that. I was going for a man that has made a choice, out of patriotism or blind belief in an ideal. He just couldn't get out of the way now. He was done. He was trapped by it. Poor Londo is probably the least present for one of the most beautiful speeches. There's so many, and G'Kar had a ton of them. But Londo was probably the least present for that freedom speech. He was in his own mind!

B: *So, obviously you got many amazing scenes over the five seasons of the show, thanks to Joe's words and your performance, and the performance of Andreas, Stephen, and everyone else. I know there were talks of you coming back as Londo when Joe Straczynski tried to resurrect* **Babylon 5** *with* The Lost Tales. *Do you know what the details were of the story that Joe had planned for you?*

P: No, I don't. I was pretty sure I didn't want to go forward, into a new thing. Again, once you accept that it was five seasons, I put that cap on the back. I always said, listen, if Joe's going to write something completely different, and I get to play somebody different, I'll do that. I didn't know where it was going because I didn't want to explore it.

By that point in my life, my son had come along. So, my life had changed. I was not only married, but I was also a father, and I had to get back to work! It took me a long time and my wife reminds me of it occasionally. Boy, did we do bad, money-wise, the year after Ben was born! But that speaks to my values, and what was important. I was a lot more interested in going forward as a person, and as a father, than I was in doing a different version of Londo in a different story.

I'm not making fun of it. But as I said, there was never any hope for me, as we got into the fourth season, that we were ever going to jump the shark, and Londo and G'Kar were going to, you know, open a dry cleaners! It wasn't going to happen.

B: *I don't know, that could have been fun!*

P: Possibly! But really, I didn't want to do it, and now when I hear people talking about rebooting *Babylon 5*, I think, I'm just too old. I actually would love to see any good actor play the role of Londo from the top, if they wanted. I would watch that. That would be of interest to me to see another actor make choices. I know how the process works. I know what I would do, in terms of interpretation. It doesn't change the script. Joe would hand a good actor that script, and they would just move differently. I mentioned a little about working from the outside in. He would walk and talk differently. It's interesting to think about somebody else doing it.

So, I wasn't that interested, and I didn't engage for that reason.

23. A Chat with Peter Jurasik (Part 2)

B: *At the time we're doing this interview, there's still talk of a new* **Babylon 5** *reboot, which is not the same as what came before. If Joe asked you to come back, and play a different role, what kind of role would you like to play?*

P: I can only say so much about it. But what I can say is that I would if Joe really wanted me to. Joe has already talked about some other ideas. But I'm already 72 years old now, and not to put myself in any corner, but as you become older, the roles become a lot more limited. I worked a ton between the age of 35 and 55 and did a *lot* of different characters. But that's because you can fill a script up with that.

But I don't know who I would like to play. I still look back at my career and what I liked about Sid the Snitch was that he had a good heart. But he was a weasel of the highest order, and would do anything for 20 bucks, A super untrustworthy person. But he had a heart, and I loved that. And Londo was, in a lot of ways, that too. He was a patriot first. He had his own heart, and his own loves. But he was also villainous and untrustworthy. So, that's the kind of character I like to play.

Excellent being, I think that's what my acting teacher called it. I'm reminded of Bruce Boxleitner as Captain Sheridan. Captains are always excellent people! You know, you and I aren't excellent people, and we don't hope to be excellent people. People who present themselves as excellent beings—that's the phrase—there's no such thing, as you know. No man or woman. No priest, or nun, or Mother Teresa. The Dalai Lama? No. Excellent beings, they don't exist! That's the nature of where we exist

But I like to go the other way. Let me play the meanest, most corrupt, most lost, most troubled individual. That's what I'd like to play for Joe.

B: *Final question. What does* **Babylon 5** *mean to you?*

P: As a man, a father and husband, I'm Peter. But as an actor, it became a major piece of my career. I love what it has done for me in terms of security and money. It gave me all those years of work. But the most important thing of all was all the personal relationships. I still have Claudia, and Pat, and Bill. That means a lot to me. As for the work, I don't think actors get lucky and get good scripts, and great characters to play. I was *really* lucky that I got two of them in my career, and Londo was certainly one of those.

So, that's what *Babylon 5* means to me. It's a wonderful piece of luck that I played into. I did what I did with it. As you look back, you ask could I have done this better, or that better. But your life is filled with that, and you try not to do that. So, it means everything to me. I'm really glad I got it. I had a great time doing it.

And I treasure the people, and the fans. People who love it along with me, and got it, and really thought about it. Who felt it. That's who we did it for. It had something in it that JMS wanted us to bring to life, and for some people, we did that. We did bring it to life. That brings great joy to my life.

24

The Canonization of Novels

All big franchises have spin-off material that explores characters and stories from TV and film off screen. There are countless universes of *Star Wars* and *Star Trek* adventures in book and comic book form, while *Doctor Who* has multiple timelines featuring the Doctors and their companions. The latter even has hundreds of audio adventures at Big Finish Productions, most featuring the original cast reprising their roles for new adventures in time and space.[1]

Spin-off material is rarely considered canon, and generally the rule is whatever happens on screen will also override a story that took place in book, comic, or audio form. With Disney's acquisition of Lucasfilm and the creation of new *Star Wars* films and series, over 20 years of carefully crafted novels were repurposed under the *Star Wars Legends* banner.[2] A similar thing happened with *Star Trek* when the TV franchise took a step into the future with *Star Trek: Picard* and rendered all the books centered on the continuing adventures of the *Enterprise, Deep Space Nine* and *Voyager* contradictory to the events we witnessed.[3]

Even Big Finish, with its hours of *Doctor Who, Blake's 7* and other material, will also find itself playing second fiddle to any new adventures on screen. There is certainly a concerted effort to play within the realms of the televised *Doctor Who* mythology, but the continuing TV series will always trump anything that took place in audio. If you were to treat all Big Finish stories as 100 percent canon, the *Doctor Who* universe would be full of chronological inconsistences. Did Mary Shelley meet the Eighth or 13th Doctor at Villa Diodati?[4] Both of them, if audio and TV have equal canon footing.

In some instances, material might be commissioned that is designed to enhance new on-screen canon. With the debut of *Star Trek: Picard*, new books were written that fleshed out the events touched upon in the revival series; these are much closer to canon than the hundreds of books written before 2020. But as a rule, if it doesn't happen on screen, it was an alternate reality and not part of the main narrative.

Babylon 5 was something of an exception. A number of novels released in the '90s through 2001 were all largely based on outlines written directly by J. Michael Straczynski. As such, they were endorsed by the showrunner himself and considered to be canon within the *Babylon 5* universe.

These books help fill in the missing pieces surrounding the fate of the *Icarus*, or Sinclair's mission to Minbar during *Babylon 5* season two. Other stories were set up by the show but never explored on-screen, such as Emperor Londo's subjugation under the Drakh or the rise of Bester and the tyrannical Psi Corps. Most interesting is the Techno-Mages trilogy, which delves into Galen's mysterious people in a way that Straczynski was never able to achieve with the cancellation of *Crusade*.

The canonization of novels in the *Babylon 5* universe was certainly unique—the *Star Trek* and *Star Wars* franchises may have explored in-canon spin-offs in more recent years, but again, Straczynski and *Babylon 5* got there first. These stories were as important to the overall story as the TV series and movies that were created.

Accompaniments to the Show—From the Icarus *to Sinclair's Journey on Minbar*

Between 1995 and 1997, Del Rey Books released nine books to accompany the TV show. Like most spin-off material, there was an attempt to stay true to the internal chronology of the show.

John Vornholt would write the first and third books in the *Babylon 5* range, both set during the events of season two. *Voices* would focus on Talia and Bester, as a terrorist attack on the station during a Psi Corps convention finds Talia a suspect, and Garibaldi and Ivanova are forced to work with Bester to hunt her down. Garibaldi and Ivanova would also be heavily involved in his other book, *Blood Oath*, the third in the series, which would see them hunt down G'Kar's "killers," with the help of his aide Na'Toth, after a Chon'Kar, or blood oath, is declared upon the Narn ambassador.

Lois Tilton wrote the second book in the series, *Accusations*, also set in season two and involving Ivanova's search for the murder of an old friend. *Clark's Law*, the fourth book and the first released in 1996, was written by Jim Mortimore. It sees Sheridan forced to defy the new President Clark's orders when an alliance is sought with the mysterious Tuchanq, after they are discovered to be hiding a mass murderer among them. Neal Barrett, Jr.'s, *The Touch of Your Shadow, the Whisper of Your Name* sees Sheridan confide in Kosh after the inhabitants of Babylon 5 are plagued by nightmares. Finally in 1996 was *Betrayals* by S.M. Sterling, which sees Sheridan, G'Kar and Londo placed in danger when negotiations between two warring forces of the same planet erupt into violence.

Three books were written in 1997, wrapping up the Del Rey range, two of which were considered canon by Straczynski. Only book eight, *Personal Agendas* by Al Sarrantonio, didn't receive the same accreditation, as this offered an alternate take on an alliance between Londo and G'Kar— presumably during the events of season three—to eliminate the mad Centauri emperor, Cartagia. Not only did this book deviate massively from the show's actual season four storyline, it was also a book that Straczynski had significant issues with, noting that the characterization was off and tried "way too hard to be funny, ignoring the notion that if everything is funny then *nothing* is funny."[5]

Across the first six novels, it is clear that the writers have taken inspiration from *Babylon 5* episodes and themes running through the second and third seasons of the show: the Chon'Kar blood oath, first seen in season one's "Deathwalker," or the growing corruption of Clark's regime on Earth. Like many franchise novels, *Star Trek* in particular, they attempt to work within the confines of the show's chronology but are overridden by events that happen on screen.

While Straczynski was involved in the reviewing of these books, there were elements that contradicted the show, such as the use of artificial gravity on Narn ships in *Blood Oath*[6] to the more obvious mistake of Lyta being deaf in *Clark's Law*.[7] Timelines are also an issue; *The Touch of Your Shadow, The Whisper of Your Name* is set during early season three, yet features G'Kar as an ambassador and Delenn a member of the Grey Council. Straczynski openly accepted that keeping continuity was difficult. Despite reading the manuscripts, his time as showrunner on *Babylon 5* was limited and "short of him adding Editor and Publisher to his list of hats" it was impossible to have full control over other people's work.[8] In the case of the massively contradictory *Personal Agendas*, Straczynski didn't actually get the manuscript until it was too late to change the publication.

However, the seventh and ninth books by Del Rey Books are different, in that they develop two key narratives that took place off-screen, using Straczynski's notes to provide more context to these characters and events. *The Shadow Within*, by Jeanne Cavelos (who would go on to write the officially canon Techno-Mage trilogy), was considered 90 percent canon by Straczynski, while *To Dream in the City of Sorrows*, by his then wife Kathryn M. Drennan (and writer of season one's "By Any Means Necessary"), was 100 percent canon within the *Babylon 5* universe.[9]

Set prior to the events of *The Gathering*, *The Shadow Within* deals with the voyage of the *Icarus* to Z'ha'dum, the awakening of the Shadows and the fate of Anna Sheridan, wife of John Sheridan. Mr. Morden gets plenty of focus here too, as his backstory and decision to join the Shadows is explored in great detail. The secondary plot sees John Sheridan take command of the Earthforce ship *Agamemnon* and attempt to foil a Home Guard plot to destroy Babylon 5 before it goes live.

With Straczynski's endorsement, *The Shadow Within* becomes an essential piece of world-building for *Babylon 5* and was later repackaged with a new cover as "a thrilling prequel to *The Passing of the Techno-Mages*" by Cavelos.

To Dream in the City of Sorrows is set in 2259, the second season of *Babylon 5*, and focuses on Sinclair's mission to Minbar as the human ambassador. There, he learns the truth about the Shadows and rises to become the leader of the Rangers, preparing for the coming fight against the Shadows. His fiancé Catherine Sakai also features heavily, surviving a Shadow attack to join Sinclair on Minbar and train with the Rangers with Marcus Cole, prior to his debut on the TV series in season three.

Again, there is a massive amount of contextual world-building in this story that enhances the overall narrative of *Babylon 5*. It picks up the unseen story of Jeffrey Sinclair after Michael O'Hare was forced to leave the show (along with Julia Nickson's recurring character Catherine Sakai), while also giving Jason Carter's Marcus Cole plenty of backstory too.

As with the later "in-canon" books, *The Shadow Within* and *To Dream in the City of Sorrows* are essential reading for any *Babylon 5* fan. Like the later trilogies, they are out of print; fortunately, they are considerably easier to find online than the stories that followed.

The Psi Corps Trilogy

The Telepath War was teased throughout *Babylon 5*, most notably in the Byron arc that dominated the first half of the show's fifth season. Each season before that had featured at least one episode with Alfred Bester and the nefarious Psi Corps. A fundamental presence in *Babylon 5*, it seemed only appropriate that the telepaths were the focus of the first trilogy of stories written as the original five-year run came to an end.

Based on three 10-page outlines from outlines from Straczynski, J. Gregory Keyes wrote the Psi Corps trilogy, dealing with the founding of the Psi Corps, Bester's rise to power, and his eventual defeat on the back of the Telepath War. Perhaps learning from some of the issues faced with the original Del Rey books, Straczynski worked closely with Keyes and a reference editor to make sure the books made canonical sense with the rest of the series. As with the subsequent Centauri and Techno-Mage trilogies, these books are considered 100 percent canon.

Dark Genesis: The Birth of the Psi Corps was published by Del Rey in September 1998, shortly before the final five-episode run of *Babylon 5*'s fifth season. In a first for the franchise, it was not set in the main *Babylon 5* timeline, instead dealing with the rise of the telepaths on Earth a century before the show.

> This is probably one of the best B5 novels ever done, and it takes quite a risk, because even though you see ancestors of some of our characters (the books cover about 80 years), there are none of the regulars in it. It's our first attempt to really flesh out the B5 universe and future history.[10]

Straczynski's praise for *Dark Genesis* was deserved. Keyes's book deals with the paranoia and bloodshed that arose from the emergence of telepaths, dealing with Holocaust themes as it explores the persecution of human telepaths that led to their becoming the second-class citizens that we see in *Babylon 5*. It also taps into the themes of government control and lust for power with the emergence of the Psi Corps, using the organization's offer of protection for humanity as a mask for its own ambitions.

Deadly Relations: Bester Ascendant was published in February 1999 and explores the face of the Psi Corps in *Babylon 5*: Alfred Bester. Like the first book in the trilogy, this is an origin story, dealing with Bester's childhood and rise to the nefarious Psi Cop we see in the TV show.

Finally, *Final Reckoning: The Fate of Bester* was published in October 1999, but does not deal with the Telepath War, as expected. Instead, Keyes, working from Straczynski's notes, picks up after the conflict. Bester has been tried and convicted as a war criminal and is on the run. Where *Final Reckoning* triumphs, however, is how it deals with Garibaldi and Bester's twisted relationship, pitting them together and offering a final fate for one of *Babylon 5*'s best villains.

Not all answers are provided by this trilogy. The oft-mentioned Telepath War remains forever an enigma, poised to be explored in the unmade movies and *The Lost Tales* that Straczynski was never able to bring to the screen. However, as a rich exploration of Alfred Bester, it offers the deep characterization and focus that he never really got on the show.

Legions of Fire *and the Fate of Centauri Prime*

"The Fall of Centauri Prime" at the end of *Babylon 5*'s fifth season left Londo in a very dark place, with the Centauri crippled by the Drakh's act of revenge. Jumping forward 19 years to "Sleeping in Light," we saw a

Centauri that was free again, with Vir now emperor. But what happened in between?

Outside of the Drakh attack on Earth in *A Call to Arms* and the unfinished Drakh War storyline of *Crusade*, fans knew the Drakh would try to ensnare Sheridan and Delenn's son David with a Keeper. This would ultimately fail, as seen in the future of season three's "War Without End," an episode that also saw Londo and G'Kar die at each other's hands.

Much of this story took place off-screen in a trilogy of novels by Peter David, again based on Straczynski's outlines, and are officially considered part of the *Babylon 5* canon. The Legions of Fire trilogy was published by Del Rey Books in 1999 and 2000 and dealt with Vir's attempt to raise the Legion of Fire, a secret resistance group on Centauri Prime intent on driving the Drakh out.

The first book, *The Long Night of Centauri Prime*, was published in December 1999 and followed Londo's journey into darkness on Centauri Prime as he adjusted to life under the Keeper's control. Despite some dating errors in the novel, the first book charts the events between his coronation and the Drakh attack in *A Call to Arms*, four years later.

Armies of Light and Dark, published in May 2000, follows these events over a seven-year period as Vir leads the underground movement with help from Garibaldi and the Interstellar Alliance. The final book, *Out of the Darkness*, published in October 2000, deals with the final five years of Londo's tragic reign as Vir continues to lead the resistance, while the Drakh try to capture David, and Sheridan and Delenn find themselves prisoners on Centauri Prime.

Like the Psi Corps trilogy, it does leave *Babylon 5* fans with many unanswered questions. The trilogy was written at a time when *Crusade* was still a planned five-year narrative by Straczynski. The fate of the Drakh War and Earth's freedom from the plague are set up but never truly explored in the novels, leaving fans with more unanswered questions. However, they do offer closure on Londo, G'Kar and the fate of David Sheridan, all events hinted at in the TV show, and given plenty of focus in the pages of David's novels.

The Passing of the Techno-Mages Trilogy— Galen Takes Center Stage

The final trilogy of novels produced by Del Rey Books turned their attention to the long-neglected techno-mages. These space wizards had featured heavily early in Straczynski's plans for *Babylon 5*, before getting a single episode appearance in season two. The debut of Galen in *A Call* to Arms marked their return to the universe, but the limited run of *Crusade* cut their continued presence short. Straczynski clearly wanted them to play a bigger part in the franchise, given Galen's encore appearance in *The Lost Tales*.

Having impressed with *The Shadow Within*, Jeanne Cavelos returned to write the Passing of the Techno-Mages trilogy, again based on notes from Straczynski himself. The first of these books, *Casting Shadows*, was published in February 2001. Set in *Babylon 5* late season one and early season two, *Casting Shadows* acted as a prelude to "The Geometry of Shadows" and saw Galen and his lover Isabella investigate rumors of the Shadows, while Elric unifies the techno-mages to decide whether they will be a factor in the war ahead. Perhaps unsurprising, given her work on the *Icarus* mission in *The Shadow Within*, Morden and Anna Sheridan also play a part in the story.

The second book, *Summoning Light*, was published in July 2001, and picks up from *Casting Shadows*, as Galen is dispatched to Z'ha'dum to uncover the Shadows' plans. Elric and the techno-mages prepare to depart, tying directly into the events of their arrival on Babylon 5 in "The Geometry of Shadows."

The trilogy concluded with *Invoking Darkness*, published in November 2001. Set during the back half of *Babylon 5* season three though to the start of season four, the final entry in the Techno-Mages trilogy sees Galen sent on a secret mission during the height of the Shadow War. It features elements from this period of the show, including Kosh and his replacement Ulkesh, Sheridan and Garibaldi, and Babylon 5 itself.

The Passing of the Techno-Mages trilogy expands on the culture of the techno-mages and weaves in their involvement—or lack of—in the Shadow conflict. While the previous two canon trilogies expand on story elements only hinted at in the show, the techno-mages story serves as a fascinating piece of world-building that adds greater context to Galen's involvement in the *Babylon 5* universe. While he may have had limited screen time, Galen at long last received the character focus to put him alongside the other *Babylon 5* greats.

The Unpublished Babylon 5 *Novels from Mongoose Publishing*

Founded in 2001, Mongoose Publishing was a British manufacturer of role-playing games, miniatures, and card games that obtained the rights to produce material related to *Babylon 5*. *The Babylon 5 Roleplaying Game* was published in 2003 and won a Silver Ennie Award for

Best Licensed Product in 2004.[11] A second edition of the game followed in 2006.

The game was followed by *Babylon 5: A Call to Arms*, which was originally envisioned as an expansion pack to *The Babylon 5 Roleplaying Game* before being published by Mongoose as a tabletop game in its own right in 2004. *Babylon 5: A Call to Arms* received a second set of core rules in 2007. It won the Academy of Adventure Gaming, Arts & Design Gamer's Choice Award in 2004. However, production of miniature games under the *Babylon 5* banner eventually ceased in 2009.

During this period, Mongoose Publishing also looked to continue the adventures of the *Babylon 5* novels through a series of six novels, including one penned by Claudia Christian. However, unlike the previous books from Del Rey Books, these were not endorsed by Straczynski, and the plans were shelved, despite the first three books already being written.

Ranger Dawning was the first novel, written by Richard Ford and set during the second season of *Babylon 5*. The protagonist was Earthforce officer James Vance, one of the first humans to be recruited by the Rangers for the coming war with the Shadows. The narrative dealt with his rigorous training and prejudice from the Minbari as he prepared for his first mission.

Baptism of Fire was written by Claudia Christian and picked up Susan Ivanova's story after she left Babylon 5 at the end of the fourth season. Now the captain of the *Titan*, a new Warlock-class destroyer, Ivanova is sent to hunt down a mysterious alien race after they attack Babylon 5. The title of the novel was very apt, dealing not only with Ivanova's new position as a ship's captain, but also with a distrustful crew following her leading role in the rebellion against President Clark in the Earth civil war.

The third book, written by Matthew Sprange, returned to the theme of the Rangers. *Visions of Peace: A Rangers Novel* dealt with their new role in the Interstellar Alliance, upholding peace in the galaxy. The human protagonist of this novel was Michael Shaw, a Ranger involved in the discovery of a weapon dating back to the Dilgar War and tied into the Centauri's fall from grace in *Babylon 5*'s fifth season.

Mongoose Publishing did attempt to involve Straczynski in order to legitimize the novels and make them officially canon. However, he felt the quality of these stories was not up to scratch (rumors that the amount they offered was minimal also fueled the rift between the publisher and Straczynski). The first three novels were published as a PDF document entitled *Deconstruction of Falling Stars* in 2008, but this is no longer available.

Details on the other three novels are scarce. Bruce Graw, who wrote some of the material for the Mongoose Publishing RPG *Babylon 5* games, was set to write the fourth novel, *Ashes of the Past*, while M.J. Dougherty would have written the fifth novel, *Actions of Many*. The final novel, *Birth of Heroes*, would have been written by Bryan Steele, who, like Graw, wrote some of the material for the *Babylon 5* games at Mongoose.

Unlike *Star Trek*, *Star Wars* or *Doctor Who*, the *Babylon 5* franchise didn't have an expansive range of written stories. However, given Straczynski's involvement in Del Rey's content (and refusal to approve apparently inferior stories at Mongoose Publishing), the quality of these stories remained high. As with the rest of *Babylon 5*'s legacy, the attempt to continue the franchise in novel form was something of a struggle and triumph. The stories might be limited, but—as proven by the like of the Psi Corps, Centauri and Techno-Mage trilogies—what fans got only enriched the universe that Straczynski had created.

25

The *Babylon 5* Community

In 2023, *Babylon 5* celebrated its 30th anniversary. Surprisingly for a show three decades old, the show was still very much in the public consciousness, thanks in no small part to the passionate fanbase that kept the dream alive. If anything, that interest in *Babylon 5* hit something of a resurgence as it headed toward its 30th birthday.

By the start of 2023, there were at least 15 active *Babylon 5* podcasts, all talking about their love of the show—including my own podcast, *A Dream Given Form*, which I started in 2022. Online articles were continuing to revisit and reevaluate the show. With the critical success of the *Star Wars* series *Andor* in late 2022, *Babylon 5* featured in two articles from *Looper*[1] and *Lifehacker*,[2] both recommending the 30-year-old show as something fans might want to watch next. *Babylon 5* was recognized as "helping pioneer long-form television storytelling," mixing politics and spectacle.

Suddenly, everyone was excited to watch *Babylon 5* again. The HD remaster on HBO Max[3] (and digital download through iTunes and Amazon) was another exciting step in the reengagement with fans. The show's original camera negatives were scanned in 4K and downscaled back to HD, with color correction, a dirt and scratch clean-up, and CGI upscale. This HD remaster took six years to develop, and eagle-eyed fans were quick to pick up on the rumors of the *Babylon 5* upscale before any official release was announced.

The upscale, while not perfect—it was still a show that was limited in its ambition by its '90s budget—was still met with great enthusiasm from fans, new and old. People who hadn't watched the show since its original run were watching again and recognizing just how ahead of its time *Babylon 5* was. Facebook groups popped up in abundance, with new posts almost daily from people who hadn't watched the show in years, talking about introducing friends and family members to it for the first time.

The legacy of *Babylon 5* is stronger than ever. It is supported by the engagement of the cast and crew of the show with wider fandom. J. Michael

Straczynski has his own Patreon for fans,[4] which ranges from sharing tidbits from the show to full support of developing writers, and he engages daily with fans on Twitter, just as he did with the online forums and message boards in the '90s. Patricia Tallman, Claudia Christian and other members of the cast continue to share their experiences with the fandom. Tallman told me that *Babylon 5* is family, and that has never been truer.

The love for the show is bittersweet. So many of the wonderful cast have passed on. In the last decade, Stephen Furst, Jerry Doyle, and Mira Furlan have joined the tragic list of so many wonderful *Babylon 5* actors who are no longer with us. It makes rewatching the show and all those wonderful performances bittersweet, knowing the legacy they left behind; a legacy that fans continue to embrace.

People are still talking about *Babylon 5*, which isn't bad for a show that ran for five seasons decades ago. In the current TV and film age, where geekdom is part of everyday life, fans don't have to choose between *Star Trek* and *Babylon 5* anymore (not that they ever did), and those who might have dismissed it the first time around are finally starting to see what all the fuss was about.

Babylon 5 is as loved now as it was 20 or 30 years ago.

The Podcast Phenomenon

Everyone's podcasting these days. Podcasts have been around for years, and indeed, *Babylon 5* podcasts existed long before the 30th anniversary, but as the show moved closer to that big three-zero, so did the number of people eager to talk about it.

Podcasts really took off during the COVID-19 pandemic in 2020 and 2021 as a new way for people to share common interests and connect with others. I certainly discovered that I could geek out over my favorite shows in a time when the world wasn't great. Before I knew it, I was on podcasts talking about *Star Trek* and *Alias*, *The Lord of the Rings* and *Doctor Who*. But what I really wanted to talk about was *Babylon 5*.

The interesting thing about the *Babylon 5* podcast phenomenon is just how many fans there are out there, willing to engage. I launched *A Dream Given Form* in early 2022 with my cohost and friend Luke Winch, and suddenly we were getting people from Australia to Sweden, Russia to Colombia, all listening to us talk about a show that hadn't been on the air for over a quarter-century. The number of downloads for *A Dream Given Form* have been much higher than any other podcast I've worked on.

And we weren't alone. We were joined by the *Yum Yum* podcast, *The Last Best Babylon 5 Podcast*, *Babylon 5 for the First Time*, and *Grey 17*.

Some were more successful than others. We hit nearly 5,000 downloads in the first year. *Grey 17*, with its mix of veteran fans and newbies to *Babylon 5*, struck the right chord with nearly 30,000 downloads. When I chatted to the hosts of *Grey 17*, Scott and Blake, they were astounded by the interest in their podcast.[5]

In our first year, Patricia Tallman and Marshall Teague came on *A Dream Given Form* to chat *Babylon 5*, and they had lost none of their passion for the show after three decades of talking about it. *Grey 17* followed suit with Marshall and Claudia Christian popping up on the podcast to connect with the fans over a show that meant so much to them.

By the time *Babylon 5*'s 30th anniversary rolled by, the podcast phenomenon was in full swing. It seemed there were thousands of fans out there eager to listen to what fans like Luke and I had to say.

From first-time watchers to veteran fan discussions, actor interviews, deep dives into themes and characters from the show, and a whole lot more: there was plenty to be said about *Babylon 5* and it was wonderful to be part of that conversation.

A Dream of Things to Come:
The CW Babylon 5 *Reboot*

After the confirmation in 2016 that the planned *Babylon 5* reboot movie had been delayed, the franchise entered a period of limbo. The 2007 release of *The Lost Tales* remained the last installment in the franchise and Straczynski moved onto other projects, like the Netflix series *Sense8*, which ran for two seasons and a wrap-up movie.

On September 27, 2021, Deadline broke a story that *Babylon 5* would be rebooted at the CW network: a "from-the-ground-up reboot" of the critically acclaimed series, from original series creator J. Michael Straczynski and Warner Bros. Television.[6]

This was quickly followed by a confirmation from Straczynski on Twitter,[7] noting that there were serious fans at the network and that he was working on the pilot. Once again, he would act as showrunner if *Babylon 5* was picked up for a full series. He also confirmed the reasons for doing a reboot—there would be no fun or surprises in telling the same story twice. Instead, it would follow the approach of successful reboots like *Battlestar Galactica* and *Westworld* and use "original elements that are evergreens and put them in a blender with a ton of new, challenging ideas, to create something fresh yet familiar."

The other reason for a reboot was obvious, but one that Straczynski called out nonetheless.

25. The Babylon 5 Community 215

To those asking why not just do a continuation, for a network series like this, it can't be done because over half our cast are still stubbornly on the other side of the Rim. How do you tell a continuing story of our original Londo without the original Vir? Or G'Kar? How do you tell Sheridan's story without Delenn? Or the story of B5 without Franklin? Garibaldi? Zack?

The reboot of *Babylon 5* would use his years of experience as a screenwriter and reflect the world in which we live now. Just as humanity had moved on in the three decades since *Babylon 5* first aired, so would the stories Straczynski wanted to tell. He had campaigned for a trans character, and a bisexual relationship, and come up against the challenges of '90s network television. But times had changed—Straczynski had changed—and the world was ready for greater representation.

The allegorical approach Straczynski had used in storylines such as the rise of Clark's xenophobic Earth during the show's original run was still just as valid. In world that had suffered through Trump, Brexit, COVID and the invasion of Ukraine, there were greater and more harrowing influences to draw upon in his writing as he imagined a realistic depiction of humanity's future.

The fans at the CW network Straczynski spoke of included none other than the network's president Mark Pedowitz. He had been a fan of *Babylon 5* since the show's original run and would often receive sneak VHS advance copies of episodes from Straczynski before they even aired.

Many of the original elements of the show would be different. Indeed, there was no Sinclair in this new reboot. The reboot synopsis (from the Babylon 5 Wiki) centered on "John Sheridan, an Earthforce officer with a mysterious background, who is assigned to Babylon 5, a five-mile-long space station in neutral space, a port of call for travelers, smugglers, corporate explorers and alien diplomats at a time of uneasy peace and the constant threat of war. His arrival triggers a destiny beyond anything he could have imagined, as an exploratory Earth company accidentally triggers a conflict with a civilization a million years ahead of us, putting Sheridan and the rest of the B5 crew in the line of fire as the last, best hope for the survival of the human race."

Planned as a new five-year arc that would be as innovative as the original, the *Babylon 5* reboot had fans excited for the possibilities to come.

A Call to Arms: #B5onCWin23

But there was trouble brewing at the CW network. On January 5, 2022, the *Wall Street Journal* reported that WarnerMedia and ViacomCBS were exploring a potential sale of the CW.[8] Despite its commitment to producing successful scripted shows like *The Flash* and *Riverdale*, the CW had never been profitable since the merging of UPN and Warner Bros. in 2006. Nexstar Media Group Inc., one of the largest shareholders in the CW and the owner of 199 U.S. domestic TV stations, was confirmed as the frontrunner to buy the CW outright.

This seismic shift at the network affected the development of new and existing shows, including the proposed *Babylon 5* reboot, which was up for consideration for the 2022–23 broadcast season. On February 3, *Deadline* announced the new pilot pickups for the 2022–23 season. *Babylon 5* was not on the list.[9]

On the same day, Straczynski announced on his Patreon that the *Babylon 5* reboot was on hold.[10] He has heard from inside Warner Bros. that conversations were taking place with the CW on the logistics of picking up new pilots during the transition, with focus on preexisting deals and commitments.

Straczynski also assured fans that the situation with *Babylon 5* was unique (99.999 percent of the time, a pilot not being picked up to production means the script is dead). He had received a call from Mark Pedowitz ahead of the *Deadline* piece, who had called Straczynski's pilot "a damned fine script." The CW president had taken the highly unusual step of rolling the project and the pilot script into the following year. The aim was to keep *Babylon 5* in active development while the dust settled on the sale of the CW network.

With the reboot of *Babylon 5* deferred, attention turned to the state of scripted content at the CW. Changes were clearly afoot, with the popular Arrowverse a big casualty in the change. *Batwoman* and *Legends of Tomorrow* were canceled, and *The Flash* was picked up for a final season.[11]

While many fans assumed this was the latest failed attempt to continue the *Babylon 5* franchise, Mark Pedowitz confirmed in May 2022 that the *Babylon 5* reboot was still "very much in active development" and a perfect fit for the CW.[12] Straczynski continued to engage with the fandom on Twitter and through his Patreon. News on the reboot continued to be elusive, even with the confirmation in August that Nexstar had sealed the deal to buy a 75 percent stake in the CW.[13]

And then Straczynski took to Twitter in September 2022, asking for a "call to arms" from fans to demonstrate their support for the *Babylon 5* reboot and show Nexstar that the sci-fi show would be big business.

> The fate of the #Babylon5 pilot may be decided end of this month. Though much of @TheCW was bought by @NXSTMediaGroup the decision also rests heavily with @WarnerbrosTV. If fans want to show their support for B5 & let them know you want this to happen, now is the time #B5onCWin23.[14]

25. The Babylon 5 Community

The *Babylon 5* fandom took up the cause in spectacular fashion, showing their unadulterated support for a new reboot. #B5onCWin23 trended at number one in the U.S. on September 19, 2022. It even trended at number two in the U.K. (It would have likely reached number one if it hadn't been for the funeral of Queen Elizabeth II taking place on the same day.)

While the Twitter storm did not yield immediate results, it showed that the *Babylon 5* community was still just as passionate and devoted to the show all these years later. From people sharing stories of how innovative the show had been, to expressions of their favorite moments, characters, and episodes, #B5onCWin23 was a massively positive experience that showed that people really wanted the franchise to continue.

Nexstar, Warner Bros. and the CW took note. This was a reboot everyone wanted. There was a whole community of fans excited to see a new *Babylon 5* with J. Michael Straczynski at the helm. But as 2022 came to an end and the 30th anniversary began, news remained scarce. Fans everywhere wondered whether—hoped—*Babylon 5* would find a way to continue.

26

Objects in Motion and the Possibilities to Come

On February 22, 2023, *Babylon 5* celebrated its 30th anniversary. This was a show that—the various TV movies and *Crusade* aside—hadn't been on-screen regularly for almost 25 years, yet people were still talking about it like it had gone off the air yesterday. J. Michael Straczynski was still interacting online, talking *Babylon 5* with fans old and new, while the surviving cast members were still excited to reminisce about their experiences on the show.

Most significantly, fans were still waiting for confirmation of the reboot. Would *Babylon 5* finally return, or would all the behind-the-scenes changes with the CW see this dream come crashing down?

On February 16, 2023, just a week before the show's 30th anniversary, Straczynski offered one final glimmer of hope to his Patreons. The CW had told him that it wasn't a no, and it wasn't a yes, but he had received an explanation of why it had taken so long to hear anything. Straczynski was encouraged by what he had been told and promised to reveal more when he spoke to the network to discuss next steps. For the first time he could "see a glide path in front of us that may be going somewhere pleasant."

This was a glimmer of hope for *Babylon 5* fans. After all this time, no one had said no to a reboot—and why wouldn't they, if they had no intention of picking it up? As the 30th anniversary of the broadcast of *The Gathering* took place, fans were celebrating not only the show they had loved so much, but the distinct possibility of what might come.

It was a hope that sustained those fans as the year progressed. Even the CW's continued cancellation of scripted content, and the strike by the Writers Guild of America in 2023, which put any talk of the reboot on hold, couldn't quash their hopes for the future of the franchise.

It was no longer a question of whether the franchise was dead.

26. Objects in Motion and the Possibilities to Come   219

Instead, fans began to wonder what might materialize as *Babylon 5* headed into its next 30 years.

The Road Home

As it turned out, the reboot wasn't the only thing Straczynski had brewing. The CW reboot of *Babylon 5* was referred by Straczynski as B5 project B. Which meant there was more than one project that he had been developing as the show reached its 30th anniversary. Project A was far more secretive, with vague details known only to Patreons until September 4, 2022, when Straczynski announced to the world on Twitter that it had already been completed.[1]

> The great thing is that the secret B5 project isn't one of those "maybe it'll happen/maybe it won't..." it's done, it has a '23 release date, and it's the closest thing to the original B5 in tone of anything we've done since. As if no time has passed at all. 100% crescent fresh.

The announcement of project A—with the original cast involved—sent the *Babylon 5* fandom into a flurry of excitement. Was this a TV movie like *Legend of the Rangers*, or a series of stories like *The Lost Tales*? Was it an audio book or play, akin to the work Big Finish did with original *Doctor Who* actors? Or perhaps it was a documentary, not unlike *Deep Space Nine*'s *What We Left Behind*, which was released on the 25th anniversary of that show?[2]

The majority of the surviving cast were certainly involved—Peter Jurasik was coy about it when I interviewed him in late 2022. Claudia Christian let slip the potential core cast involvement, when she released a photo from late 2021, reuniting her with Bill Mumy, Peter Jurasik, Pat Tallman, and Bruce Boxleitner. Fans soon assumed this was taken during production of project A, but this was never confirmed by the cast or Straczynski himself.

It wasn't until November 2022, when the showrunner finally gave an indication of when fans would learn more—San Diego Comic-Con 2023—which would take place in the summer of the 30th anniversary year.

But even then, fans did not have to wait long. There were hints from Straczynski that news might come sooner than expected. Patreons were told to prepare for details to appear in May 2023, and to await a second surprise *Babylon 5* project that would "make fans very happy." There were even the first hints at a title. It was no longer project A. It was B5:TRH.

Those details would finally be revealed in May 2023, with the surprise announcement of an animated movie by Straczynski, describing it as the "the most B5-ish of anything we've done since the original show."[3] Furthermore, fans were told that if this animated movie did well, Warner Bros. might even commission more to follow.

This was followed by an official announcement in *The Hollywood Reporter* a week later,[4] confirming that the film, now titled *The Road Home*, would feature the return of Bruce Boxleitner as Sheridan, Claudia Christian as Ivanova, Tracy Scoggins as Lochley, Bill Mumy as Lennier, Peter Jurasik as Londo, and Patricia Tallman as Lyta.

"Travel across the galaxy with John Sheridan as he unexpectedly finds himself transported through multiple timelines and alternate realities in a quest to find his way back home. Along the way he reunites with some familiar faces, while discovering cosmic new revelations about the history, purpose, and meaning of the Universe."

Furthermore, *The Road Home*, a multiverse-spanning event movie, would include new actors taking on the roles of actors that had passed. This was a movie that would feature the likes of G'Kar, Delenn, Franklin, Garibaldi and even—most surprisingly—Sinclair. This was bigger than fans could have imagined. The news set the online community alight.

The wait was almost over. Even if the reboot didn't happen, the *Babylon 5* fandom knew they were getting at least one very special 30th anniversary birthday present. *The Road Home*, released in summer 2023, was the first *Babylon 5* release since *The Lost Tales* in 2007. The story wasn't over yet.

The Next 30 Years of Babylon 5*?*

The return of *Babylon 5* was inevitable. Straczynski had promised that when he told fans of plans to make a big-budget feature film. The original story would no longer continue—project A aside—but a reboot would happen, whether it was on the small screen or the big.

On February 22, 2023, the 30th anniversary of *The Gathering*—and the first broadcast of *Babylon 5*—the world was ready for more of Straczynski's vision. The long twilight struggles—and triumphs—would continue. Even if the CW reboot died or failed, fans were as loyal and as passionate as ever, and the appetite for more *Babylon 5* was stronger than ever, as proven by the reaction to *The Road Home* a few months later.

What would the next 30 years look like for the franchise? The passing of the baton to new actors, a new Captain Sheridan, and a new Babylon 5 space station? Whether Straczynski managed to bring the beloved franchise back or someone else took it on—like Ronald D. Moore with *Battlestar Galactica*—this franchise was rich for reinvention.

26. Objects in Motion and the Possibilities to Come

Babylon 5 had started out as the underdog. A show that many unfairly dismissed as a *Star Trek* clone. It soon became something greater. Its influence on story arcs and long-form storytelling revolutionized television. It opened the door for other science fiction shows to thrive.

It wasn't the most popular science fiction show to come out of the '90s, but it became one of the most important TV shows of the 20th century. What would *Babylon 5* look like in the landscape of 21st-century television? Perhaps it was destined to revolutionize television all over again. Or maybe that big-screen version was destined, as Straczynski has foretold.

As *Babylon 5* looks toward its next 30 years, the future is filled with endless possibilities.

Chapter Notes

The Lurker's Guide to Babylon 5, referenced within these notes, may be found at http://www.midwinter.com/lurk/.

Chapter 1

1. Russell T Davies was a huge fan of American screenwriter Joss Whedon and cites *Buffy the Vampire Slayer* (1997) and *Angel* (1999) as being major inspirations in his reimagining of *Doctor Who* (2005) and the spin-off *Torchwood* (2006).
2. J. Michael Straczynski wanted *Babylon 5* to delve into controversy, dealing with political, social, and religious issues that would give the universe a hard-edged, gritty texture. J. Michael Straczynski, "Paging Jessica Fletcher," *Becoming Superman* (New York: Harper Voyager, 2019), 324.
3. David Fear, "The 50 Best Science Fiction TV Shows of All Time" *Rolling Stone*, March 12, 2020.
4. Jim Vorel, "100 Best Sci-Fi TV Shows of All Time," *Paste Magazine*, September 11, 2018.
5. "100 Best Sci-Fi TV Shows of All Time," Rotten Tomatoes, 2023.
6. Richard Edwards, "Is Babylon 5 secretly the most influential TV show of the past 25 years?" TechRadar, April 25, 2021.
7. J Michael Straczynski, Twitter (https://twitter.com/straczynski).
8. Rec.arts.sf.tv.babylon5.moderated was a moderated Usenet newsgroup that focused on the science fiction television series *Babylon 5* and the works of writer J. Michael Straczynski. It was spun off from its unmoderated version, rec.arts.sf.tv.babylon5, in 1996. The newsgroup counted Straczynski as a frequent contributor and it was among the first internet-based forums where fans interacted directly with a "showrunner."
9. Ryan and Rachel Sliwinski, *Yum Yum*, a podcast where hosts try to rewatch and break down episodes of *Babylon 5* and *Star Trek: Discovery* without having a breakdown themselves.
10. Scott McFarland et al., *Grey 17: A Babylon Podcast*, where a group of *Babylon 5* super fans and complete newbies experience every episode of the landmark series.
11. Benjamin Vigeant, Stephen Winchell, Sean Rose, *The Last Best Babylon 5 Podcast*. Ben is a *Babylon 5* veteran. Steve and Sean have never seen the show before! The three of them are watching *Babylon 5* episode by episode through, starting with the pilot.
12. Baz Greenland, Luke Winch, *A Dream Given Form: A Babylon-5 Podcast* on the We Made This network, covering thematic discussions, actor interviews and episode look-backs.
13. *Medusa Cascade*—a television and film reaction YouTube channel, including first-time reactions to *Babylon 5*.

Chapter 2

1. J. Michael Straczynski, David Bossom, "Foreword," *Creating Babylon* (London: Boxtree Limited, 1996), 4.
2. J. Michael Straczynski, "JMS revisits

Babylon 5 on show's 25th anniversary," *Newsorama*, June 1, 2020.

3. A.J. Black defines mythological story arcs within modern shows like *Lost* and *The X Files* through three key forms: the monomytharc centered on a central character's journey, the divine mytharc focused on a holy of spiritual quest, and cultural mytharc that tackles social and cultural issues through its storytelling. A.J. Black, "Before The Mytharc," "The Divine Mytharc," "The Cultural Mytharc," *Myth-Building in Modern Media* (Jefferson, NC: McFarland, 2020) 22, 56, 90.

4. Joseph Campbell's concept of monomyth (one myth) refers to the theory that sees all mythic narratives as variations of a single great story. He defined the 12 stages of the hero's journey:

1. Ordinary World
2. Call to Adventure
3. Refusal of the Call
4. Meeting the Mentor
5. Crossing the Threshold
6. Tests, Allies, Enemies
7. Approach to the Inmost Cave
8. Ordeal
9. Reward (Seizing the Sword)
10. The Road Back
11. Resurrection
12. Return with the Elixir

Joseph Campbell, *The Hero with a Thousand Faces* (Princeton: Princeton University Press, 1948).

5. German playwright and novelist Gustav Freytag wrote *Die Technik des Dramas*, a definitive study of the five-act dramatic structure, in which he laid out what has come to be known as Freytag's pyramid, in which the plot of a story consists of five parts:

- Exposition (originally called introduction)
- Rise
- Climax
- Return or Fall
- Catastrophe, dénouement, resolution, or revelation

Gustav Freytag, *Die Technik des Dramas*, 1863.

GamesRadar, https://www.gamesradar.com/jms-babylon-5-25-anniversary/.

Chapter 3

1. J. Michael Straczynski, "Re: ATTN JMS: Why Accelerate t" rec.arts.sf.tv.babylon5.moderated (Usenet), January 21, 1995.

2. J. Michael Straczynski, "jms speaks, In The Beginning," *The Lurker's Guide*, 1998.

3. J. Michael Straczynski, "Into the Zone," *Becoming Superman* (New York: Harper Voyager, 2019), 307.

4. J. Michael Straczynski, "Paging Jessica Fletcher," *Becoming Superman* (New York: Harper Voyager, 2019), 316–320.

5. J. Michael Straczynski, "JMS revisits Babylon 5 on show's 25th anniversary," *Newsorama*, June 01, 2020.

Chapter 4

1. James Marsters talked about the original plan to kill Spike off—murdered at the hands of Angelus in order to form a romance with Drusilla. "I know that the original plan was to break Buffy's heart, which is always the plan. Angel and Buffy sleep together, Angel turns evil and he was gonna kill me off and take up with Drusilla so Buffy could get shattered." James Marsters, "How Spike Was Originally Supposed to Die on 'Buffy the Vampire Slayer,'" *Toofab*, November 28, 2017.

2. When the staff writers of *Star Trek: Deep Space Nine* came up with the idea that the third season episode "Defiant" would establish a military build-up which the Obsidian Order was involved in and which was so mysterious that even Cardassia's Central Command had no intel on it, the writers likewise had no idea it would lead to a battle later the same season. "We had a vague idea of a first strike, but I don't think we knew more than that…. It wasn't until the writers were plotting the story for subsequent third season episode 'Improbable Cause' that they realized they could make the military escalation be in preparation for a pre-emptive attack by not only the Obsidian Order but also the Tal Shiar against the Dominion. However, even at this point, the actual battle itself wasn't planned; in fact, the Cardassians were to have been halted in their plans to combat the Dominion, due to Garak essentially blackmailing Tain." Terry J. Erdmann,

Paula Block, René Echevarria, "Improbable Cause," *Star Trek: Deep Space Nine Companion* (New York: Pocket Books, 2000), 226–228.

3. J. Michael Straczynski, "JMS revisits Babylon 5 on show's 25th anniversary," *Newsorama*, June 1, 2020.

4. J. Michael Straczynski, *Babylon 5: The Scripts of J. Michael Straczynski, Vol 15* (NJ: Synthetic Worlds, 2008).

Chapter 5

1. Peter Jurasik won Universe Reader's Choice Award Best Supporting Actor in a Genre TV Series for Londo Mollari in *Babylon 5* in 1996.

2. Peter Jurasik guest-starred in the 18th episode of *Scarecrow and Mrs. King*, "Wrong Number," alongside Bruce Boxleitner in 1986.

Chapter 6

1. J. Michael Straczynski, "Paging Jessica Fletcher," *Becoming Superman* (New York: Harper Voyager, 2019), 307, 311–314, 321–322.

2. The "revelations" from Steven Hopstaken about Paramount using *Babylon 5* material for *Star Trek: Deep Space Nine* can be found in the comments thread of the following article: Jason Shankel, "The Strange, Secret Evolution of Babylon 5," *Io9*, February 21, 2013.

3. Christopher Brooker, *The Seven Basic Plots: Why We Tell Stories* (New York: Continuum International Publishing Group Ltd, 2004).

- Overcoming the monster: The protagonist sets out to defeat an antagonistic force (often evil) that threatens the protagonist and/or protagonist's homeland.
- Rags to riches: The poor protagonist acquires power, wealth, and/or a mate, loses it all and gains it back, growing as a person as a result.
- The quest: The protagonist and companions set out to acquire an important object or to get to a location. They face temptations and other obstacles along the way.
- Voyage and return: The protagonist goes to a strange land and, after overcoming the threats it poses or learning important lessons unique to that location, they return with experience.
- Comedy: Light and humorous character with a happy or cheerful ending; a dramatic work in which the central motif is the triumph over adverse circumstance, resulting in a successful or happy conclusion.
- Tragedy: The protagonist is a hero with a major character flaw or great mistake which is ultimately their undoing. Their unfortunate end evokes pity at their folly and the fall of a fundamentally good character.
- Rebirth: An event forces the main character to change their ways and often become a better individual.

4. Straczynski and Bryce Zabel wrote a 14-page treatment for *Star Trek: Re-Boot the Universe* in 2004. Due to the development of the "Kelvin" *Star Trek* movie reboot, this was never pitched to Paramount.

Chapter 7

1. Only the second season of *Star Trek: The Next Generation* was unable to produce 26 episodes, the result of the 1988 strike by the Writers Guild of America. Many unused scripts from *Star Trek* and the abandoned *Star Trek: Phase II* series were used, and 22 episodes were produced.

2. J. Michael Straczynski, "Paging Jessica Fletcher," *Becoming Superman* (New York: Harper Voyager, 2019), 309.

3. "How 24 Commodore Amigas helped create the Babylon 5's effects shots," *Generation Amiga*, August 30, 2020.

4. J. Michael Straczynski, "Re: Tolkien references," *The Lurker's Guide*, March 19, 1995.

5. J. Michael Straczynski talked about the concept of using Babylon as the name of the station in the DVD commentary for season one episode "Chrysalis."

Chapter 8

1. *The Wild West* was an Emmy-nominated five-part documentary series that helped launch PTEN. It was narrated by Jack Lemmon and featured an

impressive cast, including Helen Hunt, Adrienne Barbeau, Tim Curry, and Edward James Olmos.

2. *Time Trax* was one of two main shows picked up by PTEN to launch the network. It was based around a police officer sent two centuries into the past to track criminals that had escaped through time. It first aired on January 20, 1993, and ran for two seasons.

3. *Star Trek: Voyager* was the flagship show to launch UPN in 1995.

4. Many of the 1997–99 Prime Time Invasion promos are archived on YouTube. Due to transfers from VHS to DVD-R to video files, some of them have a bit of a blocky/"Venetian blind" effect that wasn't part of the original promos as aired. Earl Green, "WACY-TV UPN 32 Prime Time Invasion Pre Launch :60," *Youtube*, 1997.

5. I spoke to Stephen Hopstaken (presumably the same Stephen who commented on the "Strange, Secret Evolution of Babylon 5" article from *Io9*, though I was unable to confirm). He was a copywriter for Warner Bros and involved in the marketing of *Babylon 5* to overseas networks. He summarized the efforts required to sell the show and the appetite for science-fiction television globally.

6. The press kit for *Babylon 5* was released prior to the production and release of *The Gathering*; in fact, the casting had yet to be completed and many of the character descriptions in the kit would be changed before the pilot aired.

Chapter 9

1. J. Michael Straczynski opened up about Michael O'Hare's battle with mental illness following the actor's death, during an interview with Karen Herman. This took place prior to Straczynski telling O'Hare's story to the world at a fan convention in Phoenix in 2013. J. Michael Straczynski, Karen Herman, "Interview with J. Michael Straczynski, Writer / Show Creator—Chapter 2," Television Academy Foundation, May 15, 2013.

2. J. Michael Straczynski, Doug Netter and John Copeland spent almost five years pitching *Babylon 5* to every network, studio and production company in town, only to be told that there was no room for a space-based science fiction series other than *Star Trek*. J. Michael Straczynski, "Paging Jessica Fletcher," *Becoming Superman* (New York: Harper Voyager, 2019), 307.

3. J. Michael Straczynski discusses the narrative decision to replace Sinclair with Sheridan for season two of *Babylon 5*. This was the public reason for O'Hare's departure, due to the secrecy surrounding the actor's mental health struggles. J. Michael Straczynski, David Bossom, "A Vision of Babylon," *Creating Babylon* (London: Boxtree Limited, 1996), 28–29.

4. J. Michael Straczynski cited contractual differences between Patricia Tallman's agent and Warner Bros as the reason for her departure after *The Gathering*. J. Michael Straczynski, "Boarding Babylon," *Becoming Superman* (New York: Harper Voyager, 2019), 323.

5. I interviewed Patricia Tallman about her time on *Babylon 5* on my podcast *A Dream Given Form* for the We Made This Network in February 2022. The episode was released in April 2022. When I asked her about not returning after *The Gathering*, her answer took me by surprise. Tallman now feels free to discuss the real reason; a producer who she would not sleep with and who had her fired from the show.

6. J. Michael Straczynski, "The Christmas Ambush," *Becoming Superman* (New York: Harper Voyager, 2019), 333–334.

Chapter 10

1. J. Michael Straczynski responds to a tweet in May 26, 2018, celebrating that Delenn was a female ambassador in a position of power and his plan to bring the first transgender character to sci-fi.

2. J. Michael Straczynski, "jms speaks, Divided Loyalties," *The Lurker's Guide*, 1998.

Chapter 11

1. My cohost Luke Winch and I interviewed Marshall Teague about his time on *Babylon 5* on my podcast *A Dream Given Form* for the We Made This network in October 2022. The episode was released in October 2022.

2. "Infection" was the first regular

episode of *Babylon 5* filmed after the show was picked up for a full first season. It was broadcast fourth in the season one running order.

3. Marshall Teague played alien Haluk in the 23rd episode of *Star Trek: Voyager* season three, "Distant Origin."

4. Marshall Teague played alien Temo'Zuma in the third episode *of Star Trek: Deep Space Nine* season four, "Hippocratic Oath."

5. Marshall Teague played Jimmy in 1989's *Roadhouse*, starring Patrick Swayze. The actors became firm friends thereafter and Marshall still has a voicemail that Swayze sent a week before he died.

6. Marshall Teague appeared in eight episodes of *Walker, Texas Ranger*. He also became firm friends with the series' star, Chuck Norris.

Chapter 12

1. The alternate 1988 pilot of *The Gathering* is the original version Straczynski shopped to Warner Bros. when he was trying to get the series picked up. This version was contained in *The Scripts of J. Michael Straczynski Volume 1*. Here's what he said about the original pilot:

"When we went to sell *Babylon 5*, I wrote a pilot screenplay to take around. When we made the deal, the notes process began...and the script went through considerable changes. But this is the ORIGINAL draft, the one only seen by the studio and the other producers on the show.

"What's different? How about Garibaldi trying to get hold of his dying father back on Mars...how about a shape-shifter instead of a Minbari assassin with a changeling net... Londo as a part-time pick-pocket...Dr. Chakri Mendak instead of Dr. Kyle... new scenes between Lyta and Laurel, Delenn and others that were later cut...a LOT more character scenes with Sinclair and Garibaldi...a discovery about Delenn's life stone and what that means to the Minbari...where Sinclair is NOT put on trial, but finds a whole different and more interesting way to solve the mystery of Kosh's assailant...and the introduction of Kosh's life-mate, Velana, who plays a very important role in the script. (Didn't know Vorlons had life-mates, did you?)

"This script is HUGELY different from the one we filmed—funnier in places, with more character moments—and it has been kept under lock and key all this time. Now, for the first time, it will has been officially released in the first volume of this 15 volume set."

J. Michael Straczynski, *The Scripts of J. Michael Straczynski Volume 1* (NJ: Synthetic Worlds Ltd, October 2005).

2. The 1992 version of *The Gathering* had an alternative introduction to Commander Sinclair in the "pre-title sequence," featuring him saving a man from a deadly encounter with an alien woman who eats her mates after sex and an extended meeting with new telepath Lyta Alexander. Garibaldi would identifying a man smuggling in Dust, the drug that would eventually appear in season three's "Dust" and allow non-telepaths to enter other people's minds. J. Michael Straczynski, "The Gathering," *Babylon 5: All My Words Volume 1* (NJ: Synthetic Worlds, December 2019).

3. Terry Jones compiled the Babylon 5 Historical Database, scouring each episode (and other B5 media) to pick out references to events past and future, as well as establishing dates for events within the show itself where possible—including a presentation of the episode order based on when they occurred chronologically.

This was published in *The Official* Babylon 5 *Magazine*, and again later in the book *Across Time and Space*. The latter also included a less in-depth chronology compiled independently by I. Marc Carlson, with the authorization of J. Michael Straczynski. I interviewed Terry Jones about the Babylon 5 Historical Database for my *Babylon 5* podcast *A Dream Given Form* in 2023.

4. During production of the first season, J. Michael Straczynski told *Cinefantastique* magazine that had an idea for an episode where Takashima returns to Babylon 5 from the Rim, and something was chasing her. The teaser would involve a damaged ship that the crew towed into the docking bay. The ship doors would open to reveal a bloody Takashima.

Chapter 14

1. J. Michael Straczynski, "The Christmas Ambush," *Becoming Superman* (New York: Harper Voyager, 2019), 337–338.
2. "Master And Slave Of 'Babylon 5,'" *Newsweek*, June 8, 1997.
3. Yasmin Alibhai-Brown, "We Remainers have become the silenced people of Britain," *The Independent*, December 15, 2020.
4. Clare Foges, "Don't bet on a hard winter toppling Boris," *The Times*, October 11, 2021.
5. J. Michael Straczynski, "JMS revisits Babylon 5 on show's 25th anniversary," *Newsorama*, June 1, 2020.

Chapter 15

1. Jane Killick, J. Michael Straczynski, *Babylon 5 Season by Season #4: No Surrender, No Retreat* (London: Boxtree, 1998).
2. *Ibid*.

Chapter 16

1. "TNT comes to the rescue of sci-fi series 'Babylon 5,'" *Deseret News*, July 04, 1997
2. A summary of the responses from J. Michael Straczynski and Claudia Christian that break down the two sides of Ivanova's departure from the show. J. Michael Straczynski, Claudia Christian, "About Claudia Christian's Departure," *The Lurker's Guide*, July 19–20, 1997.
3. *Variety* ran a gossip column in July 1997, claiming that Claudia Christian had already decided to leave *Babylon 5*. This was released during the Wolf 359 con and took the cast and crew by surprise, leading to Christian's departure from *Babylon 5*.

Chapter 17

1. I interviewed Patricia Tallman about her time on *Babylon 5* on my podcast *A Dream Given Form* for the We Made This network in February 2022. The episode was released in April 2022. I wasn't expecting the answer she gave me, when I asked her about not returning after *The Gathering*. Tallman now feels free to discuss the real reason: she refused to sleep with a producer, who then had her fired from the show.
2. Patricia Tallman established B5 Events in 2020 as a way to connect with fans, share insights with other *Babylon 5* actors, and even provide merchandise from the show.
3. Patricia Tallman created Quest Retreats to create global excursions, from Hawaii to New Zealand, and Scotland in 2022. Patricia described Quest Retreats as a way "to bring people together who are like me and create a fantastic life experience for us all."

Chapter 18

1. J. Michael Straczynski's comments on the TNT appraisal of *In the Beginning*. J. Michael Straczynski, *In the Beginning*, *The Lurker's Guide*, 1998.
2. *Ibid*.
3. J. Michael Straczynski, *Thirdspace*, *The Lurker's Guide*, 1998.
4. *Ibid*.
5. The original TNT publicity for upcoming TV movie *River of Souls*—TNT press release, March 23, 1998.
6. Ian McShane, Beverley Wedick, "Ian McShane: You Ask the Questions," *The Independent*, September 16, 2004.
7. J. Michael Straczynski, *A Call to Arms*, *The Lurker's Guide*, 1999.

Chapter 19

1. J. Michael Straczynski, "The Christmas Ambush," *Becoming Superman* (New York: Harper Voyager, 2019), 349–350.
2. In the DVD commentary for *A Call to Arms*, Straczynski stated that the Drakh plague would've been solved and dealt with by the midway point of *Crusade* season 2, in favor of other story arcs.
3. J. Michael Straczynski, "The Christmas Ambush," *Becoming Superman* (New York: Harper Voyager, 2019), 350–353.
4. Glen Oliver, "Crisis on Babylon 5: CRUSADE," Aint It Cool News, August 14, 1998.
5. Straczynski formally broke the news of *Crusade's* cancellation, noting that the Sci-Fi Channel had been crunching

numbers for weeks, trying to make the deal work with WB, but didn't have room in their budget. He also thanked fans and confirmed that TNT would still air the 13 episodes produced. J. Michael Straczynski, "from jms re: Crusade," rec.arts.sf.tv.babylon5.moderated (Usenet), February 26, 1999.

6. Details on the unfilmed *Crusade* scripts, season one story outlines, and other details about the show beyond its cancellation were laid out in J. Michael Straczynski, Fiona Avery, Peter Woodward, Jason Davis, *Crusade: Other Voices, Volumes 1 and 2* (NJ: Synthetic Worlds, 2011).

7. Grey Sector has published detailed analysis of *Crusade*, and the planned stories that would have followed the show's cancellation, using *Crusade: Other Voices, Volumes 1 and 2* as its main source. Grey Sector: Occasional musings on Babylon 5, a twenty-year-old TV show, 2014–2022, https://greysector.wordpress.com/.

8. In 2001, the Sci-Fi Channel aired *Crusade* for the first time since its original broadcast on TNT. They asked Joe Straczynski to select his preferred viewing order for the broadcast. He created one that has some continuity errors—particularly the costumes switching back and forth—but felt that the order would do the most justice to the overall story.

9. The Babylon Project (https://babylon5.fandom.com/wiki/Main_Page) suggests a whole number of viewing orders for *Babylon 5* and *Crusade*, including the chronological, JMS-recommended and continuity versions. "Viewing Order," The Babylon Project.

Chapter 20

1. J. Michael Straczynski talked about his difficulties as showrunner on Showtime's *Jeremiah*, an experience he described as being far worse than with TNT on *Crusade*, with a disconnect between Showtime and MGM on the show's direction. He did not allude to anything further for fear of legal repercussions. J. Michael Straczynski, "Lost in the Tall Grass with Jeremiah," *Becoming Superman* (New York: Harper Voyager, 2019), 372.

2. J. Michael Straczynski, "Swingin' with Spider-Man," *Becoming Superman* (New York: Harper Voyager, 2019), 360–363.

3. Straczynski talked about the broad details of the show as it went into production and aired but remained tight-lipped on where a TV series of *The Legend of the Rangers* would go if it were picked up for a full series. J. Michael Straczynski, "Legend of the Rangers," *The Lurker's Guide*, 2002.

Chapter 21

1. In 1997, Straczynski acknowledged the potential for a "sixth season" of *Babylon 5* as an anthology series, if he was ever to be offered it by TNT. J. Michael Straczynski, "ATTN JMS: Question regarding a 6th season," rec.arts.sf.tv.babylon5.moderated (Usenet), September 29, 1997.

2. "Our Selena Is Dying" was written for the second season of *The Twilight Zone* reboot in the late '90s. Rod Serling outlined the story just prior to his death, the only example of this happening in a *The Twilight Zone* reboot. Citing Serling as one of his icons, J. Michael Straczynski would write the teleplay.

3. J. Michael Straczynski talked about his vision for the project and his discussions with the cast:

> "Ideally, I'd like to rotate through the whole cast, preferably in a thematic fashion. One episode would concern itself with issues of command, and thus feature Sheridan, Lochley and Garibaldi; another would concern Psi Corps, and we'd have Lyta, Bester, and someone else; another would be a strong Minbari theme, so we'd have Delenn, Lennier and Sheridan (in his role as head of the Interstellar Alliance); a Centauri sequence with Londo, Vir and someone else; and we'd mix it up a bit."

J. Michael Straczynski, "Babylon 5 is back!", *Dreamwatch Magazine*, September 2006.

4. Aint It Cool News broke down the news of J. Michael Straczynski's *The Lost Tales* announcement at the 2006 San Diego Comic Con, along with Ron Howard looking to pick up his script for *The Changeling* and his comics work for Marvel. Joseph

Merrick, "Babylon 5 is back!", Aint it Cool News, July 24, 2006.

    5. The Warner Bros. press release for the DVD release of *The Lost Tales: Voices in the Dark* promised stunning new visual effects and a thrilling, original made-for-video movie in the long-running *Babylon 5* franchise. It did not market it as volume one. Gord Lacey, "Babylon 5—'The Lost Tales' press release," *TV Shows on DVD*, July 31, 2007.

    6. At New York Comic Con in February 2007, J. Michael Straczynski showed his video blog from the set of *The Lost Tales: Voices in the Dark* and was asked about the potential of future installments. He teased a possible Telepath War storyline in the future and confirmed that if the *Lost Tales* release was successful, a follow-up could follow in "early 2008 at the earliest." Brian Warmoth, "[NYCC] STRACZYNSKI ON STRACZYNSKI," *Wizard Universe*, February 23, 2007.

    7. The IGN review for *The Lost Tales: Voices in the Dark* gave the stories 5/10, video and presentation 6/10, audio and languages 7/10 and the extras and packaging a 4/10. It scored an overall rating of 6/10. Scott Collura, "Babylon 5: The Lost Tales," IGN, August 7, 2007.

    8. The Aint It Cool review of *The Lost Tales: Voices in the Dark* was largely positive, praising the production values, but noting it was for the fans only. Hercules, "Gaspode Has Our First Review Of BABYLON 5: THE LOST TALES!!," Aint it Cool News, July 20, 2007.

    9. Between November 5, 2007, and February 12, 2008, all 12,000 film and television screenwriters of the American labor unions Writers Guild of America East (WGAE) and Writers Guild of America West (WGAW) went on strike over pay. The majority of television production in the U.S. ground to a halt and the majority of seasons of TV shows were cut short. This impacted any writer who was a member of the WGA and delayed any plans for a follow-up to *The Lost Tales: Voices in the Dark*.

    10. Tim Callender, Summer Brooks, Jeffrey Willerth, Peter Jurasik, "Babylon Podcast #39: Interview with Peter Jurasik," *The Babylon Podcast*, November 1, 2006.

    11. In July 2008, J. Michael Straczynski commented on the rec.arts.sf.tv.babylon5.moderated forum in response to potential questions about a new *Babylon 5* announcement at San Diego Comic Con. He confirmed that he would not be making further *The Lost Tales*, as the budget Warner Bros would provide would not do the stories justice. The only *Babylon 5* project he would commit to from now on would be a full, theatrical release. J. Michael Straczynski "JMS at SDCC—Who's going?" rec.arts.sf.tv.babylon5 (Usenet), July 14, 2008.

Chapter 22

    1. At the height of its popularity, a feature film of *The X-Files* TV series was released in theaters. Set between seasons five and six of the show, *The X-Files: Fight the Future* brought Mulder and Scully to the big screen in the summer of 1998.

    2. *Lost in Space* was a 1998 film reboot of the TV series from New Line Cinema. It was panned critically on its release.

    3. Also released in 1998, *The Avengers* was a film reboot of the '60s sci-fi spy series and was also panned critically on its release.

    4. *Mighty Morphin Power Rangers: The Movie* was released in 1995, between the second and third seasons of the show, tapping into its popularity. It was received critically by young fans and far exceeded its budget in terms of box office takings.

    5. J. Michael Straczynski, *Artifacts From Beyond The Rim* (NJ: Synthetic Worlds, 2010).

    6. *Ibid*.

    7. In response to a 1998 rumor on the Coming Attractions B5 page, J. Michael Straczynski confirmed on *The Lurker's Guide*:

> "No posters had been created. Nor have we spoken to WB about any movie concept concerning the Vorlons' impact on Earth." He also stated: "There were some preliminary discussions about a possible storyline (none of which has been accurately reported anywhere, that info is still held only by us), but it's my feeling that a) it's best to concentrate on getting *Crusade* right first, and b) I'm loathe to compete with the new Star Wars movies, and would rather wait until that's all done, so we can also take advantage of new technologies to make the show. Simply

put...I'm in no hurry. I'd rather get it right than get it done on Tuesday."

J. Michael Straczynski, "jms speaks, The Memory of Shadows," *The Lurker's Guide*, November 21, 1998.

8. In 1998, the internet was abuzz with the anticipated release of a brand-new *Star Wars* movie—the first since 1983's *Return of the Jedi*. *The Phantom Menace* was released in May 1999 in the U.S. and became the highest-grossing movie of the year.

9. The TV movies script book features a treatment from Straczynski for *Wars of the Mind*, a *Babylon 5* feature film, focused on the Telepath War. J. Michael Straczynski, *Artifacts from Beyond the Rim* (NJ: Synthetic Worlds, 2010).

10. "On the B5 front, there has been something of rather substantial proportion that's finally gone from talk to money, such that I'm now working frantically to meet some deadlines, but there's nothing I can say about this until after January 15th, probably closer to the end of that month.

"The only thing I can say is that phase one of the new project is a go, hence the furious writing schedule at this end of things, which is why I've been silent until deciding to kick up some dust on the political discussion. I've been writing my little brains out.

I know the immediate result of this will be speculation, but if we could keep that to a low roar on the nets to avoid precluding anything, that would be a wonderfulness. But trust me: I wouldn't go on about something in this way if it wasn't a significant development. Just trust me on this one for a bit and hold fire until further word.

"(Long-time followers of the various news groups know that an eep means that something significant has happened, but that I can't talk about it... the eep is just a way of saying, on the QT, that something has, indeed, happened and it's real, not just speculation or maybe-gonna-happens. So on that basis, you may consider this an eep.)"

He would confirm that the script for *The Memory of Shadows* was written on January 29, 2004. J. Michael Straczynski, "jms speaks, The Memory of Shadows," *The Lurker's Guide*, November 30, 2003.

11. IGN responding to fan outrage that Warner Bros wanted to recast some of the *Babylon 5* actors for *The Memory of Shadows*. KJB, "Babylon 5 Movie Re-Casting?" IGN, December 18, 2004.

12. J. Michael Straczynski, *JMS News*, October 2004.

13. J. Michael Straczynski, *JMS News*, January 30, 2005.

14. J. Michael Straczynski, *JMS News*, February 25, 2005.

15. Rich Drees, "SDCC: STRACZYNSKI Writing BABYLON 5 Film Next Year, Will Produce With Or Without Warner Brothers Help," *Film Buff Online*, July 28, 2014.

16. Rich Drees, "SDCC 2016: Straczynski's BABYLON 5 Film Pushed Back, RISING STARS Officially Announced," *Film Buff Online*, July 25, 2016.

Chapter 24

1. Big Finish Productions holds the rights to produce stories set in the *Doctor Who* universe spanning the classic era of 1963–1989, the Eighth Doctor (but not the TV movie) and modern *Doctor Who*, up to the current era on television. Original actors have reprised their roles for new stories set during their eras on the show, including former Doctors Tom Baker, Peter Davison, Colin Baker, Sylvester McCoy, Paul McGann, Christopher Eccleston and David Tennant.

2. Following the conclusion of the original *Star Wars* trilogy in 1983, multiple books were released, kick-started primarily by Timothy Zahn's *Heir to the Empire* trilogy. These stories continued the adventures of Han, Luke, Leia and other *Star Wars* characters, spanning more than 20 years beyond the original trilogy.

With the acquisition of Lucasfilm by Disney in 2012, this timeline was no longer considered the official continuation of the *Star Wars* story after *Return of the Jedi*. These books were rebranded as the *Star Wars Legends* series.

3. Over 850 books, comics and other stories have been published in the *Star Trek* universe, expanding on the events of the original series and *The Next Generation*, *Deep Space Nine*, *Voyager*, *Enterprise* and other in-universe series such as the *New Frontier* books. In particular, the

relaunch series continued the stories of the *Enterprise* E, *Deep Space Nine* and *Voyager* crews after the series and films ended. These continued all the way up to 2017.

With the release of *Star Trek: Picard* in 2020, this continuation of the *Star Trek* universe was relegated to an alternate timeline, and official tie-ins have since been released that tie directly to the events of the sequel series.

4. Mary Shelley has encountered the Doctor on more than one occasion and in the same location. The Eighth Doctor series had the Doctor encounter Mary Shelley and a Cyberman that inspired *Frankenstein* at the Villa Diodati and bring her onboard the TARDIS as a companion (Big Finish's "The Silver Turk," released in 2011). The 10th Doctor also met her in later life in a *Doctor Who* comic ("The Creative Spark," 2008). And on TV, the 13th Doctor met Mary Shelley and the Lone Cyberman at the Villa Diodati ("The Haunting of Villa Diodati," 2020). While attempt have been made to tie into TV continuity at Big Finish, "The Haunting of Villa Diodati" rendered any previous attempt at canon null and void.

5. On the novel *Personal Agendas*, J. Michael Straczynski didn't get the actual manuscript until it was too late to do anything short of commissioning a full rewrite, which they wouldn't do. J. Michael Straczynski, "jms speaks, Personal Agendas," *The Lurker's Guide*, 1997.

6. On the novel *Blood Oath*, J. Michael Straczynski noted that the fact that the Narn ship had artificial gravity must have slipped past him in the reviewing of the book. J. Michael Straczynski, "jms speaks, Blood Oath," *The Lurker's Guide*, 1995.

7. On the novel *Clark's Law*, J. Michael Straczynski responded to the fact that Lyta was written as being deaf. "I don't know how that would've gotten past me...I don't recall seeing that in the draft...either I was tired when reading, or it was added later." J. Michael Straczynski, "jms speaks, Clark's Law," *The Lurker's Guide*, 1996.

8. J. Michael Straczynski, "jms speaks, "The Touch of Your Shadow, The Whisper of Your Name," *The Lurker's Guide*, 1996.

9. J. Michael Straczynski, *JMS News*, June 9, 1997.

10. J. Michael Straczynski, "jms speaks, "Dark Genesis: The Birth of the Psi Corps" *The Lurker's Guide*, 1998.

11. "The 2004 ENnie Awards," Ennie Awards History, 2004.

Chapter 25

1. Dustin Pinney, "12 Best Shows Like Andor That Fans Should Check Out," *Looper*, September 23, 2022.

2. Ross Johnson, "10 Morally Grey Sci-Fi Shows to Watch After 'Andor'," *Lifehacker*, November 30, 2022.

3. Daniel Cooper, "'Babylon 5 Remastered' now available to buy, or stream on HBO Max," *Engadget*, January 26, 2021.

4. J. Michael Straczynski created a Patreon in 2020 in order to share behind-the-scenes looks at projects old, new and yet to come, covering everything from *Babylon 5* to *Jeremiah*, *Sense8* and the many movies and comics that have already been created, to brand new TV series, film projects, audio dramas and animation projects currently on the boards that will be coming out.

5. Baz Greenland, Luke Winch, *A Dream Given Form: A Babylon-5 Podcast* on the We Made This network.

6. Denise Petski, "'Babylon 5' Series Reboot From J. Michael Straczynski In Works At the CW," *Deadline*, September 27, 2021.

7. J. Michael Straczynski, Twitter, September 27, 2021.

8. Joe Flint, "WarnerMedia and ViacomCBS Are Exploring Possible Sale of CW Network," *The Wall Street Journal*, January 5, 2022.

9. Peter White, "'Walker: Independence,' 'The Winchesters' & 'Gotham Knights' Land Pilot Orders at the CW," *Deadline*, February 3, 2022.

10. J. Michael Straczynski, "B5 CW News," Patreon, February 03 2022.

11. The cancellation of *Legends of Tomorrow* at the CW met with the biggest uproar and the #SavelegendsofTomorrow campaign, a sign that significant changes were afoot at the network. Ellise Shafer, "'DC's Legends of Tomorrow' Canceled After Seven Seasons at CW," *Variety*, April 29, 2022.

12. Nellie Andreeva, "'Babylon 5' Reboot Still "Very Much In Active Development," The CW CEO Confirms," *Deadline*, May 19, 2022.

13. Alex Weprin, Lesley Goldberg,

"Local TV Giant Nexstar Seals Deal to Buy 75 Percent Stake in The CW, Reshaping Broadcast Landscape," *The Hollywood Reporter*, August 15, 2022.

14. J. Michael Straczynski, Twitter, September 18, 2022.

Chapter 26

1. On August 30, 2022, J. Michael Straczynski publicized his Patreon on Twitter and hinted at a secret B5 project that has been completed for a '23 release. He followed this up with the Twitter announcement on September 04, 2022. J. Michael Straczynski, Twitter, September 4, 2022.

2. *What We Left Behind—Looking Back at Star Trek: Deep Space Nine* is a documentary, taking a retrospective look at *Deep Space Nine*, its influence, meaning, and legacy. The documentary was produced by 455 Films and directed by Ira Steven Behr and David Zappone. Shout! Studios released the film. It was first released to fans during the 25th anniversary of the show at Destination *Star Trek* in Birmingham, U.K.

3. J. Michael Straczynski revealed the first details of a Babylon 5 animated movie on Twitter on May 3, 2023.

> "BABYLON 5 ANIMATED MOVIE coming from Warner Bros. Animation & WB Home Entertainment! Classic B5: raucous, heartfelt, nonstop, a ton of fun through time and space & a love letter to the fans. Movie title, release date and other details coming one week from today. #B5AnimatedMovie."

4. Aaron Couch, "'Babylon 5: The Road Home' Voice Cast Unveiled," *The Hollywood Reporter*, May 10, 2023.

Bibliography

Alibhai-Brown, Yasmin. "We Remainers have become the silenced people of Britain." *The Independent,* December 15, 2020.
Andreeva, Nellie. "'Babylon 5' Reboot Still 'Very Much In Active Development,' The CW CEO Confirms." *Deadline,* May 19, 2022.
Avery, Fiona, Jason Davis, J. Michael Straczynski, and Peter Woodward. *Crusade: Other Voices, Volumes 1 and 2.* NJ: Synthetic Worlds, 2011.
Black, A.J. *Myth-Building in Modern Media.* Jefferson, NC: McFarland, 2020.
Block, Paula, René Echevarria, and Terry J. Erdmann. *Star Trek: Deep Space Nine Companion.* New York: Pocket Books, 2000.
Bossom, David, and J. Michael Straczynski. *Creating Babylon.* London: Boxtree Limited, 1996.
Brooker, Christopher. *The Seven Basic Plots: Why We Tell Stories.* New York: Continuum International Publishing Group Ltd, 2004.
Brooks, Summer, Tim Callender, Peter Jurasik, and Jeffrey Willerth. "Babylon Podcast #39: Interview with Peter Jurasik." *The Babylon Podcast.* November 1, 2006.
Campbell, Joseph. *The Hero with a Thousand Faces.* Princeton: Princeton University Press, 1948.
Christian, Claudia, and J. Michael Straczynski. "About Claudia Christian's Departure." *The Lurker's Guide,* July 19–20, 1997.
Collura, Scott. "Babylon 5: The Lost Tales." *IGN.* August 7, 2007.
Cooper, Daniel. "'Babylon 5 Remastered' now available to buy, or stream on HBO Max." *Engadget,* January 26, 2021.
Couch, Aaron, "'Babylon 5: The Road Home' Voice Cast Unveiled," *The Hollywood Reporter,* May 10, 2023.
Drees, Rich. "SDCC 2016: Straczynski's BABYLON 5 Film Pushed Back, RISING STARS Officially Announced." *Film Buff Online,* July 25, 2016.
Drees, Rich. "SDCC: STRACZYNSKI Writing BABYLON 5 Film Next Year, Will Produce With Or Without Warner Brothers Help." *Film Buff Online,* July 28, 2014.
Edwards, Richard. "Is Babylon 5 secretly the most influential TV show of the past 25 years?" *Tech Radar,* April 25, 2021.
Fear, David. "The 50 Best Science Fiction TV Shows of All Time." *Rolling Stone,* March 12, 2020.
Flint, Joe. "WarnerMedia and ViacomCBS Are Exploring Possible Sale of CW Network." *The Wall Street Journal,* January 5, 2022.
Foges, Clare. "Don't bet on a hard winter toppling Boris." *The Times* (London), October 11, 2021.
Freytag, Gustav, *Die Technik des Dramas,* 1863.
Goldberg, Lesley, and Alex Weprin. "Local TV Giant Nexstar Seals Deal to Buy 75 Percent Stake in The CW, Reshaping Broadcast Landscape." *The Hollywood Reporter,* August 15, 2022.
Green, Earl. "WACY-TV UPN 32 Prime Time Invasion Pre Launch :60," YouTube, 1997.
Greenland, Baz, and Luke Winch. *A Dream Given Form: A Babylon-5 Podcast*

Grey Sector: Occasional musings on Babylon 5, a twenty-year-old TV show (blog), 2014–2022.
Hercules. "Gaspode Has Our First Review Of BABYLON 5: THE LOST TALES!!" Aint it Cool News. July 20, 2007.
Herman, Karen, and J. Michael Straczynski. "Interview with J. Michael Straczynski, Writer / Show Creator—Chapter 2," *Television Academy Foundation*. May 15, 2013.
"How 24 Commodore Amigas helped create the Babylon 5's effects shots." Generation Amiga, August 30, 2020.
Johnson, Ross. "10 Morally Grey Sci-Fi Shows to Watch After 'Andor.'" Lifehacker, November 30, 2022.
Killick, Jane, and J. Michael Straczynski. *Babylon 5 Season by Season #4: No Surrender, No Retreat*. London: Boxtree paperback, 1998.
KJB. "Babylon 5 Movie Re-Casting?" IGN, December 18, 2004.
Lacey Gord. "Babylon 5—'The Lost Tales' press release." *TV Shows on DVD*. July 31, 2007.
"Master And Slave Of 'Babylon 5.'" *Newsweek*, June 8, 1997.
Marsters, James. "How Spike Was Originally Supposed to Die on 'Buffy the Vampire Slayer.'" *Toofab*, November 28, 2017.
McFarland, Scott, et al. *Grey 17: A Babylon Podcast*.
McShane, Ian, and Beverley Wedick. "Ian McShane: You Ask the Questions." *The Independent*, September 16, 2004.
Medusa Cascade—YouTube channel.
Merrick, Joseph. "Babylon 5 is back!" Aint It Cool News, July 24, 2006.
Oliver, Glen. "Crisis on Babylon 5: CRUSADE." Aint It Cool News, August 14, 1998.
"100 Best Sci-Fi TV Shows of All Time.". Rotten Tomatoes, 2023.
Petski, Denise. "'Babylon 5' Series Reboot From J. Michael Straczynski In Works At the CW." *Deadline*, September 27, 2021.
Pinney, Dustin. "12 Best Shows Like Andor That Fans Should Check Out." *Looper*, September 23, 2022.
Rose, Sean, Benjamin Vigeant, and Stephen Winchell. *The Last Best Babylon 5 Podcast*.
Shafer, Ellise. "'DC's Legends of Tomorrow' Canceled After Seven Seasons at CW." *Variety*, April 29, 2022.
Shankel, Jason. "The Strange, Secret Evolution of Babylon 5." *Io9*, February 21, 2013.
Sliwinski, Ryan and Rachel. *Yum Yum* podcast.
Straczynski, J. Michael. *Artifacts From Beyond The Rim*. NJ: Synthetic Worlds, 2010.
Straczynski, J. Michael. "Babylon 5 is back!" *Dreamwatch Magazine*. September 2006.
Straczynski, J. Michael. *Babylon 5: All My Words Volume 1*. NJ: Synthetic Worlds, 2019.
Straczynski, J. Michael. *Babylon 5: The Scripts of J. Michael Straczynski, Vol. 15*. NJ: Synthetic Worlds, 2008.
Straczynski, J. Michael. *Becoming Superman*. New York: Harper Voyager, 2019.
Straczynski, J. Michael. "B5 CW News." Patreon, February 3, 2022.
Straczynski, J. Michael. "DVD commentary—*A Call to Arms*." 2005.
Straczynski, J. Michael. "DVD commentary—Chrysalis." 2002.
Straczynski, J. Michael. "from jms re: Crusade." rec.arts.sf.tv.babylon5.moderated. February 26, 1999.
Straczynski, J. Michael. "JMS at SDCC—Who's going?" *rec.arts.sf.tv.babylon5*. July 14, 2008.
Straczynski, J. Michael. *JMS News*, 2004–2005.
Straczynski, J. Michael. "JMS revisits Babylon 5 on show's 25th anniversary." *Newsorama*, June 1, 2020.
Straczynski, J. Michael. "jms speaks, *A Call to Arms*." *The Lurker's Guide*, 1999.
Straczynski, J. Michael. "jms speaks, *Blood Oath*." *The Lurker's Guide*, 1995.
Straczynski, J. Michael. "jms speaks, *Clark's Law*." *The Lurker's Guide*, 1996.
Straczynski, J. Michael. "jms speaks, *Dark Genesis: The Birth of the Psi Corps*." *The Lurker's Guide*, 1998.
Straczynski, J. Michael. "jms speaks, *Divided Loyalties*." *The Lurker's Guide*, 1998.
Straczynski, J. Michael. "jms speaks, *In The Beginning*." *The Lurker's Guide*, 1998.
Straczynski, J. Michael. "jms speaks, *Legend of the Rangers*." *The Lurker's Guide*, 2002.

Straczynski, J. Michael. "jms speaks, *The Memory of Shadows.*" *The Lurker's Guide*, 1998, 2003.
Straczynski, J. Michael. "jms speaks, *Personal Agendas.*" *The Lurker's Guide*, 1997.
Straczynski, J. Michael. "jms speaks, *Thirdspace.*" *The Lurker's Guide*, 1998.
Straczynski, J. Michael. "jms speaks, *The Touch of Your Shadow, The Whisper of Your Name.*" *The Lurker's Guide*, 1996.
Straczynski, J. Michael. "Re: ATTN JMS: Question regarding a 6th season." rec.arts.sf.tv.babylon5.moderated. September 29, 1997.
Straczynski, J. Michael. "Re: ATTN JMS: Why Accelerate t." rec.arts.sf.tv.babylon5.moderated. January 21, 1995.
Straczynski, J. Michael. "Re: Tolkien references." *The Lurker's Guide*, March 19, 1995.
Straczynski, J. Michael. *The Scripts of J. Michael Straczynski Volume 1.* NJ: Synthetic Worlds, 2005.
Straczynski, J. Michael, Twitter (https://twitter.com/straczynski).
Straczynski, J. Michael, and Bryce Zabel. *Star Trek: Re-Boot the Universe.* 2004.
"TNT comes to the rescue of sci-fi series 'Babylon 5.'" *Deseret News*, July 4, 1997.
"The 2004 ENnie Awards." Ennie Awards History, 2004.
"Viewing Order." The Babylon Project, https://babylon5.fandom.com/wiki/Main_Page.
Vorel, Jim. "100 Best Sci-Fi TV Shows of All Time." *Paste Magazine*, September 11, 2018.
Warmoth, Brian. "[NYCC] STRACZYNSKI ON STRACZYNSKI." *Wizard Universe*, February 23, 2007.
White, Peter. "'Walker: Independence,' 'The Winchesters' & 'Gotham Knights' Land Pilot Orders At The CW." *Deadline*, February 3, 2022.

Index

Adams, Mary Kay 71
The Adventures of Superman 5
Alexander, Lyta 3, 8, 11, 30, 52, 63, 68–70, 91–93, 106, 114, 120, 124, 130, 132, 135, 139, 142–143, 145, 148–149, 151–152, 154, 155–159, 163, 166, 172, 184, 187, 190, 192, 205, 220
Alias 6, 18, 90, 213
Alien 2
Alien: Resurrection 2
Allan, Zack 72, 118, 136, 158–159, 166–168, 192, 215
Almost Human 17
The Amazing Spider-Man 23–24, 179
Aragorn 1, 52, 123

Battlestar Galactica 1, 7–9, 14, 16–18, 46, 74, 91, 119, 214, 220
BBC 1, 47
Becoming Superman 20, 42, 49, 116, 172
Bester, Alfred 3, 26, 29, 30, 31, 70, 96, 123, 124, 132, 133, 137, 142, 143, 145, 148, 174, 184, 187, 190, 204, 206, 207
Biggs, Richard 71, 74, 93, 124, 155–156, 166–167, 183, 190, 193
Boxleitner, Bruce 32, 36–37, 67, 83, 100, 102–104, 113, 124, 140, 152, 165–166, 169, 184, 186, 192–193, 201, 219–220
Bristow, Sidney 6
Brown, Caitlin 71, 93
Buffy the Vampire Slayer 6–7, 9, 18, 25, 50, 64, 90

A Call to Arms 137, 140–141, 144, 164, 168–173, 176–181, 185, 191, 208, 210
Captain Power and the Soldiers of the Future 19, 21
Carter, Chris 18
Carter, Jason 123, 206
Centauri 2, 8, 14–16, 25, 27–28, 32, 39, 53–54, 71, 92, 95, 100, 102–103, 105–109, 111–114, 120, 123, 127, 129–131, 133, 136, 139, 141–149, 167, 169, 171, 175, 184, 186, 189, 198, 205, 207–208, 210–211
Channel 4 1, 2
Christian, Claudia 1, 68–69, 77, 93, 123, 137, 139, 140–142, 147–148, 152, 163, 166, 184, 190, 210, 213–214, 219, 220
Cole, Gary 170
Cole, Marcus 1, 30, 52–53, 69, 96, 123–124, 129, 131–132, 137, 145, 184, 206
Conaway, Jeff 72, 140, 153, 156–167, 169, 193
Copeland, John 21, 37, 93, 153
Cotto, Vir 39, 40, 64, 71, 91, 93, 117, 121–124, 129–130, 137, 145, 166, 184, 189, 192, 198, 208, 215
Crusade 2, 23, 30, 69, 79, 88, 97, 112, 137, 140–141, 144, 146, 148, 153–154, 163, 167–169, 170–179, 181–182, 186, 189–192, 204, 208–209, 218

Davies, Russell T. 6, 18, 50, 64, 71
Delenn 3, 6, 12–13, 24, 26–32, 50–52, 63, 66, 69, 71, 74–77, 91–92, 94, 98, 101–106, 112, 114, 116, 121–124, 129, 130, 133–137, 139, 141–142, 144–145, 149, 164–167, 171, 174, 184, 189, 192–193, 205, 208, 215, 220
DiTillio, Larry 21, 175
Doctor Who 1, 6, 18, 49, 61, 77, 203, 211
Doyle, Jerry 72, 91, 124, 137, 167, 169, 184, 185, 213
Drakh 14, 25, 32, 133, 137, 141–144, 148–149, 168–172, 174–177, 179, 181, 182, 186, 204, 207–208
Drazi 149, 171, 180
A Dream Given Form 3, 10, 70, 79, 151, 212–214

Earth (Earthforce and its conflicts) 2–4, 6, 8, 12–16, 18, 27–30, 43, 48, 51, 53, 59,

239

63–66, 68, 70–71, 75, 91–92, 94–96, 100, 102–104, 106, 108, 112–118, 120–123, 125, 127–134, 136–137, 139, 142, 144, 145, 149, 163–164, 166, 168–172, 174–177, 181, 186, 189, 191–193, 205–208, 210, 215
The Event 17
The Expanse 1, 7, 8, 16, 17

Firefly 17
The Flash 6, 216
Flashforward 17
Franklin, Richard 71, 74–75, 93–94, 120, 124, 131–132, 135–136, 142, 145, 149, 156, 159, 164–167, 191, 215, 220
Furlan, Mira 64, 71, 76, 94, 104, 112, 137, 155, 156, 165, 166, 192, 198, 213
Furst, Stephen 36, 39, 40, 93, 137, 166, 213

Galen 168–170, 172, 175, 186, 191, 192, 204, 208–209
Game of Thrones 5
Garibaldi, Michael 3, 27, 28, 30, 31, 59, 65, 68, 72, 91, 92, 93, 96, 105, 113, 124, 127, 129, 132, 133, 134, 135, 136, 137, 138, 139, 145, 149, 167, 168, 184, 185, 186, 187, 192, 193, 204, 207, 208, 209, 215, 220
The Gathering 3, 11, 13, 20, 22, 43, 48, 50, 55, 61, 63, 68, 70–71, 76, 81, 91–93, 100, 120, 129, 157, 163–165, 168, 179, 206, 218, 220
Gideon, Matthew 170, 173–176, 178, 181
G'Kar 1, 3, 8, 12–13, 27–30, 32, 34, 38–40, 53, 63–64, 71, 79, 85–88, 91–92, 94–95, 100, 105–109, 112–114, 116–117, 120, 123–124, 129, 137, 143–145, 148–150, 155, 157, 164–165, 174, 179–180, 192, 197, 199, 200, 204–205, 208, 215, 220

He-Man and the Masters of the Universe 20–21

In the Beginning 13, 40, 93, 107, 140, 152, 163–167, 198
Invasion 17
Ivanova, Susan 1–3, 24, 51–52, 63, 68–69, 74–75, 77–78, 93, 96, 98, 100, 106, 111, 113–114, 123, 129, 132, 136–137, 139, 142, 145, 147, 149, 163, 166, 184, 189–190, 204, 210, 220

Jayce and the Wheeled Warriors 21
Jeremiah 23, 179, 183
Jessica Jones 6
Journeyman 17
Jurasik, Peter 32–40, 64, 71, 94, 103, 107–108, 113, 137, 148–149, 165, 187, 192, 195–202, 219–220

Katsulas, Andreas 33, 38, 71, 85, 94, 107, 109, 113, 123, 137, 155, 179–180, 183, 192–193
Keffer, Warren 58, 105–106, 111–112
Kirk, James T. 5, 13,-14, 44–45, 73, 91
Koenig, Walter 3–4, 30, 42, 70, 73, 124, 137, 143, 148, 174, 187, 190
Kosh 1, 12, 27–28, 67–70, 92–93, 105–106, 109, 112, 114, 116, 120, 122–124, 129, 163, 203, 209
Kyle, Benjamin 68, 71, 74, 92–93, 145

The Legend of the Rangers 2, 164, 174, 179, 180–183, 186–187, 190, 219
Lennier 8, 64, 71, 75, 91, 93, 112, 114, 145, 148, 184, 187, 189–190, 192, 220
Lochely, Elizabeth 68–69, 74, 139, 141, 145, 147–148, 168, 170, 178, 184–186, 191–193, 220
The Lord of the Rings 1, 8, 16, 19, 47, 49, 50, 51, 52, 53, 54, 123, 136, 141, 145, 161, 213
Lost 7, 10, 17, 18, 90–91, 119
Lost in Space 1, 14, 56, 188
The Lost Tales: Voices in the Dark 2, 164, 174, 183–187, 189–190, 193, 200, 207, 209, 214, 219, 220

The Mandalorian 1
The Memory of Shadows 3, 188, 190–194
Minbari 6, 8–9, 12–14, 26–31, 48–49, 51–52, 67, 71, 75–76, 78, 91, 96, 102–104, 106, 112–114, 116, 124, 127–128, 130, 133–135, 137–138, 141, 145, 149, 163, 164–166, 168, 171, 180, 184, 204, 206, 210
Mr. Morden 15, 32, 54, 96, 101, 104, 107, 206, 209
Mollari, Londo 1, 3, 8, 12–15, 27–29, 31–34, 39–40, 63–64, 71, 91–92, 94–95, 100--102, 105, 107–109, 112–114, 116, 120, 123–124, 127–129, 133, 137, 141, 143–150, 163–165, 184, 186–187, 192–193, 197–201, 204–205, 207–208, 215, 220
Mumy, Bill 36, 71, 93, 112, 152, 187, 219–220
Murder, She Wrote 20–21, 23

Narn 6, 9, 14,-15, 27, 30, 34, 48, 53, 71, 79, 83–84, 88, 92, 94, 100, 102–103, 105–109, 111–114, 120, 123, 127, 129, 130–131, 133, 143–144, 149, 171, 180, 198–199, 204–205
Na'Toth 71, 93, 204
Netter, Douglas 21, 37, 57, 167, 189

O'Hare, Michael 15, 26, 29, 31, 36–37, 64–68, 100, 102–105, 120, 124, 127, 165, 184, 193, 206
Orphan Black 1

Index

The Prime Time Entertainment Network (PTEN) 2, 22–23, 25, 31, 42–43, 48–49, 55–59, 62, 93, 97, 102, 126–128, 139, 153, 163, 173, 196
Picard, Jean Luc 13, 41, 64
Psi Corps 8, 12, 14, 26, 29, 53, 68–69, 70, 77, 95, 103–104, 112, 132–133, 135, 139, 142, 148–149, 158, 170, 174, 184, 189, 190, 204, 206–207, 211

Quantum Leap 1, 41

Rangers 1, 30, 51–52, 69, 105, 136, 149, 165, 179, 180–181, 206, 210
The Real Ghostbusters 21
Red Dwarf 1
Reeves, George 5
Ripley, Ellen 2
The River of Souls 112, 140, 164, 167–168

Scoggins, Tracey 69, 141, 148, 167, 169–170, 184, 186, 191, 220
Sekka, Johnny 71, 74
Sense 8 24, 76–77, 183, 214
Shadows 1, 2, 4, 6, 8, 11–14, 16, 19, 27–30, 32, 34, 43–44, 48–49, 51–52, 54, 63–64, 66–67, 69,-71, 91, 94–96, 98, 100–116, 119–125, 127–134, 136–138, 141–143, 148, 158, 164–168, 170–172, 174–176, 181–182, 191–192, 205–206, 209–210
She-Ra: Princess of Power 21
Sheridan, John 1, 3, 6, 8, 12–13, 15–16, 26–27, 29–30, 32, 43–44, 50–53, 59, 63–67, 69, 71, 85, 100, 102–106, 111, 113–116, 118–124, 127–132, 136–139, 141–142, 144–145, 148–149, 158, 164–168, 174, 184–186, 189–190, 192–193, 201, 204–206, 208–209, 215, 220
Sinclair, Jeffrey 2–3, 6, 11–13, 15, 26–31, 50–51, 63–69, 75, 92–96, 100–105, 107, 113, 116, 120, 124, 127, 163, 165, 184, 204, 206, 215, 220
Sliders 1, 32, 41
Space: Above and Beyond 1, 16–17
Star Trek 1, 3, 5–9, 11, 14–18, 20, 22–23, 41–46, 48, 55–58, 61–63, 73, 80, 90–91, 94–95, 100, 111, 120, 127, 151, 153, 159, 160, 170, 188, 197, 203–205, 211, 213, 221
Star Trek: Deep Space Nine 1, 7–8, 16, 22–23, 25, 41–44, 49, 57–58, 60, 69, 74–78, 82, 89, 94, 120, 148, 151, 153, 159, 203, 219
Star Trek: Discovery 7, 17, 74
Star Trek: Enterprise 17, 44, 74
Star Trek V: The Final Frontier 188
Star Trek: First Contact 188
Star Trek: Nemesis 188
Star Trek: The Next Generation 1, 5, 7–9, 17, 41, 45, 48–49, 57, 64, 73–74, 94, 151, 153, 159, 188, 203
Star Trek: Picard 7, 17, 74, 203
Star Trek: Re-boot the Universe 44, 45, 46
Star Trek VI: The Undiscovered Country 48
Star Trek: Voyager 1, 17, 57, 82, 89, 151, 153, 203
Star Trek II: The Wrath of Khan 48, 188
Straczynski, J. Michael 2, 4, 7–8, 10–28, 30–31, 42–59, 61–72, 74–80, 82, 85, 90–99, 101–107, 109–110, 117, 119–122, 125–134, 136, 139–143, 145–148, 151, 163–194, 196, 200, 204–211, 213–221
Stranger Things 5, 6
Summers, Buffy 6, 33, 42
Superman 24, 183
Supernatural 6

Takashima, Laurel 63, 68–69, 74, 92, 99, 106
Tallman, Patricia 3, 4, 36, 69, 70, 92, 93, 142, 148, 151, 152, 153, 154, 155, 156, 157, 158, 159, 160, 161, 162, 166, 187, 213, 214, 219, 220
Ta'Lon 71, 79, 82, 83, 84, 85, 86, 87, 88, 89, 145
Teague, Marshall 36, 71, 79, 80, 81, 82, 83, 84, 85, 86, 87, 88, 89, 214
techno-Mages 105, 171, 174–176, 181, 204, 206, 208–209
telepaths 2, 6, 8, 12, 14–15, 30, 63, 68–70, 77, 91, 94, 112, 114, 120, 130–133, 139, 141–143, 146–149, 156–159, 166, 170, 172, 174, 184, 187, 189–190, 205–207
Thirdspace 134–136, 140, 163–164, 166–167
Thompson, Andrea 30, 69, 77, 93
Thor 24, 183
Tolkien, J.R.R. 2, 47, 49, 51–53,, 114, 157
Tomita, Tamlyn 68, 92–93, 163
Turner Network Television (TNT) 2, 11, 58, 60, 93, 128, 134, 138, 139, 140, 142, 153, 163, 164, 165, 166, 167, 168, 169, 170, 172, 173, 177, 178, 179, 181, 188, 189, 196
The Twilight Zone 21, 50, 183

Valen 3, 163, 174, 184
Vorlons 11–13, 16, 16, 27–30, 48, 49, 53–54, 69, 92, 95, 104, 106, 114, 120, 129–130, 136, 141, 143, 155, 157, 159, 166, 168, 171, 176, 189–190

Whedon, Joss 6
Winters, Talia 24, 27, 30, 63, 69–70, 74, 77–78, 91–92, 106, 112, 114, 172, 204

Xenomorphs 2
The X-Files 1, 5, 7, 16, 20, 41, 45, 50, 64, 72, 90, 148, 188,-189

Z'ha'dum 2–3, 12, 51–52, 54, 66, 103–105, 110–111, 114, 120–122, 124, 127, 129, 131, 136, 165, 171, 205, 209

www.ingramcontent.com/pod-product-compliance
Ingram Content Group UK Ltd.
Pitfield, Milton Keynes, MK11 3LW, UK
UKHW041939140426
5217IPUK00014B/567